Advanced Information and Knowledge Processing

Series Editors
Professor Lakhmi Jain
Lakhmi.jain@unisa.edu.au

Professor Xindong Wu
xwu@cems.uvm.edu

For further volumes:
http://www.springer.com/series/4738

Nikolay Mehandjiev · Paul Grefen
Editors

Dynamic Business Process Formation for Instant Virtual Enterprises

Springer

Editors

Nikolay Mehandjiev
Manchester Business School
University of Manchester
Booth Street W.
Manchester M15 6PB
United Kingdom
n.mehandjiev@manchester.ac.uk

Paul Grefen
Information Systems Group
School of Industrial Engineering
Eindhoven University of Technology
P.O. Box 513
5600 MB Eindhoven
Netherlands
p.w.p.j.grefen@tue.nl

Assistant Editors

Dr Iain Duncan Stalker
Senior Lecturer in Mechanical,
Manufacturing and Design Engineering
School of Science and Engineering
Teesside University
Middlesbrough Tees Valley TS1 3BA
UK
i.stalker@tees.ac.uk

Rik Eshuis
School of Industrial Engineering
Eindhoven University of Technology
P.O. Box 513
5600 MB Eindhoven
Netherlands
h.eshuis@tue.nl

AI&KP ISSN 1610-3947
ISBN 978-1-4471-2558-7   ISBN 978-1-84882-691-5(eBook)
DOI 10.1007/978-1-84882-691-5
Springer London Dordrecht Heidelberg New York

British Library Cataloguing in Publication Data
A catalogue record for this book is available from the British Library

Printed on acid-free paper

Springer is part of Springer Science+Business Media (www.springer.com)

Preface

This book is devoted to automated support for the establishment and operation of a new kind of business organization, the process-oriented *instant virtual enterprise* (IVE). This new organization type brings a combination of business dynamism and explicit business process structure to domains where on-the-fly formation of well-organized business networks is required to deal with the complexity of new products or services under high time pressure. We use the automotive domain as our main example, but the approach presented is well applicable to many other domains (as we argue in the last chapter of this book).

In writing this book, the results of the CrossWork IST project have been used as a basis. These results have been extended and generalized, however, to provide a broader view on the subject area. Consequently, the book reflects more general developments in the use of advanced information technology in support of highly dynamic organization structures in modern day industrial supply chains and business service networks. To further underline the broad view of this book, we have included a number of invited case studies from other projects to complement our view.

A number of industrial and academic authors have contributed to this book. To obtain a well-structured presentation with a homogeneous style, the contributions were planned and edited by a small team from two of the partners in the project. As a result, we can present a balanced amalgamation of research-oriented and application-oriented elements.

The subject matter of this book covers both business and technical aspects of instant virtual enterprises. The contents have been organized into five parts:

Part I. *Introduction* provides a general introduction to the context in which IVEs are needed and to the CrossWork project as a basis for addressing this need.

Part II. *Business, Organization and Architecture* discusses how IVEs are managed and supported from business, organization and information system architecture perspectives.

Part III. *CrossWork Technology* provides a detailed elaboration of the information technology required for IVE support, based on the design of the architecture discussed in Part II.

Part IV. *Case Studies* gives an overview of the IVE case studies elaborated in the CrossWork project, as well as the invited case studies from related research efforts.

Part V. *Conclusion* concludes the book by emphasizing its main points and providing a look into the future and broader application context of IVEs.

Based on the organization of the parts, the book can be read in different ways depending on the interest of the reader. This is illustrated by the figure below, which serves as a route-map through the book.

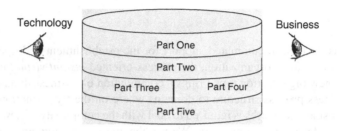

These are the four main routes through the book's contents:

- Readers mainly interested in the business side of the field are advised to concentrate on Parts I, II, IV and V.
- Readers mainly interested in the technology side of the field are advised to concentrate on Parts I–III and V.
- Readers that only want a high-level introduction into the subject area can limit themselves to Parts I and V.
- Obviously, readers who desire a complete introduction into the IVE field and the CrossWork project are warm-heartedly invited to read the entire book.

Manchester, UK, and   Nikolay Mehandjiev
Eindhoven, Netherlands, 2009   Paul Grefen

Contents

Contributors

Hamideh Afsarmanesh University of Amsterdam, Amsterdam, The Netherlands, h.afsarmanesh@uva.nl

Wolfgang Bittner Automotive Solutions GmbH, Steyr-Gleink, Austria, w.bittner@automotive-solutions.at

Luis M. Camarinha-Matos New University of Lisbon, Lisbon, Portugal, cam@uninova.pt

Martin Carpenter University of Manchester, Manchester, UK, m.carpenter@manchester.ac.uk

Rik Eshuis Eindhoven University of Technology, Eindhoven, The Netherlands, h.eshuis@tue.nl

Kurt Fessl Automotive Solutions GmbH, Steyr-Gleink, Austria, k.fessl@automotive-solutions.at

Paul Grefen Eindhoven University of Technology, Eindhoven, The Netherlands, p.w.p.j.grefen@tue.nl

Alexander Haemmerle Profactor, Steyr-Gleink, Austria, alexander.haemmerle@profactor.at

Ana Juan Atos Origin, Barcelona, Spain, ana.juan@atosresearch.eu

Georgios Kouvas Exodus, Athens, Greece, gkou@exodus.gr

Lea Kutvonen University of Helsinki, Helsinki, Finland, lea.kutvonen@cs.helsinki.fi

Nikolay Mehandjiev University of Manchester, Manchester, UK, n.mehandjiev@manchester.ac.uk

Alex Norta University of Helsinki, Helsinki, Finland, alex.norta@cs.helsinki.fi

Stefan Oppl Johannes Kepler University Linz, Linz, Austria, stefan.oppl@jku.at

Ali Owrak University of Manchester, Manchester, UK, ali@owrak.com

Peter Peherstorfer Johannes Kepler University Linz, Linz, Austria, p.peherstorfer@gmx.at

Santi Ristol Atos Origin, Barcelona, Spain, santi.ristol@atosresearch.eu

Iain Duncan Stalker University of Teesside, Middlesbrough, UK, i.stalker@tees.ac.uk

Christian Stary Johannes Kepler University Linz, Linz, Austria, christian.stary@jku.at

Georg Weichhart Johannes Kepler University Linz, Linz, Austria, georg.weichhart@jku.at

Part I
Introduction

Chapter 1
Introduction

Nikolay Mehandjiev, Paul Grefen, and Santi Ristol

This chapter provides a general introduction to this book. As such, it also describes the context of the CrossWork project that is the main source of information for this book. This project is introduced in the next chapter. We start below with discussing the business conditions for the raise of the virtual enterprise as an organization form in the modern economy. As we focus on process-oriented virtual enterprises in this book, we continue with an overview of developments in business process support technologies. Then, we introduce a framework with four aspects that can be used in a combined demand pull and technology push context – this framework is used later to structure topics discussed. In the last section of this chapter, we explain the structure of the book.

1.1 Business Conditions for the Rise of the Virtual Enterprise

The differences between the business environment at the start of the twentieth and twenty-first centuries are staggering. Take the well-known example of Ford as one of the first mass-producers of automobiles, a company which operated then and is still in business today. The first affordable automobile Ford Model T was produced for 19 years (1908 till 1927), a comfortably long life cycle. In contrast, the best-selling car in the world for 2000 and 2001, Ford Focus Mk 1, was manufactured for 6 years, a three times shorter lifespan. A shorter product lifespan is complemented by an increase in product variability and complexity. Between 1915 and 1925, Ford Model T was only produced in a single colour – black, to speed up the production, whilst throughout its lifespan, Ford Focus Mk 1 had more than a dozen different engines, including a separate set of engines for the US market, 4 body styles with 14 trim levels, and 12 special editions. The level of competition on the marketplace has also changed beyond recognition. By 1918 half of all cars in the United States were Ford Model T, and the commercial success meant Ford was working to full capacity and did not spend any advertising money between 1917 and 1923. Today's

N. Mehandjiev (✉)
University of Manchester, Manchester, UK
e-mail: n.mehandjiev@manchester.ac.uk

N. Mehandjiev, P. Grefen (eds.), *Dynamic Business Process Formation for Instant Virtual Enterprises*, Advanced Information and Knowledge Processing, DOI 10.1007/978-1-84882-691-5_1, © Springer-Verlag London Limited 2010

environment is rather different – Ford Focus Mk1 competed in the same market sector with 25 different cars by other manufacturers. These trends also hold true for other sectors of the economy, for example the average cycle of pharmaceuticals is reduced from 25 years to 7 years [16], again roughly threefold. Market opportunities are also shrinking in duration, for example a specific financial service in the pension industry had a window of opportunity of 3 months to coincide with a quirk in tax laws and interest rates [11].

The ability to reconfigure the enterprise rapidly to meet changing market needs and demands is one of the six grand challenges identified by [6]. Figure 1.1 summarizes these trends in product life cycles and market dynamics and illustrates the tension created by their opposing forces. Indeed, the developments in information and communication technology, together with general advances of science and technology, are causing the appearance of products with ever-increasing complexity, which have shorter and shorter life cycles.

Fig. 1.1 Contemporary forces in product and market development

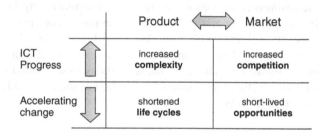

At the same time, advances in communications and socio-political developments mean organizations have to operate in increasingly competitive global markets which demand greater efficiency, developing complex products to address short-lived market opportunities. These pressures on resources and competences of individual companies have motivated an increased presence of *Virtual Enterprises* (VEs), where companies assemble forces to address a business opportunity. Once the opportunity is gone, so is the VE.

Figure 1.2 shows the life cycle stages of a VE [1] in relation to the lifespan of the business opportunity addressed by the VE. These stages are:

Fig. 1.2 Stages in the life cycle of a virtual enterprise pursuing a business opportunity

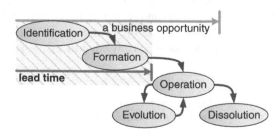

- *Identification*: This stage involves the identification, evaluation and selection of business opportunities that may be met by the formation of a VE.
- *Formation*: This stage involves partner identification, partner evaluation and selection and partnership formation, including the binding of the selected candidate partners into the actual VE.
- *Operation and Evolution*: This stage is characterized by the controlled integration of the services and resources offered by the VE partners in VE-wide collaborative processes, leading to the achievement of shared business objectives. Membership and structure of VEs may evolve over time in response to changes of objectives or to adapt to new opportunities in the business environment. Changes of VE context may necessitate contract amendment or adaptation of policy and business process enactment.
- *Dissolution*: This stage is initiated when the market opportunity is fulfilled or has ceased to exist. The major decision processes in the termination stage include operation termination and asset dispersal.

It is clear that the greater the lead time between the appearance of the business opportunity and the start of the operation of the VE, the greater the losses to earlier entrants on the marketplace or earlier bidders for the opportunity.

One industry where VEs have existed since the middle of the twentieth century is the film industry (or "Hollywood") [5] where actors and special-effect small and medium enterprises (SMEs) are joining forces to create a movie under the management of the producer and director. This project-based virtual organization model succeeded the vertically integrated large studios and is one of the earliest examples of VEs. A number of temporary formed organizations of individuals and enterprises, can of course also be found throughout Europe. The reasons for their existence range from investigating a challenging research topic to setting up a supply chain for producing the latest car. They are intrinsically linked with more permanent groupings, formal or informal, where members share interest in a specialist topic. These organizations can be either informal communities of practice or formally constituted organizations, like chambers of commerce. In relation to the virtual enterprises they play the role of Virtual Breeding Environments (VBEs), providing social and informational prerequisites for the formation of VEs.

To illustrate the difference between a VBE and a VE, let us take the example of the Automotive Clusters, or Networks of Automotive Excellence. Such organizations exist in many European countries, including Austria, Slovenia, Belgium, Hungary, etc. Their role is to support local communities of automotive suppliers, helping them bring their complementary skills and create VEs that successfully bid to develop major automotive subsystems such as engines or car doors for an automotive manufacturer such as Ford. The Automotive Clusters are playing the role of VBEs in relation to the VEs created within them.

Other examples of VBE as regional clusters seeking to facilitate project collaboration among their members are Swiss Microtech (SMT), ISOIN/Helice and Supply Network Shannon (SNS). SNS[1], for example, is an open network of

---

[1] http://www.snshannon.com

companies in the Shannon region of Ireland. It is established as a limited liability company. SNS has developed a framework for indigenous companies to collaborate in joint marketing, training development and quotation activities. SNS is a regional VBE with individual members currently creating subnetworks on a global scale. Federazione Regionale Ordini Ingegneri Pugliesi is a VBE focused on individuals rather than companies, and thus called a Professional Virtual Community (PVC). Its membership comprises the Apulian engineers, and it is established to facilitate collaboration among professionals and between professionals and SMEs in the concurrent engineering domain, again leading to project-based collaborations or virtual enterprises.

Moving to examples of VEs, one well-known example of a virtual enterprise in the high-tech industry is Airbus. Airbus consists of a number of autonomous parties that produce and assemble parts of airliners. Airbus was formed to counterbalance American forces in the airline industry. Note that Airbus is a rather stable VE; it has been in existence for a number of decades now, with a few different consortium configurations which evolved over time. An example of a VE with a much shorter lifespan (3 years) is the CrossWork project. CrossWork was organized in 2002 and 2003 in order to officially start in January 2004 as a European IST research project. It was running for 3 years and evolved over this time; individual persons came and left, as did enterprises. Dissolution was also a process that started in January 2007 and lasted for several months (till all reports and financial statements were delivered to the European Commission). Another example for such a temporary organization is ECOLEAD (European Collaborative networked Organizations LEADership initiative; for more information see http://www.ve-forum.org). ECOLEAD and CrossWork are both VEs which study the support and emergence of other VEs, used as examples in this book.

Today VEs exist in many industry and research sectors. An example in the *insurance industry* is the alliance[2] between the specialist online broker for health insurance, eHealthInsurance, and the general customer-facing financial services provider Countrywide Credit Industries, allowing Countrywide customers to shop for health insurance from a number of third-party providers via eHealthInsurance. In the *financial sector*, Special Purpose Vehicles[3] are tax-exempt companies formed for the specific purpose of buying off (or securitizing) a large pool of mortgage rights from a bank, which link together the bank, the mortgagees and its own investors in a complex financial instrument to ensure stability of the credit system.

A common feature linking the variety of VEs is that their work is often technology-mediated and geographically distributed. In a widely cited example, the Digital Media technology enables the distributed development of a new video clip for a chart-topping single. The recording session is located in London, where the singer lives, the design is done in San Francisco, the writers work from their homes (Paris and Barcelona) and the animation of the characters is outsourced to China.

---

[2] http://www.ehealthinsurance.com/content/pressNew/CountryWide.shtml
[3] http://en.wikipedia.org/wiki/Securitization_transaction

The global network and the interactive cycle of recording, writing and animation "around the clock" allow the recording of the clip to take place in a very short time, including repeated takes and rewrites.

An interesting interplay exists between VEs and supply chain arrangements. In the domain of the automotive manufacturing, for example, the large manufacturers are seeking to reduce the number of component suppliers they have to interact with. This has caused smaller companies to form VEs, which can deliver larger subsystems to the producer. This trend is reflected in several of the case studies covered by this book. The trends in product and market developments are highlighted in Fig. 1.1.

- *Developments on the product side*: Rapidly increasing product complexity is addressed by combining knowledge and skills of individual organizations in a VE. A tension is created between the increased difficulty in forming the right combinations of knowledge and skills, and the requirement to shorten the formation stage of a VE. The latter is motivated by shortening the overall product life cycles and business opportunity lifespans. Overall, a greater efficiency in forming and dismantling of VEs is needed.
- *Developments on the market side*: Market dynamics requires effectiveness in the selection of members in VEs. Currently, partners are selected from static "acquaintance" networks. Effectiveness, however, demands a more open and dynamic manner of finding the right organizations with the right skills at the point of need. Increasing competition, on the other hand, requires high speed in setup and deployment of VEs, and their efficient management.

> In an environment of increased competition and reduced life cycles for increasingly complex products, we need to find ways to effectively and efficiently compose a VE and to coordinate its operations and processes. Manufacturing is an excellent example sector but not the only one where such developments are badly needed.

1.2 Developments in Business Process Support Technologies

Management of business processes is currently supported by a number of technological developments. Below, we briefly discuss three important areas of development – workflow management (which we use as a synonym for business process management in this book), agent technology and service-oriented computing. In the following chapters of this book, we revisit these areas.

Workflow Management (WFM) technology has been around since the early nineties of the previous century and has been receiving ample attention in both industry and research. A number of general purpose WFM systems are on the market and WFM technology has been integrated into enterprise information systems, such as Enterprise Resource Planning (ERP) systems. Much of the existing WFM technology, however, focuses on intra-organizational workflows, assuming a possibly distributed, but homogeneous WFM system in a trusted environment, i.e. in the context of a single organization. When WFM is extended across organizational boundaries, the complexity is heavily increased. Early developments in the area of inter-organizational WFM have targeted the cooperation between organizations specified at process definition time. An example is the WISE project [3], which aimed at providing a software platform for process-based business-to-business electronic commerce, focusing on support for networks of SMEs. WISE relies on a central workflow engine to control inter-organizational processes (called virtual business processes). In the approach presented by WISE, a virtual business process consists of a number of black-box services linked in a workflow process. Slightly more recent, there are developments towards the dynamic integration of business processes in a workflow-based service outsourcing paradigm. An advanced approach has been developed in the CrossFlow project [7]. The CrossFlow approach uses a proprietary contract specification language to specify business relationships in two-party, dynamic virtual enterprises. A dedicated Java-based collaboration layer is used for support of dynamic business process outsourcing on top of standard workflow management software.

Agent Technology is a comparatively recent and very active field of research which has roots in general artificial intelligence research. The key idea behind agent-based technology is to form systems from communities of independently reasoning, goal-driven agents who communicate using natural language like constructs. Crucially, an agent will only take a particular action when it judges it to be in its best interests to do so. This basic structure makes multi-agent technology well suited to building systems containing multiple self-interested components. A further feature of multi-agent system is the extensive use of negotiation to enable the agents to reach mutually agreeable outcomes. This combination of features means that multi-agent systems are able to represent the interests of every company through individual agents. This is highly suitable for supporting the formation of virtual organizations [4, 15], for coordinating the work of business partners in a supply chain [12] and for controlling the scheduling and execution of detailed workflow processes [13, 14]. Agent standards are fairly mature and FIPA (http://www.fipa.org) has recently been adopted as an official standards committee of the IEEE.

Service-Oriented Computing (SOC) is a relatively new computing paradigm that promises flexible, dynamic, component-oriented interoperability between encapsulated business functionalities of autonomous organizations, called services. The functionality of a service can be quite diverse, depending on the application domain, from very simple (e.g. the functionality to convert an amount of money from one currency to another), to very complex (e.g. the functionality to invoke complex business applications). SOC as a concept is usually closely linked to Web Services as a technology. The Web Service paradigm allows the dynamic composition of application functionality using the Web as a medium [2]. A Web Service is an encapsulated piece of software functionality with a well-defined interface that is made available on the Web. Web Service technology is based on a stack of standards. The basis of the stack is typically formed by HTTP as a basic communication protocol, XML as a basic language and Simple Object Access Protocol (SOAP) as an interaction protocol on top of these two. On top of SOAP, we see languages for service interface definition (Web Service Description Language (WSDL)) and service composition (Business Process Execution Language (BPEL)). Again on top of that, there are protocols for collaboration and transaction management. Further, there are standards for various aspects of collaboration, examples of which are brokering, service level (agreement) management, and security. Recently, there are developments to integrate SOC and explicit inter-organizational process management (e.g. [8, 10]).

> Current technology developments make it possible to provide software support for near-automatic formation and coordination of virtual enterprises.

1.3 Demand Pull and Technology Push

In the domain of automated support for VEs, we see a combination of demand pull and technology push forces, which when combined enable fast developments. To analyze this domain and design a system for it in a well-structured manner, we distinguish four aspects to describe a VE e-business scenario. These aspects together form the BOAT framework [9]:

- *Business (B):* the business aspect describes the business goals of e-business, or the economic model behind its existence. As such, it answers the question of why a specific e-business scenario exists or should exist or what should be reached. Topics can include leverage of efficiency levels, access to new markets, reorientation of interaction with customers, etc. How things are conducted is not of interest in this aspect.
- *Organization (O):* the organization aspect describes how organizations are structured to achieve the goals defined in the B aspect. Organizational structures and business processes are the main ingredients here. Automated systems are not yet in scope at this aspect.
- *Architecture (A):* the architecture aspect covers the conceptual structure (architecture) of automated information systems required to make the organizations defined in the O aspect work. As such, it describes how automated systems support the involved organizations.
- *Technology (T):* the technology aspect describes the technological realization of the systems of which the architecture is specified in the A aspect. The T aspect covers the concrete ingredients from information and communication technology, including languages and protocols, software and (if relevant) hardware.

In traditional information system design practice, analysis and development of systems proceeds in a linear manner from the business to the technology side (also referred to as the waterfall model of system design). In the BOAT framework, this would mean starting from the B aspect and working stepwise to the T aspect, where each preceding aspect defines the requirements that must be fulfilled at the succeeding aspect. This leads to a design process as depicted in the left hand side of Fig. 1.3 which we call the stack model for BOAT.

Fig. 1.3 Stack and wheel models of BOAT

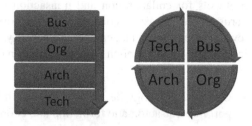

In the e-business field, the relation between business and technology is not so linear; business "pulls" technology development by stating new requirements, whilst technology "pushes" business by offering new opportunities. To model this, we need to organize the BOAT aspects such that we get a more cyclical dependency between the aspects.

This results in the picture shown in the right hand side of Fig. 1.3, which we call the "wheel model" for BOAT. With the wheel model, we can make two important observations. Firstly, a development process can, in principle, start at each aspect of the model (although B and T aspects may be most common). A new organization structure in the O aspect, for example, may be the trigger for a new e-business scenario. Secondly, the wheel model suggests a cyclical process: An e-business development process does not end after one cycle around the wheel, but is rather a continuous process of adjustment to new business and technology contexts.

> The complexity of automated VE support requires a framework to distinguish the various aspects. The BOAT framework provides the Business, Organization, Architecture and Technology aspects for this purpose.

1.4 Structure of this Book

To provide an easy overview for the reader, this book in organized in five parts, of which you are currently reading the first. Each part contains a number of chapters.

Part I provides the introduction to the book and the European research project on which its contents are mainly based. The current chapter covers the introduction. The next chapter in this part introduces the notion of an "Instant" VE as a target for the research in automated support for VEs, and introduces several influential efforts in this dimension, including details of the CrossWork project. The chapter explains the goals of this project and places it against the background of related work. Parts

II and III of the book present the ingredients of the CrossWork approach, following the BOAT framework outlined in the previous subsection.

Part II discusses the conceptual side of the approach described in this book. It covers the business, organization and architecture aspects of the BOAT framework – each aspect in one chapter. As such, it goes in three chapters from the business goals to the structural blueprint of the means, which will be made concrete in the next part.

Part III discusses the technical side of the approach, covering the technology aspect of the BOAT framework. The chapter structure of Part III is based on the main architectural clusters of the architecture described in Part II. Five chapters describe the information technology used for the realization of the five main clusters in the architecture.

Part IV presents the real-world case studies that have been conducted in the CrossWork project. These case studies show how the concepts and technology described in Parts II and III are actually deployed in the context of the automotive industry. To embed the CrossWork approach in a broader context, we also briefly present approaches and results of related research efforts here.

Part V concludes the book. Its first chapter gives an overview of the main observations with respect to the concepts and technology covered in this book. Its second chapter provides a look into future developments. Finally, a bibliography detailing the references found throughout the book is presented.

This introductory chapter has shown that

- We need to find ways to effectively and efficiently compose a VE and to coordinate its operations and processes.
- Manufacturing is an excellent example of a business sector for VEs, but not the only possible one.
- Current technology developments make it possible to provide software support for near-automatic formation and coordination of VEs.
- The BOAT framework illustrates the interplay between business and technology considerations underpinning this book.

References

1. Afsarmanesh, H., Camarinha-Matos, L. M., A Framework for Management of Virtual Organizations Breeding Environments in Collaborative Networks and their Breeding Environments, Springer, New York, pp. 35–48, 2005.
2. Alonso, G., Casati, F., Kuno, H., Machiraju, V., Web Services – Concepts, Architectures and Applications, Springer, New York, 2004.
3. Alonso, G., Fiedler, U., Hagen, C., Lazcano, A., Schuldt, H., Weiler, N., WISE: Business to Business E-Commerce, Proceedings of the 9th International Workshop on Research Issues on Data Engineering, Sydney, Australia, pp. 132–139, 1999.

4. Camarinha-Matos, L. M., Afsarmanesh, H., Virtual Enterprise Modeling and Support Infrastructures, Applying Multi-agent System Approaches, Springer-Verlag New York Inc, New York, USA, pp. 335–364, 2001.
5. Cohen, J., Integrated Practice and the New Architect: Keeper of Knowledge and Rules, The Architect's Handbook of Professional Practice, John Wiley & Sons, New York, 2004.
6. Committee on Visionary Manufacturing Challenges and Board on Manufacturing and Engineering Design and Commission on Engineering and Technical Systems and National Research Council, Visionary Manufacturing Challenges for 2020, Washington, DC, USA, 1998.
7. Grefen, P., Aberer, K., Hoffner, Y., Ludwig, H., CrossFlow: Cross-Organizational Workflow Management in Dynamic Virtual Enterprises, International Journal of Computer Systems Science and Engineering, Vol. 15(5), pp. 277–290, 2000.
8. Grefen, P., Ludwig, H., Dan, A., Angelov, S., An Analysis of Web Services Support for Dynamic Business Process Outsourcing, Information and Software Technology, Vol. 48(11), pp. 1115–1134, 2006.
9. Grefen, P., *Mastering E-Business*. Routledge, 2010.
10. Grefen, P., Service-Oriented Support for Dynamic Interorganizational Business Process Management, Service Oriented Computing, MIT Press, Cambridge, MA, pp. 83–110, 2008.
11. Hammer, M., Champy, J., Reengineering the Corporation: A Manifesto for Business Revolution, HarperBusiness, New York, 1996.
12. Huhns, M. N., Stephens, L. M., Automating Supply Chains, IEEE Internet Computing, Vol. 5(4), pp. 90–93, July/August, 2001.
13. Jennings, N. R., Faratin, P., Norman, T. J., O'Brien, P., Odgers, B., Alty, J. L., Implementing a Business Process Management System using ADEPT: A Real-World Case Study, International Journal of Applied Artificial Intelligence, Vol. 14(5), pp. 421–463, 2000.
14. Norman, T. J., Preece, A., Chalmers, S., Jennings, N. R., Luck, M., Dang, V. D., Nguyen, T. D., Deora, V., Shao, J., Gray, A., Fiddian, N., CONOISE: Agent-Based Formation of Virtual Organisations, Proceedings of the 23rd SGAI International Conference on Innovative Techniques and Applications of AI, Cambridge, UK, 2003.
15. Oliveira, E., Rocha, A. P., Agents Advanced Features for Negotiation in Electronic Commerce and Virtual Organisations Formation Process, Lecture Notes in Computer Science Vol. 1991/2001, Springer-Verlag, New York, pp. 78–97, 2001.
16. Wacker, J., Driving Forces Propelling the Next Big Thing in IT #5 – Accelerating Rate of Change. Electronic Data Systems Corporation, Available at http://www.eds.com/sites/cs/blogs/eds_next_big_thing_blog/archive/2005/06/29/84.aspx last accessed 15 Nov, 2008.

Chapter 2
Towards New Frontiers: CrossWork

Nikolay Mehandjiev, Alexander Haemmerle, Paul Grefen, and Santi Ristol

This chapter gives a general introduction into the CrossWork project and the relation to the context in which it has been set up (as explained in Chapter 1). It explains the goals and structure of the project and positions CrossWork with respect to related research efforts.

2.1 The World of the "Instant Virtual Enterprise"

Picture a world where companies are formed "on demand" to address a market opportunity, and then reformed as needed. Constituents of such companies could be individuals, small companies or project teams from bigger enterprises. Faster formation of such a VE would mean shorter delay in addressing the market opportunity, and better chances of success.

In contemporary VEs, formation activities involve a number of face-to-face meetings and negotiations, making the formation stage far too long. A compelling example is the automotive industry, where Original Equipment Manufacturers (OEMs) tend to outsource development activities to (Tier 1) suppliers. A single supplier might not be able to fulfil such a development activity. The challenge for suppliers in the automotive industry (a vast majority of them being SMEs) is to instantly form a development team (i.e. a VE) to be able to quickly react to the OEM request. For example, one of the main activities of the Upper Austrian Automotive Association is the formation of dynamic and project-oriented teams of different companies from different countries. The establishment of such teams is based on a pool of more than 280 association member companies with links to other European automotive clusters. The team formation process is very time-consuming, involving several steps from analysis of OEM requests to so-called "innovation workshops" with potential team members.

At present OEMs are typically procuring system suppliers by sending out a "request for quotation". Potential suppliers have to prepare a concrete quote within

N. Mehandjiev (✉)
University of Manchester, Manchester, UK
e-mail: n.mehandjiev@manchester.ac.uk

N. Mehandjiev, P. Grefen (eds.), *Dynamic Business Process Formation for Instant Virtual Enterprises*, Advanced Information and Knowledge Processing, DOI 10.1007/978-1-84882-691-5_2, © Springer-Verlag London Limited 2010

5 days. Currently, a typical Automotive Cluster has difficulty in supporting the creation of such teams and bids, and can only manage to support around seven such quotes per year. Imagine the effect of the economy of Upper Austria if they could support the creation of 50–70 such teams? Looking in the detail at where the time is taken, introducing software-based automation can introduce significant savings in time and effort and speed up the formation processes to the level of "Instant" VE.

Figure 2.1summarizes the differences between the "instant" and "conventional" virtual enterprise in relation to the main stages of VE life cycle shown in Fig. 1.2 and aligned with [1]. Detailed description of each stage follows.

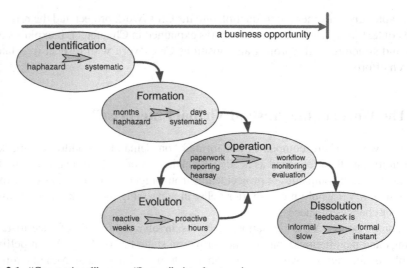

Fig. 2.1 "Conventional" versus "Instant" virtual enterprises

An Instant Virtual Enterprise (IVE) is distinguished by a systematic support for the identification, analysis and selection of business opportunities in the *Identification* stage.

It also brings about a significantly faster *Formation* stage where the time to analyse the business opportunity and form a consortium is reduced from *months* to *days*, thus ensuring rapid reaction to a business opportunity. This reduction is made possible by software automating the formation activities such as matchmaking and negotiation using advanced reasoning mechanisms. A sy*stematic* search for partners replaces the existing *haphazard* search mechanisms.

During the stage of *Operation*, the coordination of cross-organizational processes, which is conventionally based on sending documents such as shipping notes and invoices, is replaced by *workflow*-based coordination and ordering based on genuine dependencies between activities. Traditional periodic *reporting* is replaced by run-time *monitoring* of processes and exceptions. The *hearsay* channels for appraising partner performance are complemented by formal and systematic *evaluation* mechanisms.

The availability of real-time monitoring information and systematic evaluation mechanisms allows an instant VE to also excel at the stage of *Evolution*, where it can be *proactive* in optimizing its membership and performance rather than follow the conventional *reactive* approach of "firefighting" when changes occur. The systematic mechanisms for search and evaluating new replacement partners, and for exploring new opportunities of coordinating work between the current set of partners reduce the time taken to reform from *weeks* to *hours*.

During the *Dissolution* stage, the same mechanisms for systematic and formal performance evaluation help the instant virtual enterprise to retain *formal feedback* about the performance of team members and of the team as a whole, which is then retained for improving future formation stages.

These characteristics of the IVE are brought together by the combination of technology with new business practices and coordination mechanisms. Indeed, all VEs have technology at their core as a main enabling factor; achieving "instancy" requires that the latest technology achievements are combined with innovative business elements. In terms of the BOAT model introduced in Chapter 1, this denotes that the world of IVEs operates in "wheel mode". It is driven by new technological possibilities towards new business models as much as it demands new technological solutions to cater for new business models. The fusion between technology and business is what characterizes our work and this book.

Summarizing, we can define an IVE as follows:

> An instant virtual enterprise is a temporary virtual enterprise forged with support of automated systems to fulfil a specific business goal and subsequently operated with support of automated systems.

This definition highlights the main differences with traditional B2B e-business collaboration:

1. An IVE has a temporary, explicit goal-oriented character (accounting for the I);
2. The organizations participating in an IVE operate as a single business entity (accounting for the VE);
3. The creation and operation of the IVE relies on automated support (to obtain the required levels of efficiency to deal with 1 and 2).

In the "brave new world" of the IVE, companies will use software matchmaking and negotiating on their behalf to form consortia bidding for market opportunities. These consortia will be evaluated by the client in the same automated and transparent manner. Once a consortium is selected, the same software will coordinate the activities of different partners creating an IVE. A company will never have to miss an opportunity because it did not have sufficient time to prepare a bid or because it was not visible to other consortium members on the marketplace.

2.2 Introduction to CrossWork

The impetus for this book and the majority of material and examples in it were inspired and sourced from an EC-funded project called *CrossWork,* which aims to bring the vision of IVE closer to reality. The focus of CrossWork is illustrated in Fig. 2.2. It covers the Formation, Operation and, to a lesser extent, the Evolution stage of the VE life cycle, but does not cover the Identification or the Dissolution stages.

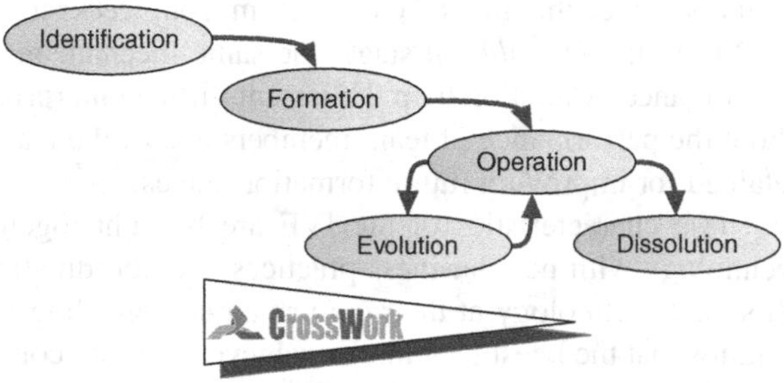

Fig. 2.2 Focus of CrossWork within the IVE life cycle

CrossWork seeks to deliver the key characteristics of the IVE idea by fusing together the advances in IT reviewed in Section 1.2 with innovative business processes:

- *Workflow modelling and management* captures existing business practices within the IVE partners and uses advanced algorithms to create a global workflow, which coordinates work performed (enacted) by different partners during the *Operation* stage of the IVE.
- *Software agents* represent individuals and organizations, mapping the social nature of the VE formation into artificial societies and thus handling the reasoning and negotiation aspects during the *Formation* and *Evolution* stages of an IVE life cycle.
- *Service-based infrastructures* join existing systems of the partners with the global workflow engine to enable seamless and efficient coordination of activities and monitoring of work across partners during the *Operation* and *Dissolution* stages of the IVE.

Following the feedback principle illustrated by the "wheel" version of the *BOAT* framework described in Section 1.3, CrossWork uses input from leading European automotive manufacturers and organizations regarding their needs and current practices. Grounding CrossWork in the needs of the *automotive manufacturing sector* reflects the acuteness of the problems which can be addressed by the concept of the IVE in this sector, and its importance for the European economy. However, the results of the project are applicable to other sectors such as the financial services.

The reader may notice that many case studies and examples in the following chapters of this book are written from the perspective of SMEs. Indeed, the increased complexity of technology demands narrow the specialization required from SMEs. When this is combined with the increased complexity of products and services, participating in IVE becomes a competitive necessity rather than luxury for this type of companies.

CrossWork did not develop its concepts in a vacuum, but interacted with a thriving community working in the area of virtual enterprise and business networks. Some members of this community contributed information about their approaches to Chapter 12. Over and above this, some of the ideas in this book were formed during the multitude of informal discussions with members of this community and we would like to acknowledge this influence and these contributions.

CrossWork brought together four academic and six industrial partners for a 3-year collaborative effort financially supported by the European Commission, which was designed to build upon the results of several other projects and existing know-how. Most influential were the following projects:

- *MaBE – IntLogProd* investigated the use of agent technology to achieve run-time optimization of a Virtual enterprise taking different locations and manufacturing/logistics costs/time into account [8].
- *CrossFlow* investigated the use of contracts and workflow modelling for enabling the coordination across participants in a VE [5].

Within CrossWork there were three groups of partners; academic, software developers and end users. Research-wise CrossWork integrated know-how from agent-based business systems (The University of Manchester), workflows and business outsourcing (Eindhoven University of Technology), information logistics (University of Växjö), and human–computer interaction, usability and learning organization research (Johannes Kepler University Linz).

CrossWork was created with a clear remit of bringing the vision of IVE closer to reality. Initially it targeted the automotive sector since the trends described in Chapter 1 are clearly at play there, and the need to support SMEs and make them competitive is very strong. Indeed, the need to support SMEs is greater since they need collaborative networks to deal with the complexity of contemporary products.

2.3 CrossWork and the IVE Formation Stage

An IVE is enabled by the confluence of advanced IT and innovative business methods, and CrossWork sets out to develop software and business mechanisms, which can bring the IVE vision closer to reality by automating the formation of an IVE and support its operation and evolution. Automating the formation of the IVE is challenging in both technical and business sense, and the dearth of systems and even published research in this area focused CrossWork on this stage of the IVE life cycle.

The Formation stage of the IVE life cycle can be described as comprising the following five intertwined activities, illustrated in Fig. 2.3:

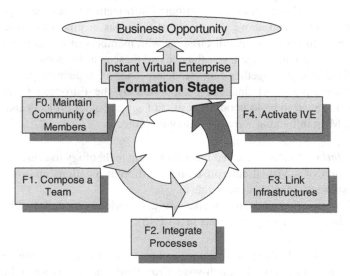

Fig. 2.3 Five activities within the formation stage of the IVE life cycle

The activity "F0. Maintain a Community of Members" is an ongoing maintenance activity, transcending the life cycle of a single IVE. The Community of Members (often called "VE Breeding Environment (VBE)" [4]), can be organized in a number of ways ranging from a closed club to a fully open marketplace. In the automotive manufacturing sector, one particular form of such organization gathering momentum is the Automotive Cluster, with examples in Upper Austria, Slovenia and Hungary. To ensure effective collaboration within such a community, its members should subscribe to a *common framework for representing and sharing knowledge*, and implement *a common software platform*. Developing such a framework and a platform are two of the main objectives of CrossWork.

The activity "F1. Compose a Team" analyses the target *Business Opportunity* and the existing Community of Members and produces a team, which is to form the IVE. Automating this activity is also one of the main objectives of CrossWork. After studying a number of approaches, CrossWork developed a *design-led dynamic team formation mechanism driven by software agents*, which is based on the knowledge representation and sharing facilities provided by the common framework and platform.

The activity "F2. Integrate Processes" composes the relevant publicly visible processes of the selected team members and, after dealing with any potential conflicts, creates a global workflow model to coordinate the operation of the IVE. CrossWork's main objectives include automating this activity using *Petri-net-based algorithms* and *developing sophisticated formalisms for modelling* not only the workflow dependencies, but also other enterprise aspects relevant to cross-enterprise coordination.

The activity "F3. Link Infrastructures" connects the systems of the IVE participants with the global workflow system in preparation for deployment. Automating this activity using *service-based infrastructures and processing of knowledge about participants and their systems encoded in ontologies* are also two of the main objectives of CrossWork.

The activity "F4. Activate IVE" is the final deployment activity before the IVE starts to operate. To support this activity, CrossWork's main objectives include the development of *open deployment platform using service-based infrastructure.*

Further details about the contributions developed in pursuit of these objectives are provided in Chapters 4 and 6–Chapter 10.

CrossWork has set an ambitious goal to enable IVE by automating their design and the composition of the workflow, which will coordinate the work across a newly created IVE. Achieving this goal requires new theoretical results as well as advanced development work at both the levels of business mechanisms and software prototyping.

We have selected appropriate technology for the different stages of the IVE life cycle, mapping the social nature of the cross-organizational team formation into a multi-agent system, where software agents represent individual companies and handle the negotiation and reasoning aspects typical for the formation and evolution stage. The formally founded workflow composition work ensures consistency and smooth flow of work across organizational boundaries, and deployment architecture based on cutting-edge Web-service standards ensures standard-compliant open deployment of the workflow coordination system.

2.4 Extending State of the Art

A number of research and development projects aim to support the efficient formation of VEs. Comprehensive reviews are available elsewhere [4], so this section focuses on several projects and systems which we consider to be most similar to CrossWork and compare their features with the corresponding aspects of the CrossWork goals. After having discussed the details of the CrossWork approach in the sequel of this book, we revisit the comparison in Chapter 13, where we analyse the contribution of CrossWork to the state of the art.

Table 2.1 Comparison framework

Stage/activity	Relevant aspects
F: Formation	General support for formation processes
F0: Maintain Community	Support and degree of openness
F1: Compose a team	Level of automation possible, underlying mechanisms
F2: Integrate processes	Level of automation possible, underlying mechanisms
F3: Link infrastructures	Level of automation possible, underlying approaches
F4: Activate VE	Support for deployment of VE and software
O: Operation of VE	Run-time support such as coordination and monitoring
O1: Process support	Support for explicit business process management
O2: Back-end integration	Support for coupling to back-end systems
E: Evolution of VE	Approach to supporting the evolution of a VE
D: Dissolution of VE	Approach to supporting the dissolution of a VE

We start with a generally accepted life cycle model of a VE [1] shown in Fig. 1.2, and detail the "formation" (Fig. 2.3) and "operation" stages of this life cycle. The resultant set of steps comprises our comparison framework shown in Table 2.1. The framework includes the four main life cycle stages. The "formation" and "operation" stages also show their major aspects to be supported.

The WISE project (Workflow based Internet SErvices) at ETH Zürich aimed at providing a software platform for process-based business-to-business electronic commerce. The approach focuses on support for networks of small and medium enterprises. A virtual business process in the WISE approach consists of a number of black-box services linked at design time into a workflow process [3]. A service is offered by an involved organization and can be a business process controlled by a workflow management system local to that organization – but this is completely orthogonal to the virtual business process (as it is a black box). As such, WISE does provide process integration, but only to a rather limited extent. The software platform used in WISE is based on the OPERA kernel [2]. The WISE system relies on a central workflow engine to control cross-organizational processes (called virtual business processes). Using this infrastructure, VE operation is supported.

In the CrossFlow project, concepts and technology for workflow support in dynamic virtual enterprises have been developed [5, 7]. In the context of this project, the formation of VEs is based on bilateral dynamic service outsourcing. Service offerings and service requests are specified in electronic contract templates [9]. These are matched in the VE formation stage by a service matchmaker to arrive to electronic contracts between two organizations. The contract model is reflected in a dedicated, XML-based contract specification language [9]. An established contract specifies how processes are integrated and is the basis for the dynamic generation of a service enactment infrastructure [6]. This infrastructure links the workflow management infrastructures at the VE partners. It performs the synchronization of their respective local business processes based on an abstracted common process specification included in the contract. The CrossFlow approach pays specific attention to inter-organizational transaction management, management of quality of service attributes of processes and the execution flexibility aspects of services. As such, there is broad support for VE operation. Once the contracted service has been completed, the generated infrastructure is automatically dismantled, thus supporting dissolution of the VE.

The MaBE project (Multi-agent Business Environment) set out to deliver an agent-based technology infrastructure suitable for implementing business support systems. MaBE was a 3-year European research project supported by the EC within the GROWTH programme. End-user scenarios from the manufacturing and logistics areas served as a basis for development. The project resulted in an easy to configure agent-based infrastructure, which provided the means for a community of organizations to stay connected, search available services and get informed automatically about changes.

The work on MaBE was conducted in close collaboration with Agentcities, another research project funded by the European Community, which set out to build a world-wide distributed agent infrastructure. This collaboration materialized in IntLogProd [8], a sub-project of Agentcities, which delivered a proof-of-concept demonstrator focused on selecting a team of partners in a VE to minimize the combined costs of logistics and manufacturing. Both MaBE and Agentcities-IntLogProd were thus focused on composing a team and linking the infrastructure of a VE, and provided tools for the operation of a VE and for reflecting the evolution of services and skills in the underlying ontologies. As such they are listed together in Table 2.2 below.

Table 2.2 Summary comparison

	WISE	CrossFlow	MaBE/ IntLogProd	TrustCom	CrossWork
F: Formation of VE	✓	✓	–	–	✓
F0: Maintain community	–	–	✓	–	✓
F1: Compose a team	–	–	✓	–	✓
F2: Integrate processes	✓	✓	–	–	✓
F3: Link infrastructures	–	✓	✓	✓	✓
F4: Activate VE	–	✓	–	–	✓
O: Operation of VE	✓	✓	✓	✓	✓
O1: Process support	✓	✓	–	–	✓
O2: Back-end integration	–	–	✓	✓	✓
E: Evolution of VE	–	–	✓	–	–
D: Dissolution of VE	–	✓	–	✓	–

The check sign indicates "support for activity developed in project".

TrustCom was similar to MaBE in that it also focused on the infrastructural support for virtual organizations, but software agents were not the main implementing technology. Instead TrustCom contributed to security, contract management and software support for maintaining trust and creating stable support infrastructures. It focused on issues of middleware rather than on team formation and community maintenance, with main contributions enabling the infrastructure integration and supporting the stable operation of a VE.

CrossWork aims at supporting the entire life cycle of a VE. In doing so, it provides extensive support for both formation and operation stages of a VE. For the formation stage, a community of potential VE partners is maintained in a knowledge base. From this knowledge base, team members can be selected in a team composition process. The integration of local processes of team members into a global process is explicitly covered by CrossWork. Also, the project aims at linking the infrastructures of team members, both with respect to process execution and with respect to coupling of back-end (legacy) systems. Given the linked infrastructure, operation of the VE is supported in a strongly process-oriented fashion, using a combination of a VE-level infrastructure and the infrastructures of the members of the VE. CrossWork is, however, not explicitly geared towards run-time evolution of a VE. It does provide ample flexibility in designing a VE during the formation stage (even with backtracking in formation steps), but after the formation stage, a VE is considered stable. Dissolution of a VE is supported implicitly only in CrossWork; in the project, dissolution is coupled to completing process execution.

CrossWork is clearly an ambitious undertaking – automating workflow design has not been done at the time of undertaking the project and writing this book.

2.5 CrossWork Summary

CrossWork was created with a clear remit of bringing the vision of IVE closer to reality. Initially it targeted the automotive sector since the trends described in Chapter 1 are clearly at play there, and the need to support SMEs and make them competitive is very strong. Indeed, the need to support SMEs is greater since they need collaborative networks to deal with the complexity of contemporary products.

CrossWork has set an ambitious goal requiring new theoretical results as well as advanced development work. It aims to create the software necessary for automatic design of virtual enterprises and composing the workflow, which will execute their cross-organizational business processes on the run.

- Effective team formation requires autonomous reasoning, automating this means using software agents.
- Effective coordination of activities requires workflow models.
- Both raise issues of interoperability.
- Deployment is facilitated by service-based infrastructure.

The CrossWork consortium was designed to integrate scientific know-how with user experience and system development excellence. It builds on two main previous projects: CrossFlow and MaBE.

References

1. Afsarmanesh, H., Camarinha-Matos, L. M., A Framework for Management of Virtual Organizations Breeding Environments in Collaborative Networks and their Breeding Environments, Springer, New York, pp. 35–48, 2005.
2. Alonso, G., Hagen, C., Schek, H. J., Tresch, M., Distributed Processing Over Stand-Alone Systems and Applications, Proceedings of the 23rd International Conference on Very Large Databases, Athens, Greece, pp. 575–579, 1997.
3. Alonso, G., Fiedler, U., Hagen, C., Lazcano, A., Schuldt, H., Weiler, N., WISE: Business to Business E-Commerce, Proceedings of the 9th International Workshop on Research Issues on Data Engineering, Sydney, Australia, pp. 132–139, 1999.
4. Camarinha-Matos, L. M., Afsarmanesh, H., Elements of a Base VE Infrastructure, Computers in Industry, Vol. 51(2), pp. 139–163, 2003.
5. Grefen, P., Aberer, K., Hoffner, Y., Ludwig, H., CrossFlow: Cross-Organizational Workflow Management in Dynamic Virtual Enterprises, International Journal of Computer Systems Science and Engineering, Vol. 15(5), pp. 277–290, 2000.
6. Hoffner, Y., Ludwig, H., Gülcü, C., Grefen, P., Architecture for Cross-Organisational Business Processes, Proceedings of the 2nd International Workshop on Advanced Issues of E-Commerce and Web-Based Information Systems, pp. 2–11, Milpitas, CA, USA, 2000.
7. Hoffner, Y., Field, S., Grefen, P., Ludwig, H., Contract Driven Creation and Operation of Virtual Enterprises, Computer Networks, Vol. 37(2), pp. 111–136, 2001.
8. Karageorgos, A., Mehandjiev, N., Weichhart, G., Hämmerle, A., Agent-Based Optimisation of Logistics and Production Planning, Engineering Applications of Artificial Intelligence, Vol. 16, pp. 335–348, 2003.
9. Koetsier, M., Grefen, P., Vonk, J., Contracts for Cross-Organizational Workflow Management, Proceedings of the 1st International Conference on Electronic Commerce and Web Technologies, pp. 110–121, London, UK, 2000.

References

Part II
Business, Organization and Architecture

Chapter 3
Business Aspect

Nikolay Mehandjiev, Paul Grefen, Kurt Fessl, Wolfgang Bittner, and Santi Ristol

This chapter discusses the business requirements of technology to be developed in support of VEs. It first describes new business directions that have come into existence in the manufacturing industry like the automotive domain. Next, it treats new criteria that have to be met by industries to become or remain successful in new market situations. Finally, new business structures are discussed that (have to) emerge as a consequence of the new directions and criteria.

3.1 New Business Directions

To succeed under the competing market forces discussed in Chapter 1, businesses need to develop strategies delivering cost-effective market advantage based on low costs and guaranteed standards of quality. Figure 3.1 (copied from Chapter 1 for convenience) shows the conflicting nature of changes in product complexity and accelerating change.

Indeed, Galbraith [4] highlights Speed and Change as two of his "Organization Shapers", forces which shape the contemporary organization. The other four are Buyer Power, Variety and Solutions, the Internet and Multiple Dimensions. Out of these four, we focus on the Buyer Power, since it has given rise to several influential trends in recent years.

One of the most vivid examples of such a trend is found in the domain of automotive manufacturing, where OEMs are attempting to simplify supply chains by dealing with fewer providers of larger systems, as shown in the MAN case study in Chapter 11. The general supply chain shape of the automotive industry is shown in Fig. 3.2. It is often seen as a pyramid with the OEM (Original Equipment Manufacturer – e.g. BMW) on top. The OEM assembles cars by putting systems like the cockpit, motor, etc. together. These systems are manufactured by Tier 1 suppliers which get the components from Tier 2 suppliers.

N. Mehandjiev (✉)
University of Manchester, Manchester, UK
e-mail: n.mehandjiev@manchester.ac.uk

N. Mehandjiev, P. Grefen (eds.), *Dynamic Business Process Formation for Instant Virtual Enterprises*, Advanced Information and Knowledge Processing,
DOI 10.1007/978-1-84882-691-5_3, © Springer-Verlag London Limited 2010

Fig. 3.1 Contemporary
forces in product and market
development

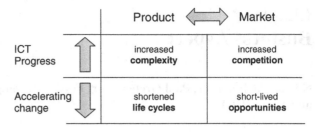

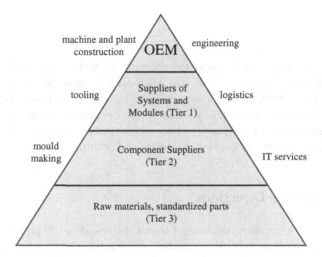

Fig. 3.2 General setup in automotive manufacturing

This is an idealized description, since the OEMs do not actually interact with Tier 1 suppliers only, but also with many suppliers from the lower tiers, providing some components which are part of the final assembly at the OEM.

The increased competition and the importance of variety and configurability cause OEMs to move towards the idealized situation where they are outsourcing more and more of their activities to Tier 1 suppliers. In the process they are reducing their interactions with suppliers from the lower tiers, and only dealing with Tier 1 suppliers. This trend is illustrated in Fig. 3.3.

Because the OEMs are Buyers in relation to the Tier 1 and Tier 2 companies and exercise their Buyer Power, proximity to them is seen as vital in the long term for the automotive manufacturers at all levels. This has the effect of increasing both competition and the complexity of the systems delivered by the "chosen few" suppliers. Becoming one of these "chosen few" is hardly feasible for an SME, since it requires an ever-increasing level of up-front investment.

One way to reduce these up-front investment costs is to share them with a set of peer companies, each company specializing in a narrow area of technology and the set of companies acting as a single VE. This solution addresses the "increased complexity" dimension in Fig. 3.1, yet the current timescales involved in setting up

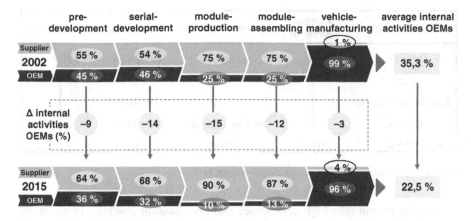

Fig. 3.3 Shift of activities from OEM to suppliers (taken from [6])

a VE are too long. This has negative effect on the company's ability to successfully address the "shortening of the life cycles" and the "decreasing windows of opportunity" dimensions of the matrix.

> There are thus two trends, which pull in opposite directions: Increased complexity and costs stimulate the *formation of VEs*, whilst the need to ensure agility and rapid reaction to business opportunities implies *delegating control and flattening communication and decision-making structures*. The formation of a VE is delaying the addressing of a new market opportunity compared to the swift reaction possible within a single company, so we need to speed up the creation of flatter and more agile enterprises.

3.1.1 Formation of Virtual Enterprises

VEs combine expertise by specialized companies, but forming them is comparatively slow and costly to set up under the current state of practice. The costs of setting up and operating a set of carefully designed collaboration patterns, processes and rules to coordinate the work of independent companies can reverse the cost–benefit equation of setting up a VE. To alleviate the negative effects of these "transaction" costs, we can automate the search for new partners and coordinating their work, making these two activities both faster and cheaper in an IVE.

The type of inter-organizational integration which is appropriate for a VE is determined from the strength of the coordination and the degree of dependence between the VE participants, as visualized in Fig. 3.4. This is used by Galbraith [4] to determine the appropriate type of relationship (from market-based interaction to outright ownership) for a VE.

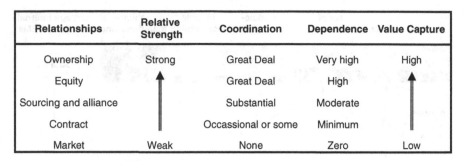

Relationships	Relative Strength	Coordination	Dependence	Value Capture
Ownership	Strong	Great Deal	Very high	High
Equity		Great Deal	High	
Sourcing and alliance		Substantial	Moderate	
Contract		Occassional or some	Minimum	
Market	Weak	None	Zero	Low

Fig. 3.4 Virtual corporation relationships (taken from [4])

Keeping in mind the high dependence and coordination observed in the cooperative work of VE partners, we can see that the appropriate type of relationship would be sourcing and alliance for the central core of companies, or contract-based collaboration for companies at the periphery of the VE.

To determine if forming a VE would be preferable to other means of achieving the same output, for example one company purchasing another, we need to model the balance between costs and benefits as a function of the expected duration of the opportunity to supply the output to the markets. Companies may indeed join forces by one of them buying the other one, thus establishing the "ownership" relation. Setting this up is a longer-term process, which is not easily reversible, yet it results in a better integration without inter-organizational transaction costs. At the other extreme, market-based interactions and contract-based relations are geared towards shorter-term partnerships and opportunities, yet they are characterized with fairly high transaction costs.

3.1.2 Delegation of Control

To speed up decision making, control and decisions should be delegated further down the control hierarchy. The idea is that individuals or companies who are closer to the work being performed and the problems being faced can be empowered to make decisions without engaging in long communications with people or organizations at the higher levels of the control hierarchy. At the same time we need to ensure consistency of any local decisions with overall strategic goals of the company. IT support can help to speed up communications, or it can be used to check consistency of local decisions with global policies.

The effects of IT support on facilitating communication and coordination activities across VE partners have been a subject of academic discourse for a while now, for example, the work of MIT on coordination [7]. Reducing coordination costs and barriers to effective inter-organizational transactions is expected to favour the shift to flatter coordination structures, for example, moving to electronic markets and away from hierarchical forms of organization. Naturally these effects are moderated by the attributes of the target service or product to be delivered by the VE, and complex products with highly specific means of production (machines and conveyor belts for automobiles) are unsuitable for market-based coordination.

The developments in IT support for cross-organizational transactions and coordination activities would influence decisions about the architecture of an IVE. The results indicate an overall move to flatter, peer-to-peer communication and coordination structures to increase agility and speed up VE setting up and evolution.

> New market conditions and increased product complexity demand collaborative business networks and models with delegated control. This is of particular relevance to SMEs, which by nature need collaborative networks to deal with the complexity of contemporary products.

3.2 New Business Criteria

The business forces described above inform the current trends in business strategy and organizational structures by setting high requirements towards the company's *effectiveness* and *efficiency*.

In terms of *effectiveness*, companies are expected to become global players by increasing their geographical reach and to continuously explore new opportunities and market niches by developing new product lines and new service offerings. Small and medium companies aim to establish themselves as the provider of choice in a particular market niche, whilst larger enterprises aim to capture market segments. A key element of this is maintaining constantly high standards of quality. In certain industry, achieving high quality standards is not only the best guarantee of continuous return custom, but also a basic qualifying parameter – those who do not maintain the highest quality will be replaced as supply chain partners.

In terms of efficiency, companies are expected to reduce their overall production and service delivery costs and also their reaction times to market changes. If companies succeed in increasing their throughput whilst keeping the product or service quality at a high level and their fixed costs stable, this will result in reducing of the "per unit" production costs and in competitive advantage for the company when larger quantities are required along the supply chain.

We now expand each of these in turn, and conclude by reviewing the role IT can play in supporting the achievement of these new business criteria.

3.2.1 Effectiveness Requirements

The following requirements for success have been formulated in relation to the automotive industry [2, 3], yet their relevance to the more general domain of manufacturing and even services is also quite clear:

- OEMs are opening production facilities across the globe, their suppliers also need to follow in the pursuit of well-coordinated supply networks and the search for new market coverage.
- Innovative products and services are required, which should be tuned to the needs of the target customer segments. The innovation can come from the OEM as the head of the supply chain, or it may also emerge from the suppliers proposing new materials and innovative combinations of functionality at system level.
- The role of suppliers is changing since they are asked to manage their part of the supply chain, including the integration and testing of sub-components plus organizing the logistics to the OEM. Suppliers need to increasingly develop new capabilities to satisfy the new competence requirements.
- We need to maximize the visibility and common understanding of partners about the state of the overall work and business processes.
- Companies need to maintain high quality standards in order to participate in the contemporary manufacturing supply chains, with very high accuracy and reliability parameters and documented quality processes.

Overall, the developments point at increasing requirements to Tier 1 and Tier 2 suppliers in terms of developing new competences and opening up new facilities, whilst having to compete on costs under strict quality thresholds. It is thus no surprise that suppliers seek collaborations within VEs to address these requirements. In creating these new business partnerships, the dimensions of collaboration and trust are becoming increasingly important [10].

3.2.2 Efficiency Requirements

In addition to the requirements for developing new capabilities and undertaking new responsibilities, suppliers are also expected to reduce their production costs and to establish processes allowing them to shorten their reaction times to market changes.

- Minimizing the production costs should not adversely impact maintaining the quality of production.
- Indeed, suppliers are expected to deliver best results with the lowest possible cost, and this means gathering a team of sub-suppliers, which is optimized in terms of complementarity, effectiveness and costs of services.
- Speeding up the response to market changes means we should minimize the setup time for a partnership to underpin a dynamic virtual enterprise.
- Increasing the agility and decreasing operation costs both require devolving of decision making and minimizing inter-organizational synchronization during enactment to reduce coordination overheads and transaction costs.

In conclusion, if a company succeeds in increasing their throughput whilst keeping the product or service quality at a high level and their fixed costs stable, this results in reducing the "per unit" production costs and in competitive advantage for the company when larger quantities are required along the supply chain.

3.2.3 The Role of IT

IT has a clear role in addressing the effectiveness and efficiency requirements above, in terms of supporting operational efficiency, seamless communication and the systematic formation and evolution of VEs. Overall, the following factors are amongst those known to have contributed to successful collaborative relationships [10]:

- Innovative business models involving profit sharing between collaborating organizations;
- End-to-end visibility of mutually agreed performance objectives;
- Open communication between and within partners in terms of continuous performance review and process optimization;
- Joint planning and business systems supported by transparency in information access.

IT can support innovative business models by streamlining communication and enabling close relationships with customers and their precise profiling. It also allows VE participants to explore alternative configurations of processes and logistic dependencies using simulation and optimization techniques.

In terms of visibility and communication, the role of IT in supporting the flow of data and measurement information is well accepted given appropriate safeguarding of business-sensitive data. IT advances in the area of service computing and e-business platforms also enable the establishment of joint planning and business control systems, providing transparency of information across the VE.

To summarize, the role of IT for success is evident, through supporting free flow of information, visibility and collaborative planning of business activities. IT can also support systematic exploration of novel team and process configurations and the testing of innovative business models.

> The new business requirements of improved effectiveness and increased efficiency inform the need to use IT in supporting the planning, formation and operation of VEs. Such support should ensure fast and systematic VE formation to increase the number of market opportunities a company may explore in a short period of time.

3.3 New Business Structures

Realizing an IVE depends upon, and also suggests, certain innovations in business structures. These are motivated by the partnering strategy and choice of external

links [4]. We observe three main new structures in the field we are addressing: dynamic partner selection, contract-driven partnerships and multi-tier business
design. We discuss each of these below.

3.3.1 Dynamic Partner Selection

Traditionally, VEs have a more or less stable character over time – partnering is
static in the sense that it takes place between fixed sets of organizations under
conditions stated in long-term contracts. In modern e-business settings, however,
organizations have to shift their priority to flexibility and ability to change if they
want to survive [8]. In a market, players and competitive situations change fast.
Adaptation to change is crucial, not only in the internal organization of a business
entity, but also in the choice of collaboration partners. In this context, we see the
emergence of dynamic virtual markets (or dynamic digital markets), in which partners are selected for short to medium timescale collaboration [9]. Consequently, a
highly dynamic approach is required to VE formation in order to create or retain
a competitive position for a commercial organization. This means that the business goals at the moment of setting up a business collaboration determine which
partners to use in the enactment of the business processes, so that those goals
can be acheived. We call this dynamic virtual enterprise creation, leading to IVEs.
This paradigm implies dynamic selection, contracting, coupling and executing of
business processes of the selected partners.

The dynamic VE creation implies that many more tasks need to be performed
with respect to business setup than in the "old-fashioned" static VE case; this is
for two reasons. Obviously, the setup stage is performed more frequently – possibly
much more frequently depending on market circumstances. But, the setup stage also
needs to be more explicit; as collaborations become more flexible, organizations
can rely less on pre-established knowledge of their partners. This means that the
information exchanged and processed in the setup stage must be more self-contained
than in a static virtual enterprise context. Both effects lead to a more demanding
setup stage that has to be completed faster. Hence, there is a clear need for automated
support for this stage.

Often, the dynamic selection of partners presumes the presence of a special
"association" of companies, where skill sets are formally specified and communication between members is encouraged by workshops. The Automotive Association of
Upper Austria, for example, sets up workshops amongst its members – SMEs from
Upper Austria that supply automotive parts and systems to larger manufacturers and
Tier 1 suppliers. In its approach to this from 2004, for example, the Automotive
Association facilitated the formation of consortia by analysing requests for quotations provided by OEMs, shortlisting candidate SMEs and selecting a "system
integrator" organization. This organization will then gather suppliers in a workshop
so that the details of such a quote can be organized and the list of companies to be
involved in the quote can be finalized.

3.3.2 Contract-Driven Partnerships

As we have seen above, dynamic setup of VEs implies explicit, self-contained setup of partnerships. The partnerships need to be described precisely, not only in operational terms, but also in business and legal terms. The operational terms specify what has to be done when (and possibly how). The business and legal terms specify the conditions under which the operational aspects are performed. To obtain this complete specification, contracts are used as the basis for the partnerships. In other words, they drive the execution of a partnership.

An example of contract-driven partnership is when an organization outsources one of its functions, for example, the cleaning function [4]. The activities of the cleaning contractors can be specified precisely, and since the time periods are often disjoint, there is no need for close operational coordination of activities between the client organization and the cleaning organization. The contract provides a clear and formal basis for the partnership and allows the organization providing cleaning services to be continuously assessed and replaced, if necessary. This example is paper-driven, yet the speed of setting up contemporary VEs means that we cannot rely on traditional, paper-based contracts that are established between lawyers of the involved organizations; this would imply both too much throughput time and far too high costs. Therefore, we have to take a turn to electronic contracting, which offers both contracts in digital form as well as (partly) automated processes for establishing contracts [1].

Electronic contracting, or e-contracting in short, provides several paradigms to allow fast contracting, cheap contracting, precision contracting and enactment contracting [5]. Fast contracting allows the formation of just-in-time virtual enterprises. Cheap contracting allows the establishment (and disposal) of large numbers of contractual relationships (such as virtual enterprises) without much contracting overhead in terms of costs. Precision contracting is required when contracts do indeed become more complex because of the fact that they need to be completely self-contained. Enactment contracting does not only support establishing a contract by automated means, but also provides automated means for the subsequent enactment of that contract based on the operational information contained in it.

In an example from the automotive industry, Magna Intier manages relationships with its numerous suppliers using specially assigned procurement managers and strict contracts embedded in project definitions. When a business opportunity appears, Magna advertises it to its own branches and to external suppliers, and the responses are considered on their merit and match to the specifications.

3.3.3 Multi-tier Business Design

Contemporary products are often so complex that they cannot be produced by a single organization, but require a complex supply chain structure. In this structure, we can often observe multiple business tiers. Each tier is responsible for a part of the overall production process, may get input from a lower tier and supplies output to a higher tier.

The nature of the target product to be produced (i.e. its structure and functionality) determines the structure of its manufacturer. The business structure in the automotive industry shown in Section 3.1 can be matched to the structure of the car as the final product – OEMs manufacture cars, Tier 1 suppliers manufacture car subsystems and suppliers of Tiers 2 and 3 manufacture the components of subsystems.

One contemporary trend in this area referred to earlier is driven by the "Buyer Power" factor shaping this multi-layer business design. In the automotive industry, OEMs such as MAN are trying to reduce the interactions they have with Tier 2 and 3 suppliers by redesigning the processes in their supply chains. Tier 1 suppliers are made responsible for a complete subsystem; so they do not only assemble the subsystem but are also responsible for the supply chain feeding their production, including selection and even training of suppliers, organizing the logistics, etc. To achieve this, MAN runs supplier development workshops, where the skills of Tier 1 and Tier 2 suppliers are analysed, improvement actions are identified and supply chain processes are redesigned to accommodate the new organizational shape.

3.3.4 Integrating the Three Principles

The dynamic partnering and contract-driven partnership principles are illustrated in Fig. 3.5, which introduces the concept of a "role". A role is a set of responsibilities and obligations within an organization, which requires a number of competences (skills). A role acts as a placeholder, and is used to implement dynamic partner selection by matching the competences required by a role with the competences of potential candidate organizations. The main two types of roles are supplier and integrator [4].

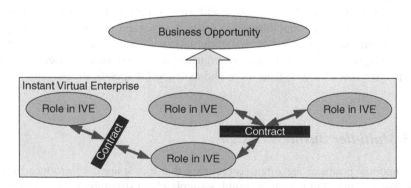

Fig. 3.5 Designing IVE as a network of roles and contracts to ensure flexibility

The figure 3.5 also illustrates the organizing role of the contracts in implementing IVEs. Contracts determine inter-role interactions and thus define material dependencies and communication routes through the organization. In principle, IVEs can be formed at multiple levels of a multi-tier business structure as outlined in the third principle above. In that case, an "upper-level" IVE may provide a business opportunity for a "lower-level" IVE.

> The target product determines the business structure, and the speed of operations allows partners to be selected at the point of need.

3.4 New Business Forms for the New Business World

The new business environment motivates trends of increased organizational agility and devolution in decision making. It also stipulates a number of effectiveness and efficiency criteria, which can be addressed by the use of IT systems to facilitate operations and communications (better flow of information, visibility across the supply chain), and also the design and formation of a virtual organization.

These trends and success factors give rise to three new business structures: dynamic selection of partners; contract-driven partnerships and multi-tier business design. In our interactions with companies within the automotive domain, we have observed the emergence of these new business structures and the importance of IT-based support for their effective and efficient operation.

> New market conditions and increased product complexity demand collaborative business networks with delegated control. This is more so for SMEs, which by nature need collaborative networks to deal with the complexity of contemporary products.
>
> VEs emerge to deal with these challenges. To increase the number of market opportunities a company may explore and use in a short period of time, VEs must be formed faster, better and with less human intervention.

References

1. Angelov, S., Foundations of B2B Electronic Contracting, Dissertation, Technology University Eindhoven, Faculty of Technology Management, Information Systems Department, 2006.
2. Billington, J., Christensen, S., Hee, K. V., Kindler, E., Kummer, O., Petrucci, L., Post, R., Stehno, C., Weber, M., The Petri Net Markup Language: Concepts, Technology, and Tools, Proceedings of the 24th International Conference on Applications and Theory of Petri Nets (ICATPN), pp. 483–505, Eindhoven, The Netherlands, June 23–27, 2003.

3. Dudenhöffer, F., Automobil-Zulieferer im Wachstumsstreß, in GAK: Gummi, Fasern, Kunststoffe, Vol. 55, Jg., Heft 1, pp. 16–19, 2002.
4. Galbraith, J. R., Designing Organizations, Wiley, New York, 2002.
5. Grefen, P., Angelov, S., On τ-, μ-, π-, and $\acute{\epsilon}$-Contracting, Proceedings of the CAiSE Workshop on Web Services, e-Business and the Semantic Web, Toronto, Canada, 27–28 May, 2002.
6. Kurek, R., Erfolgreiche Strategien für Automobilzulieferer, Springer, Berlin, 2004.
7. Malone, T. W., Yates, J., Benjamin, R. I., Electronic Markets and Electronic Hierarchies, Communication of ACM, Vol. 30(6), June, 1987.
8. Pieper, R., Kouwenhoven, V., Hamminga, S., Beyond the Hype – e-Business Strategy in Leading European Companies, Van Haren Publishing, Zaltbommel, 2001.
9. Timmers, P., Electronic Commerce – Strategies and Models for Business-to-Business Trading, John Wiley & Sons, New York, 1999.
10. Wilding, R., Playing the Tune of Shared Success in Undertaking Collaboration, FT, 8th November, 2006.

Chapter 4
Organization Aspect

Paul Grefen and Nikolay Mehandjiev

Following the BOAT framework discussed in Chapter 1, this chapter describes the organization aspect of the CrossWork approach. It shows how the business requirements identified in the previous chapter can be fulfilled by dynamic organization structures and business processes in Networks of Automotive Excellence (NoAE). It explains why business processes require explicit attention, i.e. why business process engineering is the pivotal point around which modern business management rotates. Next, based on the observations in Chapter 3, the chapter zooms in on processes for the formation of instant virtual enterprises and for their enactment (execution).

4.1 Explicit Business Process Management

To make an IVE work, explicit business process management is required across the boundaries of the members of that IVE. As the IVE is distributed across multiple autonomous parties, visibility of process definitions (work structure) and process status (work progress) is important. As other parties in the IVE are doing work which enables your own processes to start, and since the final deliverable is time-critical, you cannot afford to start late. Visibility also delivers trust and allows companies to choose new partners. Based on inter-organizational process visibility, we require explicit enactment of the IVE processes. Explicit enactment makes sure deadlines are met or exceptions are raised and relevant parties are notified. The way visibility and enactment are organized is defined in contracts, which provide the formal business relation between IVE partners. Contracts make the performance and quality promises of your partners explicit, as well as the penalty they promise to pay if these are not met. We therefore have the following features of explicit business process management:

P. Grefen (✉)
Eindhoven University of Technology, Eindhoven, The Netherlands
e-mail: p.w.p.j.grefen@tue.nl

N. Mehandjiev, P. Grefen (eds.), *Dynamic Business Process Formation for Instant Virtual Enterprises*, Advanced Information and Knowledge Processing,
DOI 10.1007/978-1-84882-691-5_4, © Springer-Verlag London Limited 2010

- *Contracts:* as a basis for shared understanding and agreement to cooperate;
- *Enactment:* a powerful tool for coordinating work;
- *Visibility:* in support for decision making and participation.

Contracts provide a basis of explicit business process management as they can define not only *what* is exchanged between business partners, but also *how* this exchange is organized, i.e. what processes are to be enacted. To achieve this, contracts can contain explicit references to process models or the process models themselves. The use of electronic contracts can keep the costs of contracting low – both in terms of money and time [2, 8]. Contracts containing process models have, for example, been used in the CrossFlow project [7], where electronic contracts define process-oriented, dynamic service outsourcing relationships between organizations. Cases elaborated in this project are the outsourcing of logistic processes in a telecom setting and damage assessment processes in an insurance setting. In both cases, explicit contracts are the basis for creating the outsourcing relationship with minimal delay and costs. This contracting approach has been further elaborated in the 4 W framework, which distinguishes the What, Who, Where and hoW aspects of electronic contracts [1, 2].

Enactment of processes is used as an instrument of coordinating work under a distributed organizational structure with delegated control. Explicit enactment of business processes allows the synchronization of distributed activities and has the potential of speeding up processes and decreasing the coordination overhead of a virtual enterprise. In one example, a bank reduced the time necessary to add a new merchant to its own label credit card system from weeks to a day [3]. In the CrossFlow logistics and insurance cases [7], automated enactment of processes across the boundaries of the organizations in the outsourcing relationship leads to a high level of efficiency in operations management. On the one hand, this enables fast completion of inter-organizational processes. On the other hand, this allows the handling of a large number of concurrent processes and thereby the establishment of many outsourcing relationships, each optimized to the context at hand.

Visibility of processes and their status provides a powerful instrument for businesses to explicitly collaborate in a tightly linked (i.e. process-oriented) fashion. It also allows them to assert and monitor their compliance to the plethora of process-based standards, for example the European Union's Markets in Financial Instruments Directive (MiFID) in the financial industry. In the health service sector, for example, the UK Government targets demand that no more than 18 weeks elapse between first referral and the start of treatment. University College London Hospitals installed an explicit process-based monitoring system to alert decision makers of any cases which break this rule [3]. Clearly, in an inter-organizational setting, the visibility of processes to the outside world must be chosen with care, such that no sensitive information is disclosed and no unnecessary information (noise) is provided. The use of well-defined process views [5] is a way to achieve this.

The Instant Virtual Enterprise requires visibility, monitoring and control of business processes across organizational boundaries.

4.2 Formation of Virtual Enterprises

The process of forming a VE follows a set of steps, which have different formulations in different studies. A good reference list of the steps is formulated in Deliverable 23.1 of the Ecolead project [6], a European research project looking specifically at the topic of forming VEs:

1. Collaboration Opportunity Identification
2. Draft VE Planning
3. Partner search and selection
4. VE Composition and Negotiation
5. Detailed VE Planning
6. Contracting
7. VE Set up

Step 1 is equivalent to the "Identification" stage of our model presented in Fig. 2.2, whilst the other six steps are equivalent to the "Formation" stage of our model.

To provide software support for these processes, we need to analyse the activities in each step and identify core concepts, which would then serve as cornerstones for our information structures underpinning automated search and composition mechanisms. Two core concepts are that of *team* and *role*, which are intrinsically linked to the concepts of *goal* and *actor*. Steps 1–3 from the list above construct a VE from a *goal*, by producing an ideal *team* comprising a set of abstract *roles*, and then filling these abstract roles with appropriate *actors*. Once the concrete actors are recruited for each role, a process of detailed negotiation of cooperation processes and mechanisms can commence, which will produce contract-governed cross-organizational network.

Figure 3.5 in the previous chapter provides a high-level view of a VE as a network of roles connected by contracts. This idea is extended in Fig. 4.1 to show the association of actors with roles, and the fact that this association brings into the frame a set of concepts associated with an actor as an independent (autonomous) entity. Indeed, an actor will have a set of aims, which would contain both aims associated with their participation in the VE and aims which may be in conflict with this participation. An interesting example is the appearance of "co-opetition" as a business practice, where competitors join forces in development or even production. For example, VW and Ford designed jointly their MPV platform, which was then produced and marketed as VW Sharan, Ford Galaxy and Seat Alhambra. Recently, Ford and Fiat will share a factory in Tychy, Poland, where the new Ka and the Fiat's 500 model will both be made [9]. In an example outside automotive production, Heineken and Diageo have jointly developed a brewery in Africa to manufacture their competing brands Heineken and Amstel.

The role in a VE will be consonant with the aims of a particular actor playing this role. Roles can be divided into two basic role types: supplier and coordinator. The qualifications required for playing the role will be matched to the actor's capabilities, which will in turn be determined by their internal processes

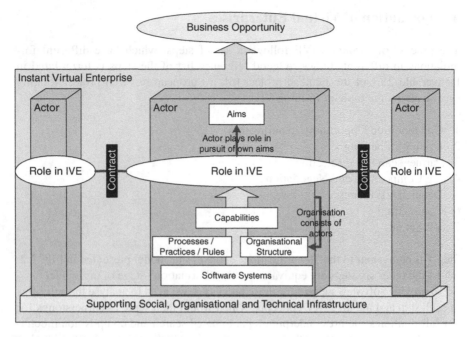

Fig. 4.1 Appointing actors to fulfil roles in the IVE

and their organizational structures. The actors will also have internal software systems supporting their operations, and effective integration of business processes should include integration of information and eventually integration of the supporting software systems. The creation of a VE is thus closely related with issues of interoperability at the following levels [4]:

- *Goal Level*: alignment of goals organizations have in relation to the VE;
- *Process Level*: alignment of internal processes and their coordination through an inter-organizational process, supported by workflow coordination;
- *Semantic Level*: alignment of concepts and terminology across organizations;
- *System Level*: alignment of software systems of partners to accommodate inter-operation between them.

Having seen the core concepts and their relationships, a closer look is warranted into the processes involved in the formation of the team. Fig. 2.3 has illustrated the decomposition of the formation process into five core steps: maintain a community, compose a team, integrate processes, link infrastructure and activate IVE. Of these, we focus on the second and third step, which are expanded in Figs. 4.2 and 4.3.

The process of composing a team, shown in Fig. 4.2, contains five steps: *Analyse Opportunity*, *Consider General IVE rules*, *Create an Abstract IVE*, *Match Members to Requirements* and *Evaluate Choices*. Analyse opportunity provides a set of goals and aims which should be fulfilled by the roles and their relationships. After considering general rules for forming an IVE, such as guarantees of governance

Fig. 4.2 The activities
involved in developing a team

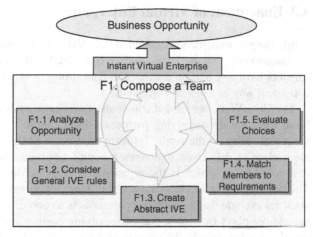

Fig. 4.3 Activities involved
in integrating processes

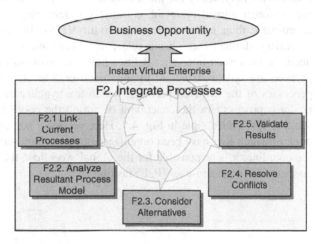

and accountability, we can proceed to create an abstract IVE, comprising roles and contracts linking these roles in the context of a set of aims. We can then proceed to match candidate members' capabilities to the skills required by each role. The interdependencies between possible allocations of actors to roles would constrain the space of possibilities, and alternative assignments will be evaluated in the fifth step. Figure 4.3 shows details of integrating processes, which comprise the steps of linking existing processes, analysing the resultant process model, considering alternatives, resolving any conflicts and validating the results.

Starting from the requirement for product-driven team structure and dynamic selection of partners described in Chapter 3, we have designed a mechanism and process, which allows these requirements to be fulfilled by a software system in an effective and efficient manner.

4.3 Enactment of Virtual Enterprises

While the previous section explained how VEs can be formed, this still leaves open the question of how the VE should be organized in its operation. In particular, the partners have to agree on a way of collaborating in order to act in a coherent and consistent way as a virtual enterprise.

For CrossWork, we have distinguished two basic roles in the operation of a VE. First, there are the supplying partners, which can be considered as the organizations that really do the work. Typically, these are SMEs that are not large enough themselves to deliver on their own a complete product to a client. Second, there is a coordinator, which is the organization responsible for the work undertaken. The coordinator merely coordinates and does not do anything itself. Note that this does not exclude that a supplying partner acts as coordinator. In that case, the partner simply plays two roles: one of supplying partner and one of coordinator. The coordinator is typically the main contractor of the VE, as is the party with whom the customer agreed upon the contract for delivering a product or service. The coordinator, then, is also the interface to the VE for the customer.

Having defined these basic roles, an organizational communication structure needs to be agreed upon that defines how the business processes of the involved partners are synchronized. At the organizational level, we have the local business processes of the involved partners, which are synchronized by means of a global business process (for the enactment of which the coordinator is responsible). We see a simplified example in Fig. 4.4. Here we see a market of seven possible partners, of which four have been organized into an instant virtual enterprise. Although the coordinator is responsible for the global workflow, the partners are in principle connected in a peer-to-peer (P2P) fashion.

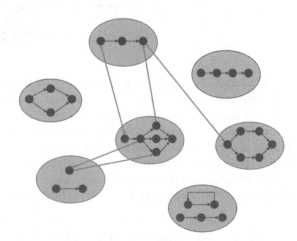

Fig. 4.4 Example of an instant virtual enterprise in a market

Note that this does not mean that a P2P technical implementation is indeed required. As explained in the next chapters, the organizational P2P model of CrossWork is supported by a technical architecture with a hub-and-spoke topology.

The organizational model is thus independent from the technical implementation. There are, however, several requirements that are important for the IT solutions:

- *Cost*: Typically, SMEs have already invested great sums of money in IT infrastructure, which supports them in doing their own local business processes in an efficient way. Given these sunken costs, it is not realistic to expect that organizations will switch to an IT infrastructure that is solely dedicated to B2B collaboration. Also, huge IT investments for a single collaboration are too risky. These considerations lead to the requirement that the IT solution for collaborating with other partner organizations should be of low cost.
- *Time*: VEs are typically short-lived, existing for a single product or single service only. Given this short time span, it is vital that the IT infrastructure supports the operation of a virtual enterprise in a timely way.
- *Flexibility*: VEs operate in dynamic environments, which are fluid and susceptible to change. Consequently, partners can be replaced with other partners, new partners can join. Such changing organizational structures need to be supported by the IT system.
- *Privacy*: Each partner should be able to shield its internal private details from its co-workers. This way, partners can keep their business secrets to themselves while collaborating with other organizations.
- *Trust*: A VE cannot always be formed with partner organizations that know each other. Some partners can be new to each other. A critical issue then is how well the partners trust each other. Trust can be managed in various ways. For example, organizations can be member of a cluster organization that guarantees the trust level. Or there can be dedicated trust agents that can inform parties about the past performance of organizations.

The above observations have a number of implications for the architecture that is discussed in Chapter 5:

- *Monitoring*: Each partner should inform the VE, so that its partners and the coordinator are aware of the progress made. This way, the global process enactment can be optimized and adapted to changes.
- *Control*: Each partner should allow the VE coordinator to partially control its process.
- *Legacy*: The enactment of a VE should use existing legacy systems of partners as much as possible.

To support SMEs in collaborating with each other in an IVE, a formed IVE needs to be enacted in a fast, cheap and flexible way by means of automated support.

4.4 Processes and Structures in IVEs

In this chapter, we have discussed the organizational aspect of the CrossWork approach. We have seen that formation and enactment of IVEs are the two main overall subprocesses in this approach. The formation subprocess consists of a number of steps that lead to the definition of an IVE. We have also seen that these processes and their underlying organizational structures are of substantial complexity and have many aspects that we need to deal with. One of the main ingredients of an IVE is the specification of its global process, which synchronizes the operation of the participating members. This implies that both formation and enactment of IVEs call for an explicitly process-oriented approach. The information structures that the processes work on contain knowledge about formation and operation of an IVE. This implies that these structures need to be paid explicit attention to also. Concluding, one can say that the CrossWork approach is process-oriented with explicit information (knowledge) structure support.

The processes and structures discussed in this chapter are the basis for the design of the automated system that supports the CrossWork approach. This system needs to be explicitly process-oriented, needs to have information structure support, needs to support both formation and enactment of IVEs, and must comply with all the additional requirements discussed in this chapter (like interoperability of legacy systems). Consequently, the system will have considerable complexity too. The design of the system is elaborated as the architecture of the CrossWork system (which covers the A aspect in the BOAT framework discussed in Chapter 1). This design is discussed in the next chapter, where we will see how a top-down design is used to obtain a modular architecture reflecting the requirements from this chapter.

The new ways of doing business described in the previous chapter require novel organizational structures and processes to implement both business formation and drive business operation. This calls for explicit business process management, product-driven role-based team design and dynamic selection of partners when forming VE.

References

1. Angelov, S., Grefen, P., The 4 W Framework for B2B e-Contracting, International Journal of Networking and Virtual Organisations, Vol. 2(1), pp. 78–97, 2003.
2. Angelov, S., Foundations of B2B Electronic Contracting, Dissertation, Technology University Eindhoven, Faculty of Technology Management, Information Systems Department, 2006.
3. Cane, A., Making Complex Business Simpler, Financial Times, 14th May, 2008.
4. Chen, D., Jaekel, F. W., Li, M. S., Mehandjiev, N., Ruggaber, R., Wilson, M., Zelm, M. Enterprise Interoperability research roadmap: Annex I – Indicative Research Challenges. V4. 31st July 2006. Available from ftp://ftp.cordis.europa.eu/ in the following directory: pub/ist/docs/directorate_d/ebusiness/ei-roadmap-final-annex1_en.pdf last accessed 25th November, 2008.

5. Eshuis, R., Grefen, P., Constructing Customized Process Views, Data and Knowledge Engineering, Vol. 64(2), pp. 419–438, 2008.
6. European Collaborative Networked Organisations Leadership Initiative, ECOLEAD Project, http://ecolead.vtt.fi, 2008.
7. Grefen, P., Aberer, K., Hoffner, Y., Ludwig, H., CrossFlow: Cross-Organizational Workflow Management in Dynamic Virtual Enterprises, International Journal of Computer Systems Science and Engineering, Vol. 15(5), pp. 277–290, 2000.
8. Grefen, P., Angelov, S., On τ-, μ-, π-, and ε-Contracting, Proceedings of the CAiSE Workshop on Web Services, e-Business and the Semantic Web, Toronto, Canada, 27–28 May, 2002.
9. Reed, J., Manufacturers Adapt with Smaller Vehicles, Financial Times, 1st October 2008, Available from www.ft.com, last accessed 20th November, 2008.

Chapter 5
Architecture Aspect

Paul Grefen, Rik Eshuis, Iain Duncan Stalker, and Georgios Kouvas

This chapter discusses the architecture of the CrossWork approach, i.e. it explains the information system structure required for the support of the organizational structures described in the previous chapter. As such it represents a change of direction. Whilst the previous chapters discussed the business and organizational domains, this chapter is concerned with structuring a software system that can support and even automate activities in these domains.

We start this chapter with a brief introduction into the concept of architecture. Then, we discuss the requirements to the CrossWork architecture and its logical design view in two sections. The logical design is the core of this chapter and hence receives most attention. In the next three sections, we move our attention to implementation aspects: software development, technology aspects and mapping to a network topology. In the last section of this chapter, we summarize the main findings and take a look at "automating the instant virtual enterprise".

This chapter provides the bridge between Parts II and III of this book and also supplies enough high-level information about technology so that Part IV can be understood without reading in detail the work presented in Part IV.

5.1 Introduction to Architecture

This section briefly introduces the basic notions of architecture and architecture design in the context of information systems. It provides the conceptual background for the next sections of this chapter.

5.1.1 What Is Architecture?

In the "distant past" (which for information systems means a few decades ago), information systems were usually of limited complexity. They were also of limited

P. Grefen (✉)
Eindhoven University of Technology, Eindhoven, The Netherlands
e-mail: p.w.p.j.grefen@tue.nl

N. Mehandjiev, P. Grefen (eds.), *Dynamic Business Process Formation for Instant Virtual Enterprises*, Advanced Information and Knowledge Processing,
DOI 10.1007/978-1-84882-691-5_5, © Springer-Verlag London Limited 2010

connectivity with respect to other information systems. They typically supported the basic operation of an also limited set of business functions, like general ledger and payroll administration. They were typically connected to other information systems in a very simple way (if at all), often using off-line connections (e.g. using magnetic tape as a transport medium). In the present time, however, individual information systems are of far greater complexity as they support far more aspects of an extended set of business functions. To support end-to-end business processes, they are often connected to a myriad of other information systems, both within the same organization and across organizational boundaries. Individual information systems are arranged into an "information system landscape" – together they form a complex information system (an enterprise information system or even inter-enterprise information system).

To design complex information systems and to support change in existing complex information systems, the concept of *architecture* has emerged in the information system field. An architecture of an information system (or a CIS) can be seen as the high-level, structural blueprint of that system. The concept of architecture of software systems originates from the domain of software engineering, i.e. the field in which the detailed structuring of computer programs is the focus. The following is a definition of the term *architecture* from a well-known book in this domain [13]:

> The architecture of a software system defines that system in terms of computational components and interactions between those components.

In this chapter, we are interested in the structure of a complex information system; the system that supports the establishment and enactment of IVEs (as described in the previous chapters). This means that we don't look at small details of computer programs, but at larger structures of complex systems. The complexity implies that we have to focus on specific aspects of the system, that we have to distinguish between multiple levels and that we need structuring principles to understand the complexity. Hence, we use the following definition of the term architecture [8] (which is an extension of the definition above):

> The architecture of a (complex) information system defines that system in terms of functional components and interactions between those components, from the viewpoint of specific aspects of that system, possibly organized into multiple levels, and based on specific structuring principles.

An information system architecture thus defines the structure of that system in a well-organized manner. We now turn our attention to the process of designing architectures.

5.1.2 Designing Architectures

The architecture of a complex information system usually consists of several views, since a single view to understand a complete system all at once is too complex and too difficult to understand. Each view captures one or more aspects of a system. Therefore, to design an architecture, several views need to be modelled.

Several view-based approaches for designing software architectures exist. A well-excepted standard approach is the 4+1 approach by Kruchten [11], which has been adapted in the Rational Unified Process (RUP). Kruchten proposes the following views [11]:

- *The logical view* specifies the object/module models of the design, i.e. the structure of the application logic in abstract terms;
- *The process view* specifies the concurrency and synchronization aspects of the software design, i.e. the way objects or modules in the logical view dynamically collaborate in parallel;
- *The development view* specifies the organization of the software in development environment, i.e. the way the software development is supported;
- *The physical view* describes the mapping(s) of software onto hardware, thereby reflecting the distribution aspect (what runs where?).

The four views have a temporal relationship indicated by the arrows in Fig. 5.1. The *logical view* defines what the information system does, i.e. its functionality – clearly this is of prime interest to the end users of the system described by the architecture. As such, this is the starting point for an architectural design. From this, the *process* and *development views* can be elaborated, which are succeeded by the design of the *physical view*. Each view has its prime stakeholder type and its major concerns.

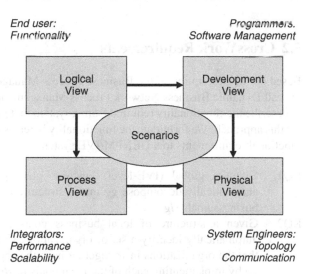

Fig. 5.1 The 4+1 views of Kruchten (taken from [11])

The four basic views are illustrated by the *scenarios* element of the 4+1 framework, which describes a few selected use cases that illustrate the four basic views. The *scenarios* create a concrete platform and a basis for discussions between the various groups of stakeholders in the architectural design or analysis stage. The *scenarios* do not form a fifth view, but complement the other four views (hence the "4+1" indication instead of "5"). In the design of the CrossWork architecture, we have adopted this 4+1 framework as follows:

- The logical view contains the abstract design of the CrossWork system. The design consists of modules and their interactions, and is guided by several structuring principles.
- The process view details the choices we that have been made regarding technology platforms, i.e. the middleware that is used to technically integrate the modules defined in the logical view.
- The development view describes how the software is developed using a software engineering approach suited for building complex prototypes: the empty shell approach. In this approach, first the interfaces of the modules are implemented, and next the application logic for each module is realized.
- The physical view builds on the process view and the development view by detailing how modules are actually deployed in a distributed setting.
- The scenarios are formed by several industrial case studies that have been performed to develop and validate the CrossWork approach.

In the next two sections, we begin the discussion of the design of the CrossWork architecture by focusing on the logical view. We first provide a systematic list of requirements, following the discussion in the previous chapters. These requirements are then used to design the logical structure of the CrossWork architecture.

5.2 CrossWork Requirements

Based on the description of the Business Process Management within IVEs, which we call Dynamic Business Network Process Management (DBNPM), we can begin to describe the functionality required from a system that provides automated support for this approach. We formulate the functionality in terms of the following high-level functional requirements to a DBNPM/IVE system:

RQ1.   Given a global (IVE-level) business goal gg, the system can semi-automatically decompose gg into a structure of local (organization-level) business goals slg.

RQ2.   Given a structure of local business goals slg, the system can semi-automatically identify a set of organizations so in a business market such that the organizations in so together have the capabilities required to reach gg by implementing each of the local goals in slg.

RQ3.   Given a local business goal lg and an organization o, the system can semi-automatically obtain the specification of one or more external level local business processes of o that implement lg.

RQ4.   Given a set of local business processes *slp*, the system can semi-automatically compose the local processes in *slp* into an IVE-level Business Network Process.

RQ5.   Given a Business Network Process *bnp*, the system can validate process execution characteristics of *bnp* without actually enacting it in an IVE, where validation is interactively performed by a business process engineer.

RQ6.   Given a Business Network Process *bnp*, the system can automatically map *bnp* to the distributed DBNPM system of an IVE.

RQ7.   Given a Business Network Process *bnp* mapped onto the DBNPM system *ds* of an IVE, the system can automatically enact *bnp* on *ds*, where enactment includes providing end-user interaction functions and process manager monitoring functions.

RQ8.   In the enactment of a given Business Network Process *bnp*, the DBNPM system facilitates interaction with legacy (back-end) systems of the organizations enacting *bnp*.

Some of the above requirements include the qualification "semi-automatically". The reason for this stems from the fact that fully automatic realization of these requirements is not directly feasible in most situations, as this would require a complete set of domain knowledge that is not available in machine-interpretable format. The system should, however, support the migration of knowledge from a human-oriented format towards a system-oriented format, such that the level of automation can increase as domains become more formalized. This migration takes place in the time scope of a business market (or business domain) life cycle, which typically spans the life cycle of many IVEs operating in that market (or domain). Therefore, we include the following additional requirement:

RQ9.   For those system functions that rely on reasoning on the basis of domain-based knowledge, the system supports accumulation of this knowledge into knowledge stores that can be accessed by automated reasoning mechanisms.

Note that we have not included non-functional requirements in the above discussion. Non-functional aspects do play a role, however, only when dealing with the technical details of system implementation. These are not part of the logical view of the CrossWork architecture, but of the process view (and hence of later concern).

Clearly, the above list of requirements can be further refined to obtain a software requirement specification – this is, however, not in the scope of this chapter. However, we choose to map the high-level requirements to a high-level system architecture. This is discussed in the next section. Functional details following requirements are treated later when discussing the functionality of the software modules in the architecture.

5.3 Logical View of the Architecture

Taking the system requirements identified in the previous section as a basis, we present the design of a conceptual system architecture in this section. As the requirements imply a degree of complexity, a clear design approach is essential to attaining a well-structured architecture. The design approach applied in the remainder of this section consists of two main phases:

1. A general clustering of functionalities is taken as a starting point to arrive at a structure of very-high-level modules;
2. A stepwise refinement of this structure is performed.

The general clustering of functionalities is based on a very abstract separation of concerns. This separation of concerns is not specific to the architecture under design, but is a conceptual tool aimed at obtaining a starting point for an architectural design in which these clusters play major roles. We address this phase in the first subsection below.

The stepwise refinement is based on the result of the first phase and the requirements identified in the previous section. We show three refinement steps in this chapter – a more detailed picture is presented in [6]. In the refinement steps, we apply well-accepted design principles in the form of architecture levels [8] and architecture patterns [4]. The refinement steps are presented in the following subsections.

5.3.1 Step 1: Defining High-Level Architectural Blocks

As discussed above, we begin the architecture design with a high-level functional separation of concerns, which provides a basis for an overall clustering of functionality. Such a separation of concerns can be achieved through the application of an interrogative-based clustering of issues. This approach has been successfully applied in the well-known Zachman framework [15].

Like Zachman, we use an interrogative-based separation of concerns. We apply the following simple approach with four interrogatives:

- *What* is the operationalized goal of the IVE, e.g. what products need to be produced?
- *Who*, i.e. which organizations can together form this IVE?
- *How*, i.e. through which business process(es) can this IVE attain the operationalized goal?
- *With* what automated infrastructure can this business process be enacted?

Strictly, *With* is not a true interrogative but rather paraphrases *How*. Nevertheless, it is useful since it enables us to distinguish between *How* as a process and *How* as a means. We shall refer to the above as the four interrogatives.

Note that our four interrogatives have a close relation to the four interrogatives presented in the Zachman Framework [15]. Zachman also uses *What, Who* and *How*. Our *With* interrogative can be related to Zachman's *Where*. The additional interrogatives, *Why* and *When*, do not feature explicitly in the architectural design. The motivation for the formation of an IVE, i.e. the business opportunity, constitutes the *Why*. The *When* is dealt with directly within the processes and their synchronization. Also note that we do not distinguish explicitly between stakeholder groups as Zachman does in his second dimension.

The functional clusters related to the four interrogatives correspond to four consecutive phases in the formation and enactment of an IVE. The fact that we have consecutive phases leads to the observation that the functional clusters should be embedded into a *pipe and filter* architecture pattern [4]. This leads to the architecture shown in Fig. 5.2. In this figure, we see that the creation of an IVE starts with a goal specification (specified by a client organization), which triggers a pipeline of four software modules, corresponding with the four interrogatives, covering support for activities from IVE formation to IVE enactment.

Fig. 5.2 Architecture after separation of concerns

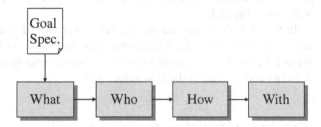

5.3.2 Step 2: Applying Architecture Levels

The architecture shown in Fig. 5.2 does not identify any levels, but places all four modules at the same level. We attain structure by applying the three-level framework for inter-organizational process-oriented collaboration [5]. This framework distinguishes between *external, conceptual* and *internal* levels for process support. The central *conceptual* level defines the logical business view of a process, i.e. the structure of a process without constraints by local technological infrastructures or external (market) requirements. The *external* level contains a projection of the conceptual level specification of a process that is meant to be externalized, i.e. made visible to other business organizations in a market. Hence, the external level is relevant for collaboration; it allows synchronization of multiple local business processes. The *internal* level specializes a conceptual process definition that is adapted to the local technological infrastructure (e.g. local enterprise information systems).

Fig. 5.3 Architecture
following the application of
the three-level framework

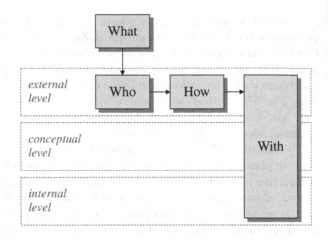

The application of the three-level framework transforms the architecture of the previous subsection into a *layered* architecture [4]. The result[1] of this transformation is shown in Fig. 5.3.

In Fig. 5.3, the layers are not yet fully crystallized; the *With* module is spread across layers (which violates the *layers* architecture pattern). Hence, a further detailing of functionality is required to obtain a comprehensibly layered architecture. This detailing is described in the next subsection.

5.3.3 Step 3: Detailing Functionality

In this subsection, we further detail the architecture presented in the previous subsection by "exploding" the identified modules where necessary. This detailing is based on the requirements that were identified earlier in this chapter. To do this, we begin by matching the requirements to the functional clusters in the architecture. The result of this match is presented in Table 5.1.

Table 5.1 Matching architecture clusters and functional requirements

	RQ1	RQ2	RQ3	RQ4	RQ5	RQ6	RQ7	RQ8	RQ9
What	X	–	–	–	–	–	–	–	X
Who	–	X	–	–	–	–	–	–	X
How	–	–	X	X	X	–	–	–	X
With	–	–	–	–	–	X	X	X	X

---

[1]Note that the "What" block is not about processes and hence is not in the scope of the three-level framework.

When analysing the results in the table, we treat RQ9 separately as this requirement refers to a very specific functional aspect (we revisit this in the next step of the logical architecture design). Looking at the other requirements, we see that the *What* and *Who* clusters each correspond to a single requirement, and hence do not need to expand this level of architecture design. The *How* and *With* clusters each correspond to multiple requirements, so we can expand these two clusters on this basis.

The functionality of the *How* module is concerned with determining the business process in an IVE to achieve the overall business goal (RQ3–RQ5). This implies obtaining local business processes of members of an IVE and weaving them into a global business process, i.e. composing a global workflow from a number of local workflows. From an architectural point of view, the functionalities related to RQ3 and RQ4 are interwoven, so we decide to allocate them into a single architectural module called *Workflow Composition*. Fulfilling RQ5 implies both static verification and dynamic prototyping of composed processes. From an architectural point of view these are two separate functionalities, which we thus place in two separate functional modules; Workflow Verification and Workflow Prototyping. The result of the "explosion" is shown in Fig. 5.4.

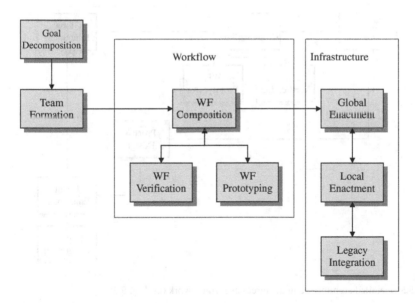

Fig. 5.4 Architecture after detailing functionality

The functionality of the *With* module concerns enactment of composed global business processes, taking into account the legacy situation at participating IVE members (RQ6–RQ8). The distinction between overall process management (inter-organizational synchronization) at IVE level and local process management within the scope of a single IVE member, leads to the observation that we need to identify both a Global and a Local Enactment module in the detailed architecture. The coupling of the DBNPM system to the back-end system implies complex functionality that we allocate to a separate module, "Legacy Integration". The general functionality of this module is to provide a common interface to execute operations in multiple, heterogeneous Enterprise Information Systems (EIS). The result of this explosion is also shown in Fig. 5.4.

We can map the detailed architecture again to the three-level framework [5], as we did earlier for the functional clusters. Here, the modules resulting from the *With* cluster require attention, as this cluster extends over multiple layers. As the Global Enactment module coordinates IVE members across their boundaries, we place this module at the external level. As the Local Enactment and Legacy Integration modules depend on the infrastructure existing at specific IVE members, we place these modules at the internal level. The result is shown in Fig. 5.5.

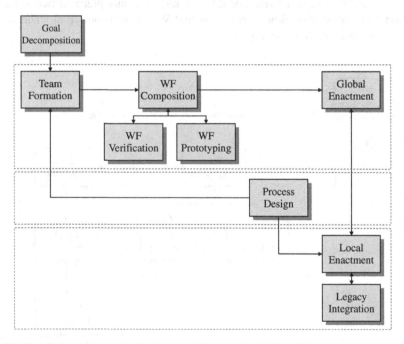

Fig. 5.5 Detailed architecture in the three-level framework (cf. Fig. 5.3)

Our architecture does not include any enactment functionality at the conceptual level, as this would require double dynamic mapping between module states. The conceptual level however is of interest; the design of local business processes within a specific IVE member takes place at the conceptual level, and is next mapped on to the external and internal levels for use within the Team Formation and Local Enactment modules. For clarity, this is also shown in Fig. 5.5. Note, however, that automated support for this design is not part of our approach (as the design of local business processes is not specific to DBNPM); therefore, we omit the Process Design module from our architectural design. In the next subsection we see that the local process specifications (the results of the design activity) are an essential element of the market knowledge required for the creation of IVEs.

5.3.4 Step 4: Adding Knowledge

An IVE-enabling system must perform complex tasks at a high level, and as a result must be able to apply knowledge of IVE markets, IVE members, their local processes and information system infrastructure, etc. Ultimately the goal is to achieve a fully automated system, but currently such a system requires the intervention of human users and access to knowledge stored in knowledge bases – this has been listed in the requirements analysis as RQ9. The knowledge in the system is accumulated across the life cycles of individual IVEs, such that the automation level of successive IVEs can increase over time.

Equipping the architecture with the means to support hybrid decision making requires three additional types of functionality:

1. Dedicated, interactive user interfaces, through which users can feed decisions to the appropriate software modules;
2. Automated knowledge bases, which accumulate formalized knowledge in the context of a specific application domain (or market) about IVE formation and enactment;
3. Advanced automated reasoning logic in system modules identified in the architecture.

The advanced automated reasoning knowledge is not visible in the architecture at this aggregation level – we address this in the next section. We extend the architecture first with the required user interfaces, and demonstrate how a single User Interface (UI) module (Formation UI) interacts with the Goal Decomposition and Team Formation modules. A process engineer should be able to interact with the Workflow Composition modules (and via this with Workflow Verification and Prototyping); for this, we include the Workflow User Interface. Finally, an operations manager in an IVE must be able to monitor and control Business Network Processes during their enactment. Therefore, we include a Monitoring User Interface. Note that the Local Enactment module also requires end-user interaction; this is however not specific for DBNPM and is addressed later in this chapter. The resulting architecture is shown in Fig. 5.6.

Note that reasoning leads to decisions, and decisions may be negative. For example, the Workflow Composition module may decide that a correct global workflow cannot be composed. In this case, the system must backtrack, i.e. go one or more

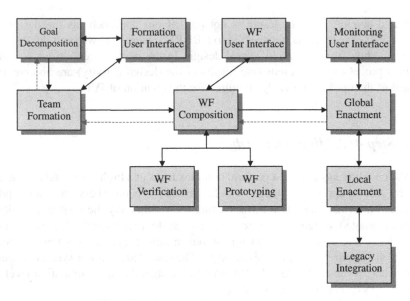

Fig. 5.6 Architecture with user interfaces added

steps back in the creation of an IVE. This is supported by interfaces between modules as indicated by the reverse dotted arrows shown in Fig. 5.6.

Next, we add knowledge bases to the architecture. We distinguish between the following knowledge bases:

- The product knowledge base contains general knowledge about the products in a specific application domain (as produced by IVEs) and their composition (comparable to a bill of materials). It is used by the Goal Decomposition module.
- The market knowledge base contains specific knowledge about organizations within a market (potential IVE members), their capabilities and their local processes. It is used by the Team Formation module to select potential members for an IVE.
- The infrastructure knowledge base contains knowledge regarding the back-end (legacy) information systems that exist at specific organizations. This knowledge is used by the Team Formation module to avoid the composition of teams that are incompatible with respect to their local infrastructures.
- The workflow pattern knowledge base contains workflow specification patterns that are used in the composition of global workflows by the Workflow Composition module.

Figure 5.7 presents the architecture of Fig. 5.6, which has been extended with these four knowledge bases. This is the final diagram in the discussion of the logical view on the CrossWork architecture. It is the basis for the process and the development views discussed next.

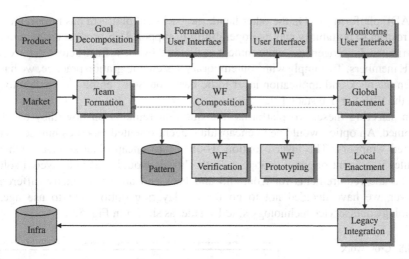

Fig. 5.7 Architecture with knowledge bases added

5.4 Process View of the Architecture

In the previous section, we discussed the logical view of the CrossWork architecture. In this section, we turn to the process view. In this view, we determine the right technology choices to realize (embody) the logical view of the architecture. We first pay attention to the choice of technology platforms for CrossWork, upon which the CrossWork functionality can be built. The enactment support of CrossWork clearly requires a high level of interoperability in order to allow process enactment within a distributed IVE environment. Therefore, we also pay explicit attention to technology choices for this part of the architecture.

5.4.1 Technology Platforms for the CrossWork Architecture

Clearly, automated support for an IVE must be highly distributed, for the simple reason that the IVE itself consists of many distributed, autonomous parties with local systems that must be integrated into the global process. Therefore, the CrossWork system must also possess a distributed disposition. The bottom-level communication infrastructure layer for the CrossWork system is internet-based. Using internet standards like HTTP as a basic infrastructure allows free choice of higher layers to implement CrossWork's application functionality.

When looking at the application level of CrossWork, we see different requirements for the IVE formation (front-end) and IVE enactment (back-end) platforms. On the one hand, the front-end has main requirements in the fields of goal-orientation and support for reasoning mechanisms needed to implement the IVE construction algorithms. For this reason, we have chosen a Multi-Agent System (MAS) platform [10] as a basis for the front-end application layer, more specifically the JADE platform [9]. On the other hand, the back-end platform has requirements with respect to portability and interoperability to support IVE process enactment in a distributed, heterogeneous environment as dictated by the infrastructure that exists at IVE members. To comply with contemporary system integration practice, we have chosen the back-end application layer to be based on SOC, employing technology from the Web Service stack [2].

On selecting these two platforms, the question remains on how they can be combined. An option would be to encapsulate agent-oriented modules into service-oriented wrappers. The inverse option would be to encapsulate service-oriented modules into agent-oriented wrappers. Both choices would lead to a layered solution. As the requirements for front-end and back-end are so distinctly different, however, we have decided not to go for the layering option, but to use agent technology and service technology side-by-side, as shown in Fig. 5.8.

Fig. 5.8 CrossWork technology stack

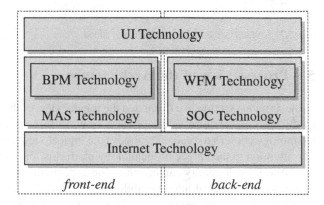

Within the MAS environment, Business Process Management (BPM) technology is embedded, required for process specification handling, most notably global process composition. Within the SOC environment, Workflow Management (WFM) technology is embedded, required for business process execution. Clearly, the side-to-side approach requires an interface between the two environments.

Next in selecting platform technologies, we needed to choose the specification languages to be used in the system. Within the front-end, we need a process specification language that is expressive enough to specify all relevant aspects of IVE configurations. For this we have developed the eSML language [12]. Extendable expressiveness and easy manipulation are the main design criteria for eSML. The language is XML-based to easily fit the internet environment. For the back-end, interoperability and portability with respect to global process engines have been the main selection criteria, leading to the necessity of a standard language. Given the internet context, BPEL [3] is the obvious choice.

Given differences in platform and specification language between front-end and back-end, we clearly require an interface to close this gap. For this purpose, we have developed a *paradigm bridge* that translates eSML specifications into BPEL and communicates them between the MAS and SOC environments. We have placed the paradigm bridge at the front-end side, which allows a direct link to the standardized BPEL back-end engines. This is presented in Fig. 5.9.

Fig. 5.9 Position of the paradigm bridge

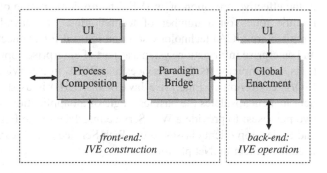

front-end: IVE construction

back-end: IVE operation

5.4.2 The Service-Oriented Back-End

The CrossWork back-end supports the execution of dynamically composed global business processes in IVEs using state-of-the-art SOC technology. We have adopted a two-level approach to process execution; global process orchestration and local process execution. Doing so, we attain both a separation of concerns between IVE-level process synchronization and local process execution, whilst also obtaining an architectural decoupling between global and local process management technology.

Global process orchestration is performed by the Global Enactment module. The basis for this module is a standard BPEL engine – we use Active BPEL [1] in our prototype system. The use of a paradigm bridge allows decoupling of dedicated process manipulation in the CrossWork front-end and standard off-the-shelf process enactment technology in the CrossWork back-end. The Global Enactment module is coupled to a user interface for IVE-level process monitoring.

The Local Enactment module provides the local process execution functionality. This module is based on a standard WFM system, for which we use the i.Perform system (www.exodus.gr) in the prototype setting. For the interface between the Global Enactment and Local Enactment modules, we use the concept of a Business Process Web Service (BP-WS) [7], which includes a business process specification and business process state that can be accessed externally. Access to specification and state are provided through a number of dedicated Web Service interfaces (ports). Four BP-WS classes are introduced in [7] following four control flow interface levels, which we use as a basis in the CrossWork system. Each IVE member may decide to expose specific details of its services by using the BP-WS classes. Local Partners specify selected internals of their business processes (a projection of the business process specification) to the outside world by using eSML (for workflow composition in the CrossWork front-end) and BPEL (for monitoring and control purposes in the back-end).

The last module in the CrossWork back-end architecture is the Legacy Integration module. This module enables flexible coupling of the CrossWork system to internal legacy systems of IVE members, such as ERP systems or planning systems. Obviously, tight coupling of these systems to IVE processes is of great importance in the effective operation of an IVE. The implementation of the Legacy Integration module relies on a number of technologies. The Java-based J2EE Connector Architecture (JCA) technology solution is used for connecting application servers and enterprise information systems as part of enterprise application integration solutions. It complements Web Services and BPEL in a Service-Oriented Architecture (SOA) environment. Enterprise Java Beans (EJB) is used as a server-side component that encapsulates the business logic of an application. Apache Axis is used for two purposes; to provide a Web Service interface to the Legacy Integration module and to develop client classes to use Web Service connectors, which are principally used to connect to .Net platforms.

5.5 Development View of the Architecture

In the previous sections, we have discussed the design of the logical and process views of the CrossWork architecture. In this section, we turn our attention to the development view, i.e. to the way the software can be constructed by realizing the functionality specified in the logical view. For the development view, we have chosen the Empty Shell Approach [14], which allows software development based on incremental prototyping. Below, we first explain the ESA. Following this, we demonstrate how an example module is realized through this approach.

5.5.1 Empty Shell Approach

For a software development approach, we choose the ESA, which is particularly suited to the distributed, incremental development of complex software prototypes. The ESA has been successfully applied to a number of projects in which complex software prototypes had to be realized in geographically distributed consortia. The ESA was first used in the PRISMA database project [14].

The main idea of the ESA is to separate the communication topology (the overall global structure of a software system) from the internal functionality of components (the *inside* of the modules in the topology).

5.5.1.1 Steps in the Empty Shell approach

Within the ESA, the Empty Shell (ES) consists of the complete specification and implementation of the externals of all modules, and the interaction between these modules. The ES is implemented first, including:

- Full outside shell of each component with all interfaces;
- Trivial implementation inside modules with all interfaces internally coupled and with hardwired (standard) responses that generate correct communication protocols;
- All connections between empty shell modules.

The complete ES is a system that works (i.e. all modules show external activity) but is completely "stupid" (i.e. the modules can only perform predefined, trivial actions). The ES can be completely tested with respect to module interaction.

After the ES has been realized and tested, the *internals* of modules can be added on a per-module basis as follows:

1. Incrementally add internal logic to a component;
2. Test the module in isolation for correct operation of the new internal logic;
3. Test the module within the ES for compliance with overall communication behaviour;
4. Distribute the new module to other partners.

The above approach in module realization keeps a working overall system throughout the entire development process, thereby supporting a flexible, distributed incremental prototyping approach. The overall system will incrementally grow from *completely stupid* to *intelligent*, whilst keeping the same interaction patterns on the architecture level.

5.5.1.2 Example Empty Shell Module

Figure 5.10 shows an example illustration of an ES module; the Workflow Composition module. The interfaces correspond with the interfaces of the Team Formation module (interfaces A and D), Global Workflow Enactment module (B and C), WorkFlow verification module (E) and Workflow Prototyping module (F) as specified in the overall architecture (Fig. 5.7). For reasons of brevity, the interface to the Workflow User Interface has been omitted here.

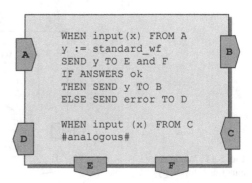

Fig. 5.10 Empty shell example of workflow composition module

Figure 5.10 clearly shows that the ES module always produces the same *output* (labelled *standard_wf*), no matter what its *input* is. Hence, it does not require actual logic to compute the output, though all interactions with its *neighbours* in the architecture are present and operating.

5.6 Physical View of the Architecture

After having discussed the logical, process and development views of Kruchten's 4+1 framework, the physical view remains to be discussed. The physical view describes how components are allocated to elements in the hardware infrastructure, i.e. to computer systems present in an IVE market (for the formation stage of an IVE) and in an IVE (for the enactment). Clearly, the CrossWork system is not designed for application in a single fixed market/IVE context, but must be generally applicable for the supports of process-oriented IVEs. Therefore, we cannot design a specific, concrete physical view of the architecture.

For this reason, we limit the discussion of the physical view to looking at how the enactment (which has the most distributed physical requirements) stage can be supported in an IVE where physical possibilities are not evenly distributed among the IVE members. In other words, we look at the situation where not all IVE members have enough IT infrastructure to support a substantial part of the enactment functionality of the CrossWork software. This is quite likely in situations where IVE members include SMEs, which is comparable to the automotive domain used in the case studies of this book.

The answer to supporting IVE members with limited IT infrastructure is the use of application service provisioning. This means that members with adequate infrastructure provide CrossWork services for those that are less well equipped. In the CrossWork system, Web-based clients are used for this purpose.

Both the Global Enactment module and the Local Enactment module support Web-based remote workflow clients. The remote client technology allows the inclusion of IVE partners with limited IT resources, thereby supporting the possible heterogeneous nature of the members of an IVE. We see an example topology in Fig. 5.11. Here we see four IVE members (A to D), three of which have workflow

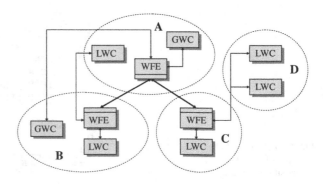

Fig. 5.11 Workflow enactment topology

engines (WFE); member A runs a Global Enactment module whilst members B and C run Local Enactment modules. The three engines serve Global Workflow Clients (GWC) and Local Workflow Clients (LWC) in all four organizations.

5.7 Automating the "Instant Virtual Enterprise"

In this chapter, we have taken a look at the design of the CrossWork architecture, which forms the basis for automating the IVE. From the discussion of the design, we can make a number of important observations:

- To provide a complete *end-to-end* support for the establishment and operation of IVEs, a complex information system is required that stretches across the members of an IVE. This complexity implies that a modular architecture with clear interfaces is needed to and to keep that software maintainable.
- The various modules in the architecture have very different functional and non-functional requirements. This implies that, to avoid re-implementing basic infrastructure functionality, different technology classes (e.g. software agents, conventional java implementation and Web Service-based technology) have been selected for the software implementations of our modules. This leads to a hybrid software platform that again increases the complexity of the system. We have introduced a dedicated module (Paradigm Bridge) to deal with the heterogeneity aspect of technology.
- The CrossWork approach aims at the gradual automation of IVE support and this is directly reflected in the designed architecture. We see explicit attention for both *automated knowledge* (in intelligent components and knowledge bases) and *human knowledge* (in rich user interfaces). This *dual design* is essential for dealing with a problem domain of this complexity.

Automating the IVE is possible on the basis of the architecture discussed in this chapter and the technologies to be discussed in the following chapters. Such support, however, implies a non-trivial level of complexity. Also, we need to increase the level of automation possible in a gradual fashion, as the system gathers more domain knowledge.

Designing software support for IVE shows that we need to address different aspects of the problem differently, using different approaches and technologies. Stability is provided by conceptual structures of information which are based on theories reviewed in the previous two chapters.

This chapter provides the bridge between Parts II and III of the book, and also supplies enough high-level information about technology so that Part IV can be understood without the details of Part III.

References

1. ActiveBPEL, Website: www.activebpel.org, 2008
2. Alonso, G., Casati, F., Kuno, H., Machiraju, V., Web Services – Concepts, Architectures and Applications, Springer, New York, 2004.
3. OASIS Web Services Business Process Execution Language (WSBPEL), Version 2.0, May 2007, http://www.oasis-open.org/committees/tc_home.php?wg_abbrev=wsbpel
4. Buschmann, F., Meunier, R., Rohnert, H., Sommerlad, P., Stal, M., Pattern-Oriented Software Architecture, Vol. 1, Wiley, New York, 1996.
5. Grefen, P., Ludwig, H., Angelov, S., A Three-Level Framework for Process and Data Management of Complex e-Services, International Journal of Cooperative Information Systems, Vol. 12(4), pp. 487–531, 2003.
6. Grefen, P., CrossWork Global Architecture, CrossWork Project Deliverable D4.1, 2006.
7. Grefen, P., Ludwig, H., Dan, A., Angelov, S., An Analysis of Web Services Support for Dynamic Business Process Outsourcing, Information and Software Technology, Vol. 48(11), pp. 1115–1134, 2006.
8. Grefen, P., Introduction to (Complex) Information System Architecture, Eindhoven University of Technology, 2008.
9. JADE, Java Agent Development Environment (2006) See http://jade.tilab.com, last accessed Dec 2007.
10. Jennings, N. R., An Agent-Based Approach for Building Complex Software Systems, Communications of the ACM, Vol. 44(4), 35–41, April 2001. DOI= http://doi.acm.org/10.1145/367211.367250
11. Kruchten, P., Architectural Blueprints – The "4+1" View Model of Software Architecture, IEEE Software, Vol. 12(6), pp. 42–50, 1995.
12. Norta, A., Exploring Dynamic Inter-Organizational Business Process Collaboration, PhD Thesis, Technology University Eindhoven, Department of Information Systems, 2007.
13. Shaw, M., Garlan, D., Software Architecture, Prentice Hall, Englewood Cliffs, NJ, 1996.
14. Wilschut, A. N., Grefen, P., Apers, P., Kersten, M. L., Implementing PRISMA/DB in an OOPL, Proceedings of the 6th International Workshop on Database Machines, pp. 97–111, Deauville, France, 1989.
15. Zachman, J., The Zachman Framework for Enterprise Architecture, Zachman International, 2002.

Part III
CrossWork Technology

Chapter 6
Goal Decomposition and Team Formation

Iain Duncan Stalker and Martin Carpenter

In this chapter we describe the conceptual framework underpinning the software solution to goal decomposition and team formation developed in CrossWork. We then elaborate on the software implementation itself. We begin with a description of the conceptual framework within which goal decomposition and team formation must operate. Following this we present the approach to goal decomposition and team formation taken within the CrossWork project.

6.1 Conceptual Framework

The challenge taken up by CrossWork was to create a software solution which brings the vision of the "instant" virtual enterprise (IVE) one step closer to reality. The essential notion is a near-instantaneous assembly of an IVE (of enterprises, individuals, etc. as appropriate) to respond to a relevant business opportunity. This demands a clear understanding of what the business opportunity entails, in particular, in terms of services needed and the matching of these needs to the "best" available service providers. A subtle aspect is that in the context of a team, the "best-in-class" is not necessarily the "best" for the team; team dynamics must be respected and matters of interoperability of systems are paramount.

In manufacturing domains, an IVE will embody a number of complementary *teams*, which together ensure that the IVE achieves its aims and responds appropriately to the business opportunity motivating its formation. For example, in CrossWork we identified production teams responsible for the realization of a physical product, and management teams responsible for the management of the project, of which production forms a part. This addresses supervening aspects of administration, compliance, quality, finance, etc. The testing ground for CrossWork was in the automotive sector and ancillary industries, where typically, an IVE forms with a specific product in mind. The realization, i.e. design, manufacture and delivery of

I.D. Stalker (✉)
University of Teesside, Middlesbrough, UK
e-mail: i.stalker@tees.ac.uk

N. Mehandjiev, P. Grefen (eds.), *Dynamic Business Process Formation for Instant Virtual Enterprises*, Advanced Information and Knowledge Processing,
DOI 10.1007/978-1-84882-691-5_6, © Springer-Verlag London Limited 2010

a specific product is the overall goal of the IVE. As such, we shall mainly consider production teams since the services needed for the realization of a given product will identify the primary or core members of the related IVE. Nevertheless, the approach is general as shown in Section 6.3.

The function of a production team is to transform the current state characterized by the incompleteness of information, a statement of raw materials, etc. into an attainment of this goal. Initially, this transformation is too abstract to match with available services, expertise, etc. and needs to be elucidated. Information about the physical product is used to rewrite the global goal as a combination of subgoals, which are matched to (known) services. Interdependencies of components of the physical product and their relations to each other are reflected as interdependencies of these subgoals, for example, as (partial) ordering on the fulfillment of these; and thus in the services associated with each. Essentially, we have at this stage an abstract process through which the global goal can be achieved.

Team formation takes this abstract process and finds particular providers for each service. That is, its primary activity is (intelligent) "matchmaking". Naturally, there is likely to be a number of candidates for a given service and some evaluation mechanism is required. Also, the user might have particular selection criteria, which must be satisfied. For convenience, we consider a supplier to be a particular type of service provider; it provides the "service" of a particular physical component. This allows us to treat the suppliers of physical products and suppliers of services in a single consistent manner. In the tradition of *Economics*, we consider a service to be an "intangible product", a non-physical item, which affords some value to its owner or a recipient. That is, a "service" is a particular type of intangible product distinguished by its active provision by some entity called a "service provider". A service can take many forms including the provision of some prefabricated item, the manufacture of a bespoke item and intangible services such as advice, consultancy or design. Thus, we associate a type with a service to reflect this. A natural consequence of this is that a service provider inherits a type from the type of service it offers.

There will be some interplay between goal decomposition and team formation. For example, additional subgoals are likely to arise during team formation, say the need for some movement of components between geographically dispersed team members.

6.2 Goal Decomposition

We sketch the model of goal decomposition (GD) underpinning our implementation. There are (at least) two complementary ways in which to decompose a product. A *physical* decomposition identifies (physical) substructures which combine to comprise a whole. A *functional* decomposition identifies how a global function (of a product) derives from an interaction and combination of subfunctions. Each perspective offers valuable information and generally which is preferred depends upon the nature of the project. Consider, a car can be decomposed both physically and functionally. Physical components include doors, windows, interiors, locks, etc. with each component often further decomposable. This is of particular use when we are assembling a team to produce and deliver a product for which a complete design exists. A functional decomposition of a car might identify support for loco-motion, passenger comfort, passenger safety, storage and accommodation. This is more appropriate to the concept design for a new car. Here, we shall focus on the case of an established design and so consider only physical decomposition.

6.2.1 Theoretical Aspects

We introduce a few of the theoretical aspects which underpin the implementation of GD. While the following is a little more formal in style, our primary intention here is to establish a little terminology.

Goal – A *goal* G is a quantifiable (desired) state pursued by some agent, or set of agents (we use the term "agent" informally here). In particular, a goal G is owned by some agent, or group of agents, and is characterized by a set of variables V_G. We can ascribe a preferred range of values to each of (at least a subset of) the variables V_G. We denote the preferred values for $v \in V_G$ by R_v and call this the range of v.

Goal Decomposition Artefact – Let $G, S_1, \ldots, S_n$ denote goals with associated variables (sets of) $V_G, V_{S_1} \ldots V_{S_n}$, where $2 \leq n \in \mathbf{N}$. We define a *goal decomposition artefact* for G, to be a rewrite of G in terms of (a conjunction of) $S_1, \ldots, S_n$; thus, $G \leftarrow S_1, \ldots, S_n$. We refer to G as a *composition* of $S_1, \ldots, S_n$ and we consider it a *top-level goal* for $S_1, \ldots, S_n$; conversely $S_1, \ldots, S_n$ are considered *subgoals* of G.

We should note that there are some technical constraints on the above definitions. For example, acceptable rewrites require that subgoals collectively share some vari-ables with the initial goal and that the ranges associated with such variables are maintained or "narrowed". These are needed to ensure relevance. However, in the interests of brevity, we omit such formalities here.

Figures 6.1 and 6.2 demonstrate two potential forms of the goal decomposition artefact. In each the goal is to move from the current state to a certain goal state. In the case shown in Fig. 6.1 each subgoal corresponds to the partial completion of part of the goal states, thus the subgoals are substates of the goal state.

In Fig. 6.2 the subgoals simply represent intermediate states between the current state and the goal state, and might not directly contribute to reaching the goal state.

Narrowing and Widening – Let G_1 and G_2 denote goals sharing associated vari-ables, i.e. $V_1 = V_2 = V_G$. Denote the occurrence of $v \in V_G$ in G_i by v_i for $i = 1,2$. Then, we call $[G_1; G_2]$ a *narrowing* of G_1 on v if $R_{v_1} \supset R_{v_2}$ and note that $G_2 \to G_1$; or a *widening* of G_1 on v if $R_{v_1} \subset R_{v_2}$ and note that $G_1 \to G_2$. Typically we use sim-ply *narrowing* and *widening*, respectively; overloading each term to apply to both the process and the result.

Refinement and Abstraction – We refer to the decomposition or narrowing of a goal, applied individually or in combination, as *goal refinement*. We refer to the

Fig. 6.1 Subgoals as
(sub)states

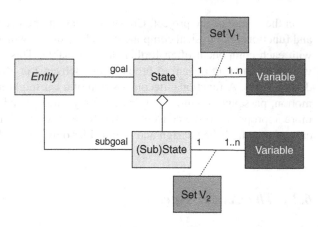

Fig. 6.2 Subgoals as
intermediate states

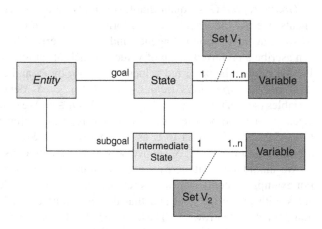

composition of a set of goals or the widening of a goal, considered individually or in combination, as *goal abstraction*. We typically drop the qualifier goal and overload each term to signify both the process and the result. Thus, more precisely, the restatement of a global goal as a combination of subgoals involves more than mere decomposition and is in fact goal refinement. However, to remain consistent with the terminology of the CrossWork architecture and indeed general usage of terms, we retain use of the less formal term *goal decomposition*.

Goal Decomposition Process – A *goal decomposition process* signifies any systematic activity which results in a goal refinement, including an implementation of such activity.

6.2.2 A Process for Goal Decomposition

We elaborate the particular goal decomposition process we have implemented through a short presentation of detail about the inputs, outputs, the process itself and conclude with a summary of implementation aspects.

Input Structures – The most important aspect of the input to the goal decomposition module is the order specification. An order specification identifies desired products with required quantities, specifies any constraints on the order (e.g. delivery in 15 days) and allows the user to give any relevant additional information, such as previous similar orders. The most important aspect, for the present discussion, is product specification.

Output Structures – The goal decomposition module outputs a goal decomposition artefact: a set of components and a set of primary services. In particular, these are instances of ontology structures from the product and market ontologies, as appropriate.

Process – Output is derived from input through an implementation of the following goal decomposition process. We analyse the product specification (or a set of these; we assume one for discussion with an obvious generalization to many) from an order specification. The product is (physically) decomposed to the finest level of detail possible according to the information and structures available in the product ontology. To facilitate this, the product specification includes a particular specification of a product concept, which can be taken or adapted from the product ontology. Such a specification is illustrated in Fig. 6.3 representing the case of a simplified water tank system (cf. Section 11.2). The "primary" services needed to fulfil the order are identified. In particular, we identify retailers for standard components, manufacturers for non-standard components and providers of intangibles for the primary services, such as assembly and financial management. Each results in a service provider request (cf. Fig. 6.5), which is represented using the vocabulary of the market ontology (complemented by that of product ontology).

PRODUCT	
Identifier	Water Tank System
ProductType	System
FunctionType	Complex
Capability	Water or Aqueous Solution Storage
Capability	Water or Aqueous Solution Deployment
BehaviorType	Complex
Structure	Complex
→ Shape	*Appropriate Geometric Information*
→ Weight	*In appropriate dimensions, e.g. Newtons*
→ Material	*Composite*
→ Component	Water Tank, Pump, Valve, Gasket, Grommet, Pipe, Hose
→ Connection	*As appropriate*

Fig. 6.3 Water tank product structure

6.2.3 Implementation Aspects

The brief exposition of theoretical aspects above is deliberately suggestive of a logic-based formalism. Indeed, this is the implementation approach. We maintain two consistent representations of our ontology structures: a java class-based representation for JADE and a representation in the W3C standard Web Ontology Language (OWL) (http://www.w3.org/TR/owl-ref). The latter allows us to obtain and manipulate conceptual structures which derive from outside of our application platform. This is especially important as we assume an open environment. Our agents are implemented using JADE (jade.tilab.com) to provide the fundamental multi-agent framework. We supplement this framework with two logic programming paradigms: a java-based Prolog engine and also the Java Theorem Prover (JTP) (www.ksl.stanford.edu/software/jtp). Respectively, these allow our agents to deal with the JADE ontology structures and also to manipulate ontology structures written in OWL. Accordingly, we equip our agents with reasoning structures, i.e. knowledge bases, comprised of rules and facts in each of these logic programming paradigms, viz. Prolog and Knowledge Interchange Format (KIF) tuples for JTP. The appropriate bases are chosen according to requirements when the goal decomposition module is initiated.

6.2.4 Example of Goal Decomposition

Recall the water tank structure of Fig. 6.3. The global goal for a team which has to manufacture, assemble and deliver this would be to deliver a water tank system. An OWL structure extract from an order specification (which imports the appropriate supporting ontology) for an instance might look like the following:

```
<Product rdf:ID="WaterTankSystemEG1">
<productType rdf:resource="#System"/>
<functionType rdf:resource="#Complex"/>
<structureType rdf:resource="#Complex"/>
<materialType rdf:resource="#Composite"/>
<component rdf:resource="#WaterTankEG1"/>
<component rdf:resource="#GrommetEG1"/>
<component rdf:resource="#PumpEG1"/>
<component rdf:resource="#GasketEG1"/>
<component rdf:resource="#ValveEG1"/>
<component rdf:resource="#HoseEG1"/>
<component rdf:resource="#PipeEG1"/>
</Product>
<Product rdf:ID="WaterTank">
    <productType rdf:resource="#Complex"/>
<component rdf:resource="#Cap"/>
</Product>
```

```
<Product rdf:ID="Cap">
<productType rdf:resource="#Simple"/>
</Product>
<Product rdf:ID="Pump">
<productType rdf:resource="#Complex"/>
<component rdf:resource="#Motor"/>
<component rdf:resource="#Pipe"/>
<component rdf:resource="#Valve"/>
</Product>
<Product rdf:ID="Motor">
<productType rdf:resource="#Simple"/>
</Product>
<Product rdf:ID="Valve">
<productType rdf:resource="#Simple"/>
</Product>
<Product rdf:ID="Pipe">
<productType rdf:resource="#Simple"/>
</Product>
<Product rdf:ID="Gasket">
<productType rdf:resource="#Simple"/>
</Product>
<Product rdf:ID="Grommet">
<productType rdf:resource="#Simple"/>
</Product>
<Product rdf:ID="Hose">
<productType rdf:resource="#Simple"/>
</Product>
```

This is parsed by JTP to give a knowledge base of KIF triples which can be directly queried. For example, the following query can be iteratively applied to return all the products of type simple:

```
(and
(|http://www.w3.org/1999/02/22-rdf-syntax-ns\#|::|type| ?X
        |http://www.crosswork.info/basic\#|::|Product|)
(|http://www.crosswork.info/basic\#|::|productType| ?X
        |http://www.crosswork.info/basic\#|::|Simple|) )
```

Such queries are embedded into the (appropriate OWL handling) decomposition behaviours of our goal decomposition agent. The above query allows all simple products extracted, which are

```
|http://www.crosswork.info/basic#|::|Pipe|
|http://www.crosswork.info/basic#|::|Valve|
|http://www.crosswork.info/basic#|::|Cap|
|http://www.crosswork.info/basic#|::|Gasket|
```

```
|http://www.crosswork.info/basic#|::|Hose|
|http://www.crosswork.info/basic#|::|Grommet|
|http://www.crosswork.info/basic#|::|Motor|
```

Each of these constitutes a component. Thus, assuming these are standard, then each would be associated with a service provider request seeking a retailer and would associate with the subgoal *obtain <component>*.

6.3 Team Formation

Having decomposed a goal to the appropriate level, we can proceed to recruit appropriate actors (organizations) for each subgoal, thus forming the team for the goal. This can be done in a top-down fashion, matching the requirements of a goal to the capabilities of a team member, or in a bottom-up fashion, where organizations offer to participate in a consortium which can together satisfy a subgoal. These are now discussed in more detail.

6.3.1 Top-Down Team Formation

In many domains, knowledge about a final product provides invaluable information for team formation. For example, the structure of a car and in particular its composition from identifiable components imposes a sequence on the tasks in the assembly process. Such dependencies on the activities of the partnership members influence the structure of the team. Of course, the need for a given component or the need for a given skill in the assembly process identifies necessary expertise which must be embodied by some partners in the network producing the car. Our top-down approach to goal decomposition and team formation makes use of these interrelations.

6.3.2 Theoretical Aspects

We introduce a few of the theoretical aspects which underpin the implementation of top-down team formation. Again, though a little more formal in style, our primary intention here is to establish a little terminology.

Essentially, top-down team formation can be summarized as follows: having clarified the team function into a set of services, find a set of candidates for each service needed, select from these to create candidate teams, and choose in each the most appropriate.

Thus, theoretically it reduces to selections over various bases in the following sense. Formally, a *selection function* is a vector, s, over a set C, called a *set of candidates* or a *basis for selection*, $s: C \rightarrow \{0,1\}$. s_c denotes the value returned for $c \in C$, called the *c-component* of the vector s. Generally, $s_c = 1$ if candidate c is chosen and 0 otherwise. We refer to s as the *selection vector*. We call a process, σ (say), used to determine the value for a particular s_c as a *selection process* or *selection procedure*.

Selection – We represent the selection of a team as a vector over the set of candidate teams "select": $T \rightarrow \{0,1\}$. In this case, "select" is called a *team selection function*, and T is called a *basis for team selection* or more usually the *set of candidate teams*. Naturally, the same formal mechanism applies to (team) members: "member": $M \rightarrow \{0,1\}$. In this case, "member" is called a *member selection function* and M is called a *basis for member selection* or more usually simply the *set of candidates*.

Selection Variable and Ranking Criterion – A *selection variable* denotes something measurable or quantifiable which is used in a given selection process. A *(selection) criterion* is a statement about the selection of variables used to inform a selection function. Selection criteria are often used to order choices according to preferences. As such, an order is induced on the candidates, referred to as a *ranking*, which allows candidates to be *ranked*. In this case a selection criterion is called a *ranking criterion*.

Selection criteria are often used to filter choices according to whether a particular condition is met. In this case, the selection criterion functions as a *constraint*. If the violation of a constraint immediately disqualifies a candidate for selection then constraint is called *hard constraint*. If the violation of a constraint merely signifies that a preference is not realized in the supplier, then the constraint is called a *soft constraint*.

Performance Measure or Indicator – By *performance measure* or *performance indicator* we mean some quantifiable aspect of behaviour associated with a candidate. Formally, a performance measure associates some item of interest i to an appropriate value v, i.e. $i \rightarrow v$; or let I denote a set of items of interest, let S denote some scale, e.g. an interval of the real line $\mathbf{R}$, then a performance measure μ is a mapping $\mu: I \rightarrow S$. Our interest in performance measures here is in their use as selection variables, thus as ranking criteria or constraints. We shall typically use the two terms interchangeably.

Acceptable Candidate – Suppose we have a selection procedure σ for a set of candidates C which makes use of a set of performance measures M. For each $\mu \in M$ identify a subset $A_\mu \subseteq D_\mu$ of values in the range of μ. Let $\mu(c)$ be the value of μ associated with the candidate $c \in C$. Then, a candidate $c \in C$ is *acceptable according to the selection procedure s* (or simply *acceptable*) if for all $\mu \in M$, $\mu(c) \in A_\mu$. That is, a candidate $c \in C$ is acceptable if the values for its performance measures fall within prescribed ranges.

Best Candidate – Suppose we have a selection procedure σ for a set of candidates C which makes use of a set of performance measures M. Let A_C denote the resulting set of acceptable candidates. Let $\subseteq_\mu$ be the order induced by the performance measure $\mu \in M$. Then:

1. the *best candidate with respect to the performance measure μ* is $c \in C$ such that $\mu(c) \subseteq_\mu \mu(d)$, for all $d \in C$.

2. if there exists $c \in A_C$ such that for all $\mu \in M$, $\mu(c) \subseteq_\mu \mu(d)$, for all $d \in C$, then c is called the *best candidate overall* or simply the *best candidate*.

Typically, performance measures are not independent, thus, changes in one cause changes in others. Furthermore, such changes are often incompatible, that is, changes "for the better" in one measure will induce changes "for the worse" in another. To accommodate this interdependence, it is common to consider some function (e.g. linear combination) of the performance measures which can be used (singularly) to rank a set of candidates.[1] Such a function is called an *objective function*. Typically, the aim is to optimize, i.e. minimize or maximize, the objective function.

Optimal Candidate – Suppose we have a selection procedure σ for a set of candidates C which makes use of a set of performance measures $M = \{\mu_1,\ldots,\mu_n\}$. Let A_C denote the set of acceptable candidates. Let $f(\mu_1,\ldots,\mu_n)$ be an objective function for the selection procedure. Let $\subseteq_f$ be the order induced by the optimization of this function. Then the *optimal candidate* (*with respect to f*) is $c \in C$ such that $f(\mu_1(c),\ldots,\mu_n(c)) \subseteq_f f(\mu_1(d),\ldots,\mu_n(d))$, for all $d \in C$.

Since we are free to choose our selection variables and performance criteria, then we can use as our (single) performance measure a suitably chosen objective function. Thus, we typically consider optimal and best candidates as equivalent. A summary of the concepts involved in resource selection and their relationships is shown in Fig. 6.4.

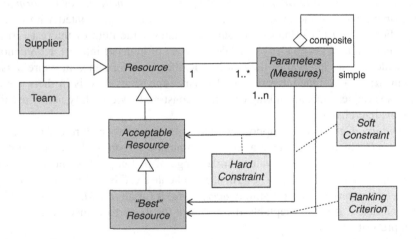

Fig. 6.4 The CrossWork approach to resource selection

---

[1] Such an approach is taken from mathematical programming approaches, where a problem (typically) takes the form: optimize (i.e. minimize or maximize) $F(\mathbf{x})$, subject to $\mathbf{G}(\mathbf{x}) \leq 0$ (constraints). Solutions satisfying the constraints are called *feasible* solutions.

6.3.2.1 A Process for Team Formation

We elaborate the particular top-down team formation process we have implemented through a short presentation of detail about the inputs, outputs, the process itself and conclude with a summary of implementation aspects.

Input Structures – Naturally, the output structures of goal decomposition provide the input structures for team formation, thus a goal decomposition artefact, a set of components and a set of primary services.

Output Structures – The primary output of team formation is an enumerated team and a structure which represents the interdependencies of the activities, i.e. services provided, by the members of the team. We capture this as (an instance of) an ontological structure which formalizes what we refer to as a shape graph. Basically, a shape graph is a directed graph, in fact, a directed multi-graph with loops. Nodes are connected when one depends upon another; the target node of an arc is dependent upon the source node. Each node identifies a team member and a purpose, i.e. service or particular activity, realized at the node. Each (directed) arc identifies source and target nodes and is typed according to the dependency, e.g. control, data, resource, physical material.

Process – We model (top-down) team formation in CrossWork as the following series of stages. In the terms of the formal framework summarized above, at each stage we develop and implement appropriate selection procedure to establish a vector of service providers to be considered further. Ultimately, this results in an optimal candidate for each service and thus an optimal candidate for our final team.

- Identify Resources. Before we consider the structures received from the goal decomposition module, we need to identify the various markets, databases, acquaintances, appropriate case libraries and so forth, which are available to the team formation module. It is from these that the team formation module will select potential service providers (*candidates*). Since we take an agent-based approach, the team formation module appeals to agents, which wrap appropriate resources such as catalogues, libraries and databases. We refer to these collectively as *CLDs*. At this stage we refer to service providers under consideration as *resources*.
- Filter Service Providers. To help us manage complexity, we make an initial filtering of available resources through a simple, shallow matchmaking. This is supported through two simple ontology structures depicted in Fig. 6.5.

The fundamental structure of the provider request concept on the left and the provider description concept are devised to be identical at this level of abstraction. This provides for a straight syntactic match on the relations, specifically if the set of relations implicit in the left structure of the figure is contained in the set of relations implicit in the right. Commitment to the same ontologies ensures a semantic match.

We create an instance of a service provider request ontology concept, which has precisely the same structure as that of service provider description concept. Accordingly the two can be directly compared to determine whether or not we have

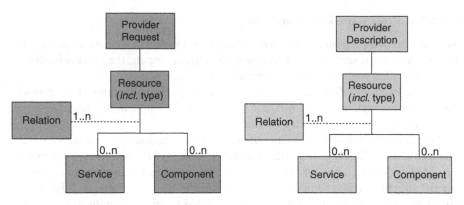

Fig. 6.5 Shallow matchmaking

prima facie service provision. This ensures that we consider in detail only relevant service providers. At this stage we refer to service providers as *nominees*.

- Pre-Select Candidates. This stage corresponds to application of hard criteria to the nominees. Thus, it reduces the set of nominees to acceptable candidates.
- Evaluate. Here, we evaluate both individuals and teams. In particular, appropriate soft constraints are considered and ranking criteria evaluated. Of particular note is that owing to the intricate interdependencies of ranking criteria, the best candidate for a given service might not be the optimal candidate in the context of the team.
- Select Team. Based on the evaluations, the optimal team is selected. At this stage there are likely to be detailed negotiations among team members. These are easily simulated in agent-based formalisms through the use of negotiation protocols.

The above series of stages is necessarily followed by a consideration of the dependencies of the services and activities of the team members. These are used to establish the structure which formalizes the shape of the graph. In particular, the team structure as reflected in the shape graph constitutes an abstract global workflow which is refined in workflow composition. Figure 6.6 offers a concise summary of the stages of top-down team formation.

Implementation Aspects – As for goal decomposition, we maintain two forms of ontology structures, java classes and OWL; we equip JADE agents with knowledge bases written in Prolog facts and rules, and KIF tuples. Of particular note, we implement the forms selection procedure identified (e.g. shallow matchmaking and evaluation) as behaviours which are independent of the team formation agent. This maximizes flexibility and allows us to distribute computational effort according to the origin of the agents involved in the activities of the team formation module. For example, if the Catalogue Library Database CLDs have been implemented to CrossWork interfaces, then we assign matchmaking duties to the appropriate wrapper agents. Similarly, if the evaluation structures are as developed for the CrossWork

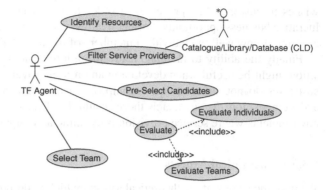

Fig. 6.6 The CrossWork approach to top-down team formation

case studies, then evaluation behaviour is embodied in an independent, internal evaluation agent. If neither case applies, and the CrossWork system communicates with external agents to achieve evaluation and pre-selection of nominees, then the necessary behaviours are assigned directly to the team formation agent.

6.3.3 Bottom-Up Team Formation

Top-down approaches assume access to appropriate syntactic and semantic structures to allow goals to be rewritten and to a level of detail which allows matching to known service providers. Moreover, to associate providers with the goal rewrites assumes that the respective sets of structures are consistent in both semantics and level of detail. Problems arise when this is not the case. Naturally, this assumes knowledge of service providers or at least some indirect access to these. Additional disadvantages include the possibility of needing to make several approaches to a number potential service providers owing to lack of information regarding workloads (cf. opportunism), and since existing automated top-down approaches often reduce to matchmaking there is a heavy computational cost which increases with scale (cf. tree-isomorphism). Naturally, approaching this in stages, as we have, can help. The bottom-up approach (in CrossWork) was devised to overcome some of these difficulties. It is intended to operate in situations where more traditional techniques as presented above struggle. A fuller discussion of the motivation behind the system can be found in [2].

The bottom-up approach assumes no centralized decomposition and does not involve matching advertised processes to potential subtasks. Instead the team formation process is driven by companies volunteering to extend existing partially formed teams with a process of their choosing. These teams then build up until they are sufficient to meet the original business opportunity. Support for this process is provided by agents that hold the information relating to a particular business opportunity.

One characteristic of this approach is that it gives the companies great flexibility in deciding which teams they want to join, and which processes they wish to contribute when doing so. In particular this caters for situations in which an agent wishes to customize its processes in order to join a team meeting an especially lucrative business opportunity. Further it allows the team formation to naturally take account of how well the individual members of the team will work together.

Finally the ability to facilitate team formation without a centralized decomposition might be useful when developing an entirely novel product, where available structures do not allow such a decomposition or when the services assumed for a decomposition do not match those available. This is highly possible in open environments where service provision is dynamic and opportunistic.

6.3.3.1 Theoretical Aspects

We introduce a few of the theoretical aspects which underpin the implementation of bottom-up team formation. Again, though a little more formal in style, our primary intention here is to establish a little terminology.

Partial Solution – Suppose that we have a consistent set of goals. A *partial solution* is any set of tasks (or activities) which satisfies a subset of our set of goals. A *complete solution* is a set of tasks (or activities) which satisfies all of our goals. We overload the term partial solution to apply more informally to any set of activities arising in the pursuit of complete solution to an identified global goal; here the subgoals are left implicit. A complete solution is necessarily a partial solution. However, a complete solution is (typically) not a unique combination of partial solutions.

We seek a team to fulfil a given order; a complete solution is a team which can do this whilst a partial solution is team which can fulfil part of the order.

Constrained Resources – A *constrained resource type*, T, consists of a type, T, together with constraints on its attributes. A *constrained resource set*, RS, consists of a natural number, Q, and a constrained resource type T. Here, Q represents the amount of the resource of the constrained resource type T present within the given set, it is important to note that this number is only the quantity needed to produce one of the requested products. A *state* is a collection C of constrained resource sets.

Types are assumed to come from some frame structured ontology. For example, a metal bar with length between 5 and 10 units, height between 8 and 9 and depth 1 is expressed as

> *"metal bar (:length (FromRange (5,10)):height (FromRange (8,9))::depth (1))"*.

A state consisting of 4 bars of this type might be expressed as

> *":ResourceSet (:Quantity (4):Type (metal bar (:length (FromRange (5,10)):height (FromRange (8,9))::depth (1))))"*.

These states are then used throughout the system.

The intention of constrained resource types is to capture, and make explicit, the way that a manufacturing process can consume/produce components of a certain type whose attributes lie within a particular tolerance level.

Declared Capability – A *declared capability* consists of a pair of states $S0_T$ and $S1_T$ together with a label, L_T, which is either a string or the reserved character "?".

L_T denotes the company providing this process, and "?" denotes that no agent has yet done so; such a declared capability is called *free*. Informally, partial solutions within a noticeboard may be thought of as a set of partially ordered declared capabilities, some of which are free. This is consistent with the external representation presented to the process agents, which is a set of *potential extensions* calculated from the internal representation. A potential extension is equivalent to a free declared capability.

Two main types of agents feature in the system: *Noticeboard Agents* and *Process Provider Agents*. Each noticeboard agent (there may be several) relates to a single business opportunity and acts as a blackboard; it centralizes the information defining the business opportunity including all of the related partial solutions. The process provider agents drive the system by locating partial solutions to extend on noticeboards, and proposing processes to extend them.

6.3.3.2 Process Details and Implementation

Input and output structures are for top-down team formation. No initial decomposition of the top-level goal into subgoals is made. Decompositions emerge from the agents proposing processes to create a solution. The first step is the creation of a noticeboard agent, to manage the creation of complete solutions. Using the information within the order specification the noticeboard agent makes public:

1. An initial partial solution calculated from the product specification, taking into account relevant constraints;
2. Utility information defining the worth of the request;
3. An (initially empty) set of partial solutions extending the initial solution;
4. Constraints on the potential solutions to the problem.

The next stage involves process agents' detecting and extending the partial solutions on the noticeboards within the system. To facilitate this, a noticeboard agent calculates a set of potential extensions for each partial solution that it owns. Process agents can then evaluate the worth of the business opportunity represented by the noticeboard, work out what types of declared capabilities they are prepared to contribute towards it and match their declared capabilities to these potential extensions. A process provider agent may also decide not to contribute a specific process, or indeed any process, on seeing which companies they would have to work with to do this.

When matching potential extensions and declared capabilities, a simple test to see if the input and output states of the two match exactly is too rudimentary. The system relies on partial matches, where an agent could produce a needed resource if it had some other resource not currently present within the partial solution. In such cases the partial solution is extended to note that the resource produced by the declared capability is produced and that the resource required is required. Similarly, if an agent can produce some resource not directly required using resources present within the partial solution, they are permitted to extend it in the indicated manner. Indeed, an agent can propose a declared capability which matches no resources either forwards or backwards, if it anticipates a later need for this. Furthermore, agents are allowed to alter the constrained resource types if they can produce a sub- or supertype of the already present type. Consider, if partial solution contained a requirement for planks of wood of length between 10 and 15 m, whereas the company could produce planks of wood of lengths between 8 and 14 m, the partial solution resulting from the extension would contain planks of wood of between 8 and 14 m. Clearly this process of altering the types has potential implications for other agents within the partial solution who might produce or consume this resource (or if any declared capabilities have functional dependencies between their input and output resources, on agents further *down/up* the partial solution). Such problems can be addressed either when the agents discuss if a proposed extension is acceptable or not, or once a complete solution has been located.

Once an agent has decided to propose a declared capability to the noticeboard it requests that the extension be made, giving both the declared capability it proposes to extend with and the potential extension it proposed to extend. Before the noticeboard allows an extension it first verifies that it is acceptable to the agents contributing to the present partial solution. Agents might choose to reject the extension for several reasons: they are not prepared to work with the company proposing the extension; the proposed extension fails to advance the partial solution in any way or perhaps another company which can do the same thing is already preferred. A protocol is used whereby the noticeboard agent contacts each agent with a declared capability within the partial solution asking if they are prepared to accept it. If the noticeboard agent then receives no refusals within a given time period the proposed extension is accepted. Otherwise it is rejected and the proposing agent informed of this. If a proposed extension is accepted the noticeboard then calculates the new partial solution produced, adding in the newly added declared capability and updating the states within the partial solution as required. This new partial solution is then put onto the noticeboard. However, the old one is still retained. Finally, a check is made to see if the new partial solution is complete, i.e. that every resource within the partial solution is produced by some agent (it is possible that *excess* resources will be produced). If it is complete then the newly generated complete solution is noted. When a complete solution is located, the agents involved in this complete solution are informed of this information and then negotiate the details of exactly how they wish to work together.

Again, we use JADE for implementation. To facilitate implementation, a third type of agent was introduced, a Noticeboard Factory Agent. This creates new noticeboards as needed and acts as a (supplementary) *yellow pages* for the noticeboards within the system. Currently, the factory creates new noticeboards only when requested, though feasibly it could subscribe to an electronic marketplace to locate new opportunities – there is only one noticeboard factory agent; however, federations or specialized types of factory agents for given classes of problems are potential extensions

Fig. 6.7 Overview of bottom-up team formation

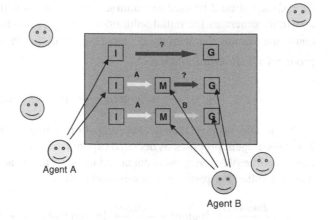

Figure 6.7 offers a pictorial summary of the development of a single complete solution during team formation. It shows several stages, starting from the initial solution being placed on the noticeboard, followed by agent A offering to extend it before agent B finally completes the partial solution. Intermediate stages such as the negotiation between agents A and B as to the acceptability of the proposed extension are omitted for clarity.

6.3.3.3 Example of Process Emergence

Again recall the water tank system from Fig. 6.3, however, to avoid repetition only four of the components are used. For simplicity, we use ontology names without constraints. Also for the purposes of clarity we use the linear representation from [1]. In this representation a partial solution is given by a set of states linked by arrows, labelled either with a ? when no agent has claimed them, or with an agent's name as appropriate. We assume the following agents and declared capabilities:

1. WaterTankSystemAssembler:
   [tank, pipes, seals, pump] *WaterTankSystemAssembler* [waterTankSystem]
2. TankMaker:
   [ø] *TankMaker* [tank]
3. PipeMaker:
   [ø] *PipeMaker* [pipe]
4. SealsMaker:
   [ø] *SealsMaker* [seals]

We assume that each agent has one, fixed declared capability. The initial order specification contains the following elements; a product specification asking for some water tank systems to be assembled, and a constraint that the company

PumpMaker should be used to manufacture the pumps within the system. The first constraint generates the initial solution of [ø] $\xrightarrow{?}$ [waterTankSystem]. The second constraint extends this with the declared capability [ø] *PumpMaker* [pump], which produces a *final initial* solution of:

$$[\emptyset] \xrightarrow{PumpMaker} [\text{pump}] \xrightarrow{?} [\text{waterTankSystem}]$$

Agents now propose their declared capabilities to extend the initial solution. The *TankMaker* agent proposes its declared capability as an extension to the partial solution. The *PumpMaker* agent is contacted to see if this is acceptable and agrees that it is. The following partial solution is produced:

$$[\emptyset] \xrightarrow{PumpMaker} [\text{pump}] \xrightarrow{TankMaker} [\text{pump,tank}] \xrightarrow{?} [\text{waterTankSystem}]$$

The noticeboard now contains both the initial solution and this partial solution. The *WaterTank SystemAssembler* proposes its declared capability here. Both the *TankMaker* and *PumpMaker* are contacted, and agree to the extension. The following partial solution is produced:

$$[\emptyset] \xrightarrow{PumpMaker} [\text{pump}] \xrightarrow{TankMaker} [\text{pump,tank}] \xrightarrow{?} [\text{tank, pipes, seals, pump}]$$
$$\xrightarrow{waterTankSystemAssembler} [\text{waterTankSystem}]$$

As can be seen, all that is required is that some method be found to manufacture some seals and pipes given a pump and a tank. The two agents *PipeMaker* and *SealsMaker* extend this partial solution. Thus:

$$[\emptyset] \xrightarrow{PumpMaker} [\text{pump}] \xrightarrow{TankMaker} [\text{pump,tank}] \xrightarrow{PipeMaker} [\text{pump, tank, pipes}]$$
$$\xrightarrow{SealsMaker} [\text{tank, pipes, seals, pump}] \xrightarrow{waterTankSystemAssembler} [\text{waterTankSystem}]$$

No free declared capabilities remain in the partial solution, so the complete solution is detected. The way that the resources have to be copied from state to state in the study above is clearly far from ideal, and indeed was one of the main motivations behind the current development of a new algorithm.

6.3.4 Hybrid Team Formation

While bottom-up team formation has some advantages over a top-down approach, as we have already noted, it does come at a price and has its own disadvantages. Where goal decompositions are available it is considerably less efficient than a top-down approach. If there are only a fixed, limited number of types of process available within the system it again can be considerably less efficient; in the worst case, that no solution can be found may take a considerable time to determine. Since it totally distributes control it is very dependent on the agents within the system behaving in an altruistic manner; it can be wide open to malicious behaviour. Thus, it assumes and requires a certain level of trust among participants. It cannot operate to extremely short timescales and so is inappropriate for some highly dynamic and opportunistic markets.

For well-defined products, a dedicated top-down approach is usually appropriate. Where novel products are being developed, a bottom-up approach is often the only option owing to a complete lack of semantics. There are occasions where a combined approach represents an exciting possibility. Consider, for concept design and early stages of product development, even when a functional decomposition is possible, bottom-up approaches can significantly enhance creativity and foster synergies which may otherwise be missed.

Many occasions call for a synthesis, for example, where many suppliers provide more than one part of an automotive system, thus a detailed decomposition can be somewhat redundant; and indeed the exact decomposition of the system is negotiated by the team members. To minimize the shortcomings of each approach and maximize the benefits of each, we typically use a top-down approach to obtain a high-level decomposition; each resulting subgoal is used to create a noticeboard to drive a bottom-up solution, thus, the remainder of the decomposition emerges.

6.4 Related Work

Several cognate areas of research underlie the discussions within this chapter. Some of these are long established and have an extensive literature. Indeed numerous systems which use such techniques to drive VE formation have been proposed.

The *bottom-up team formation* uses the idea of combining blackboard systems and agents. This idea has previously been used within several systems. These include [8], in which such a hybrid system is used to generate plans, and [3], in which the authors use their own blackboard/agent hybrid architecture to compare three different approaches to organizing teamwork within agents: contract net, cooperative problem solving and shifting matrix management. While these systems share an underlying technology with the *bottom-up team formation* system proposed within this chapter, they markedly differ in both the application area and the way in which the technology is used.

The description of *top-down team formation* within the current chapter included a theoretical treatment of the well-studied process of matchmaking. An alternative approach to matching suppliers to roles is the Contract Net protocol, originally introduced in [7]. The protocol is used after a set of roles to fill have been identified. Instead of attempting to identify appropriate suppliers from adverts, the company in charge of forming the VE sends messages to appropriate companies asking if they were prepared to supply a required service. These companies then reply with bids, from which the best supplier would be chosen. The main effect of this protocol is to place the responsibility for matchmaking on the potential suppliers. This could be advantageous in situations where the abilities of the suppliers are unknown, perhaps because they dynamically vary.

The contract net approach has been used in several systems supporting VE formation with interesting examples including [4, 5]. Systems using ContractNet decentralize the process of selecting the potential candidates for tasks. However, both goal decomposition and the final selection of the optimal candidate for each role remain centralized.

One approach to task formation which lessens the need for a centralized decomposition is presented in [6]. This chapter attempts to use agents to yield a more flexible mix of decomposition and allocation of tasks within team formation. In the paper they assume the existence of multiple different possible decompositions of the task and argue that the best one of these cannot be chosen on an a priori, centralized basis. Instead, the choice of which decomposition to use is guided by checking (with the agents) which of the atomic actions within the decompositions can actually be filled and then selecting the possible decompositions. While this system does retain some flexibility in the choice of decomposition used, it is still restricted to selecting from a globally predefined set of decompositions. In addition the need to enquire as to which atomic tasks are viable could entail a considerable performance overhead.

In contrast to this the *bottom-up team formation* system proposed within this chapter fully decentralizes all of the phases of team formation, including decomposition. As a result of this, the hybrid system proposed within this chapter can intelligently switch between existing decompositions where they are reliable, whilst allowing entirely novel solutions to be created where necessary.

6.5 Summary of Agent-Based Team Formation

This chapter discussed how we can support team formation within the context of IVEs. Detailed theoretical review of the traditional technique of top-down team formation has been complemented by the novel technique of bottom-up team formation, using goal decomposition and matchmaking, which allows for cooperative team formation.

During our investigation of team formation techniques it became clear that supporting team formation would be best implemented through an intelligent hybrid of these two approaches. This hybrid approach has been presented in this chapter.

Team formation requirements need flexibility in exploring different configurations and teams, and autonomy of team members who are independent organizations. All these suggest the need for software agents, which can use different problem-solving approaches and negotiation patterns to support the different degrees of problem specification and different circumstances.

References

1. Carpenter, M., Mejandjiev, M., Stalker, I., Emergent Process Interoperability within Virtual Organisations, Proceedings of Agent-Based Technologies and Applications for Enterprise interOperability Workshop (ATOP), 2005.
2. Carpenter, M., Mehandjiev, N., Stalker, I., Flexible Behaviours for Emergent Process Interoperability, Proceedings of the 15th IEEE International Workshops on Enabling Technologies: Infrastructure for Collaborative Enterprises (WETICE), Manchester, UK, 26th–28th June, 2006.
3. Li, G., Hopgood, A. A., Weller, M. J., Shifting Matrix Management: A Model for Multi-Agent Cooperation, Engineering Applications of Artificial Intelligence, Vol. 16(3), pp. 191–201, 2003.
4. Norman, T. J., Preece, A., Chalmers, S., Jennings, N. R., Luck, M., Dang, V. D., Nguyen, T. D., Deora, V., Shao, J., Gray, A., Fiddian, N., CONOISE: Agent-Based Formation of Virtual Organisations, Proceedings of the 23rd SGAI International Conference on Innovative Techniques and Applications of AI, Cambridge, UK, 2003.
5. Oliveira, E., Rocha, A. P., Agents Advanced Features for Negotiation in Electronic Commerce and Virtual Organisations Formation Process, Lecture Notes in Computer Science, Vol. 1991/2001, Springer Verlag, New York, pp. 78–97, 2001.
6. Ozturk, P., Gundersen, O. E., A Combined Top-down and Bottom-up Approach to Integrated Task Decomposition and Allocation, Proceedings of the International Conference on Machine Learning and Cybernetics, Vol. 1, pp. 163–168, 2004.
7. Smith, R. G., The Contract Net Protocol: High-Level Communication and Control in a Distributed Problem Solver, Distributed Artificial Intelligence, Morgan Kaufmann Publishers Inc, San Francisco, CA, USA, pp. 357–366, 1988.
8. Wilkins, D. E., Myers, K. L., A Multiagent Planning Architecture, In Artificial Intelligence Planning Systems, pp. 154–163, 1998.

Chapter 7
Business Process Composition

Rik Eshuis and Alex Norta

This chapter describes the realization of the business process composition cluster in the CrossWork architecture. Business process composition is concerned with automated means for constructing business processes in a dynamically forged virtual organization. A business process is operationalized in a workflow, which can be supported by workflow management technology. We first introduce several perspectives for business process collaborations and discuss how they relate to each other. Next, the languages used for process specification are presented. We examine the workflow composition module, which provides support for (semi-) automatic composition of global workflows from local workflows of members in a VE. Before a composed workflow can be used in practice, it needs to be tested – this is discussed in the next subsection. The interfaces used for the transfer of a composed workflow to its execution environment are subsequently discussed in this chapter.

7.1 Perspectives for Business Process Collaboration

Collaboration among business processes can be supported by linking the underlying workflow management systems that are responsible for executing the corresponding local workflows. To connect local workflows in an appropriate way, several conflicting issues have to be balanced. For privacy and security reasons, each partner wishes to shield as much as possible of its own internal local workflow. To collaborate, however, each partner has to expose some details of its internal process, to inform its team partners about the local progress so that the global progress can be tracked. Therefore, we distinguish between two *visibility levels* for local workflows; the conceptual (internal) level and the external level. The external-level workflow is visible to the partner and the outside world whereas the internal-level workflow is only visible to the partner doing the workflow. This way, the partner doing the local workflow can hide internal details from the local workflow from the outside world. However, the external-level workflow is an abstract and coarse-grained

R. Eshuis (✉)
Eindhoven University of Technology, Eindhoven, The Netherlands
e-mail: h.eshuis@tue.nl

N. Mehandjiev, P. Grefen (eds.), *Dynamic Business Process Formation for Instant Virtual Enterprises*, Advanced Information and Knowledge Processing,
DOI 10.1007/978-1-84882-691-5_7, © Springer-Verlag London Limited 2010

version of the internal-level workflow, so the external-level workflow does offer valid information on the progress of the internal workflow to other partners.

Another important concept is *workflow perspective* [23]. A perspective is a particular angle from which a workflow is regarded. Important perspectives for traditional (intra-organizational) workflows are the control flow, data flow, resource and transaction perspective. Control flow focuses on the temporal ordering of tasks, so it answers the question when each task is to be done. Data flow focuses on the various ways in which data is represented and utilized in workflows [25], i.e. how data flows between tasks. Undertaking a task involves human or non-human resources, e.g. machines, production material, office space and so on. Thus, the resource perspective deals with the way involvement of such resources is represented and utilized [26]. Finally, the enactment of a local workflow must offer a degree of certainty in cases of exceptional situations. The transaction perspective secures the effects of tasks and handles exceptional situations and compensates them if required.

For workflows spanning multiple organizations, an overarching perspective such as eSourcing [23] is needed. To explain this perspective, Fig. 7.1 shows the simplest collaboration possible. The team consists of two parties: an organization outsourcing a part of its local workflow to another organization. The outsourcing organization is called consumer, whereas the organization performing the outsourced workflow part is called provider. The four mentioned intra-organizational perspectives are shown as pillars in Fig. 7.1. Note that more perspectives may exist; however, the listed ones were considered most important for CrossWork. The inter-organizational concept of eSourcing, which is explained in the remainder of this chapter, rests on these intra-organizational perspectives.

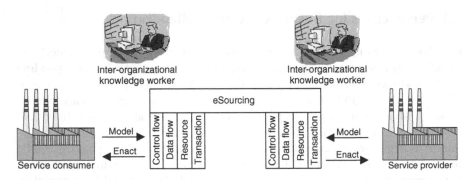

Fig. 7.1 Relating perspectives in business collaboration

As shown by Fig. 7.1, the eSourcing perspective harmonizes the local workflows of the consumer and the provider. Thus, the eSourcing perspective is specific to the external level. This harmonization is done in a global workflow, which spans the collaborating organizations. The global workflow coordinates the local external-level workflows. The global workflow itself is a workflow too, consisting of perspectives like control flow and data flow, so in this sense the eSourcing perspective is a meta perspective. For teams consisting of more than two partners, similar diagrams as shown in Fig. 7.1 can be made, where each partner is represented by a pillar and eSourcing is the roof connecting the pillars.

To specify eSourcing models, a separate language has been developed, called eSML. The roots of eSML are existing proposals for modelling electronic contracts and inter-organizational workflows. eSML deals with workflow perspectives but also with external-level issues. Thus, eSML is a language that can be used to express workflows in a B2B setting. eSML is explained in Section 7.2.

Given a set of team partners with their local workflows, all specified at the external level, the problem is how a global workflow, expressed in eSML, can be constructed. The global workflow must coordinate the execution of the local workflows. Section 7.3 outlines a semi-automatic approach for composing a global workflow from a set of local workflow models that are of a external level.

The constructed global workflow may contain errors, for example a deadlock, when two parties are waiting, each for the other, to send something. Such errors should be detected as soon as possible, as repairing them while the global workflow is being done is typically very costly, since it can involve stopping a production process or redoing some parts of a local workflow. To detect logical errors before the global workflow is done, the global workflow is analysed both mechanically, by a verification tool, and manually, by means of a prototyping tool that allows users to execute sample scenarios of the global workflow. Section 7.4 presents these tools.

Finally, Section 7.5 explains how the workflow composition module links to the workflow enactment module, by detailing how an eSML specification can be transformed into the industry standard language BPEL. Since BPEL is not as rich as eSML, we also use some BPEL extensions to configure the CrossWork enactment infrastructure.

7.2 Process Specification

We explain two XML-based languages that were used in CrossWork, eSML and XRL. eSML has been used to express business process collaborations. The part of eSML in which processes are specified, is based on the workflow language XRL.

7.2.1 eSML

The XML-based modelling language eSML is instrumental for specifying inter-organizational business processes. eSML stands for electronic Sourcing Markup Language. The design of eSML has been influenced by a pattern catalogue for eSourcing which is specified in [24]. As explained in the previous section, eSML models are global workflow models that concern the external level where business-process details are publicly disclosed. eSML contains many advanced constructs for visibility, monitoring and polling business collaborations [23], but we focus here on the basic structure of the language used for CrossWork.

7.2.1.1 Foundation of eSML

The foundation of eSML is the XML-based language ECML (Electronic Contracting Markup Language) [6], which is designed for the formulation of electronic contracts. A contract is a legally enforceable agreement, in which two or more parties commit to certain obligations in return for certain rights [12]. In B2B relationships all economic production and exchange processes are organized through contracts. Electronic contracting aims at using information technologies to significantly improve the efficiency and effectiveness of paper contracting, allowing companies to support the newly emerging business paradigms while still being legally protected.

At the highest level of abstraction a contract in eSML is reduced to answering three questions, i.e. the *Who*, *Where* and *What* question [6]. The *Who* answer concerns the actors that participate in the contract establishment and enactment. The *Where* answer specifies the context of a contract, e.g. the legal and business context. The *What* answer models the exchanged values, rules, and the exchange processes for which XRL [23] is an integral part. ECML also uses the *How* answer that specifies the contract content structuring, representation, establishment and enactment. However, the *How* answer is not part of eSML as it is already covered by the CrossWork system.

The following sections present models of constructs and their relationships that are part of the eSML definition. These models are based on the three contracting questions described above.

7.2.1.2 eSML Overview

First, Fig. 7.2 gives an overview of the structure in an eSML instantiation, which uses parts of the ECML [6] schema as a foundation. In Fig. 7.2 this fact is reflected by considering an entire eSML instance as a contract between collaborating parties and by structuring the eSML content into the blocks *Who*, *Where* and *What* that are explained in the sequel. The parts of eSML in Fig. 7.2 that are ECML-based are not explained in this case study, namely the definition of company data and company-contact data, the *Where* block and the XRL-based process definition within the exchanged-value definition.

The bold-typed eSML-definition parts in Fig. 7.2 are either extensions or modifications that are not part of the ECML foundation. In the *Who* block extensions for eSML are the resource definition and the data definition [23]. In the *What* block, the process definitions are based on XRL, however, extensions have been made to allow for integrating the non-control-flow perspectives.

The following sections present models of constructs and their relationships that are part of the eSML schema. These models are based on the three contracting questions that are described above. We highlight the *Who* dimension, since that one together with the *What* dimension, is most relevant to CrossWork. The *What* dimension is mostly covered by XRL. For a complete overview of the eSML schema, see [23].

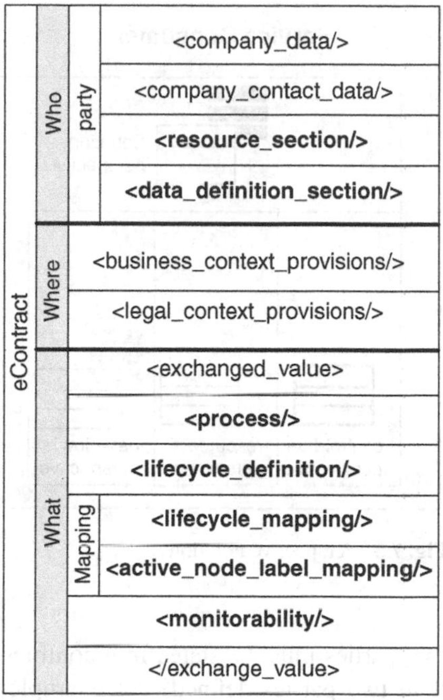

Fig. 7.2 eSML overview

		<company_data/>
Who	party	<company_contact_data/>
		<resource_section/>
		<data_definition_section/>
Where		<business_context_provisions/>
		<legal_context_provisions/>
What		**<exchanged_value>**
		<process/>
		<lifecycle_definition/>
	Mapping	**<lifecycle_mapping/>**
		<active_node_label_mapping/>
		<monitorability/>
		</exchange_value>

(eContract)

7.2.1.3 Notation Explanation

Since different perspectives are contained in eSML, it is important to visually distinguish them in the following static UML diagram [27]. The referred to perspectives are paid attention to with a special notation as depicted in Fig. 7.3.

In Fig. 7.3 some UML-class icons are visualized with background shading of different darkness variations and different boldness of lines. Since the inter-organizational concept of eSourcing rests on the three inter-organizational perspectives of control flow, resource and data flow, eSML also incorporates classes belonging to the three perspectives.

Visualizing all elements of eSML in a static class diagram results in fairly large models. In order to fit the visualization into this chapter, a way of splitting the overall model into smaller sub-models must be found. Thus, classes that are coupling points between different sub-models are grey shaded and replicated in those sub-models that are adjacent to each other.

7.2.1.4 The Who Concept

Figure 7.4 describes the classes and relationships belonging to the *Who* concept. As mentioned before, this concept clearly identifies the contracting parties by including the class "party".

Parties are actors that have rights and obligations, which are listed in the eSourcing configuration. Concerning the relationship cardinalities, it is defined that at least

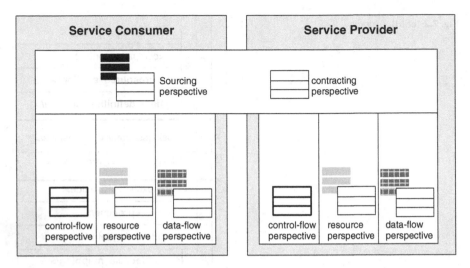

Fig. 7.3 Perspective notation

two parties must be stated in a contract. However, it is also possible to have more than two parties defined. For example, an original manufacturer can agree with several suppliers to be included in one contract.

In a contract several third parties may optionally be involved that are called mediators in the case of eSML. Mediators represented by class "mediator", participate in the enactment of an eSourcing configuration but their rights/obligations are not stated. Since mediators are not considered in CrossWork, we do not discuss them any further; more information can be found in [23].

Contracting parties and optional numbers of mediators are in a relationship with several other classes. The "company_data" comprises information like the name of a contracting party or mediator, the type of legal organization, and so on, while the "company_contact_data" refers to information related to the geographic location of the eSourcing party. That way a contracting party or a mediator is uniquely identified according to legal requirements.

The third related class termed "resource_section" is the root class of the resource perspective. A contracting "party or a mediator" may have attached resource definitions. However, in most cases it might, for example, be superfluous to define resources of mediators, unless a mediator is also primarily involved in commercial exchanges. Resources may comprise of actors and non-actors where the latter can be of a consumable or non-consumable nature. Further details are contained in [23], where figures about the resource perspective are outlined.

The classes "company_data" and "company_contact_data" are subclasses of class "only_vars_section", which contains variables and so-called snippets. The class "var_section" is a docking class belonging to the data-flow perspective that includes company description, trade registration number, VAT registration number, address of registration, etc. The class "snippet_section" references so-called

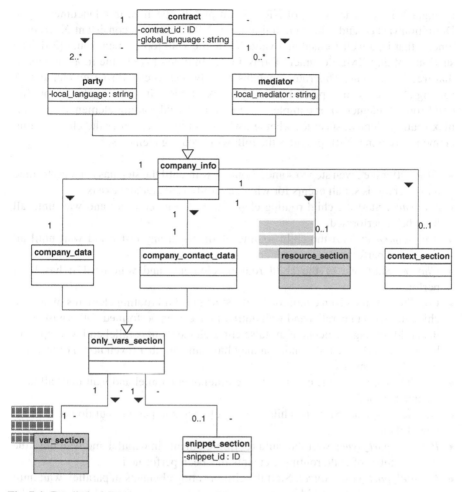

Fig. 7.4 Detailed who concept

contract snippets that can be attached to particular contract definitions, e.g. to represent general terms and conditions.

7.2.2 XRL – eXchangeable Routing Language

XRL is an instance-based workflow language that uses XML for the representation of process definitions and Petri nets for its semantics. A catalogue of control-flow patterns [1, 18, 19] is contained in the definition of XRL [3] as routing elements that results in strong control-flow expressive power of XRL. These routing elements are equipped with Petri net semantics [2], namely, every routing element stands for an equivalent WF-net snippet that can be connected with other routing elements into a bigger WF-net. The syntax of XRL is completely specified in a Document Type Definition (DTD) and schema definition. An XRL route is a consistent XML document, that is, a well-formed and valid XML file with top element route [23]. The structure of any XML document forms a tree. In case of XRL, the root element of that tree is the route. This route contains exactly one so-called routing element. A routing element is an important building block of XRL. It can either be simple (no child routing elements) or complex (one or more child routing elements). A complex routing element specifies whether, when and in which order the child routing elements are done. XRL provides the following routing elements:

- *Task*: Offer the given step to some resource, wait until the step has been performed and afterwards set all events for which a child event element exists.
- *Sequence*: Start the child routing elements in the given order and wait until all have been performed.
- *Any_sequence*: Start the child routing elements in any order and wait until all have been performed.
- *Choice*: Start one of the child routing elements and wait until it has been performed.
- *Condition*: If the given condition holds, start the child routing elements of all true child elements in parallel and wait until all have been performed. Otherwise, start the child routing elements of all false child elements in parallel and wait until all have been performed. A condition may have any number (even none) of true and false child elements.
- *Parallel_sync*: Start the child routing elements in parallel and wait until all have been performed.
- *Parallel_no_sync*: Start the child routing elements in parallel but do not wait for any of them.
- *Parallel_part_sync*: Start the child routing elements in parallel and wait until the given number of child routing elements has been performed.
- *Parallel_part_sync_cancel*: Start the child routing elements in parallel, wait until the given number of child routing elements has been performed and cancel the remaining child routing elements if possible.

The routing elements of XRL are based on a thorough analysis of the workflow patterns supported by leading workflow management systems. XRL is an instance-based workflow language that uses XML for the representation of process definitions and Petri net formalism for its semantics resulting in an unambiguous understanding of XRL. This makes XRL an interesting candidate for eSML instantiations where XRL is used for modelling the contractual spheres of a service consumer and a service provider [23].

As shown in [2], the semantics of XRL is expressed in terms of WF-nets [4, 5, 14], which permits the use of theoretical results and standard tools such as Woflan [29] for checking the notion of soundness. The Petri net semantics of XRL is realized by mapping to the Petri Net Markup Language (PNML) [20, 21], an XML-based interchange format that permits the definition of Petri net types. For that purpose, a stylesheet translator is employed that contains mapping rules to PNML for every XRL control-flow construct [2].

As pointed out by Norta [23], in the context of eSourcing, *projection inheritance* [7], originally defined on Petri nets, can be useful. Informally, projection inheritance allows adding tasks to an original process without violating the original observable runtime behaviour of the process. By establishing a projection inheritance relation between an external and an internal process, these two processes are guaranteed to behave the same for their common tasks. Thus, the processes at the different levels are consistent with each other. For a complete account of this topic, we refer to [23].

7.3 Workflow Composition

Chapter 6 elaborated how teams are formed in CrossWork teams. Each formed team is potential, in the sense that the business processes, or local external-level workflows of the team members need to be weaved together before the team can work together. The workflow composition module takes care of this by constructing a global workflow model, expressed in eSML that coordinates the local workflows of the team members. First we discuss the basic approach as implemented in the CrossWork prototype system. Next, we explain some extensions.

7.3.1 Basic Approach

The composition is done in two phases [15]. The first analyses dependencies among the local workflows, whilst the second phase constructs a global workflow, expressed in eSML, which satisfies the dependencies between the local workflows.

In the first phase, data-flow dependencies between the local workflows of the individual team members are analysed. Each local workflow is treated as a black box that needs a certain input in order to start, and upon completion gives its output, hiding the process of each local workflow. The global workflow activates the local workflows, and also takes the data-flow dependencies between the different local workflows into account, modifying the control flow if necessary. For example, if team member A requires as input a frame that is produced by member B, then the global workflow must ensure that the local workflow of B finishes before the one of A is started.

The data-flow dependencies between the local workflows can be captured in a dependency graph $(L, E, fork)$, where L is a set of local workflows and $E \subseteq L \times L$ a set of dependencies between these workflows, and function $fork{:}L \rightarrow \{AND,XOR\}$ assigns each local workflow with the branching type for its outgoing dependencies, where AND denotes that all outgoing dependencies are triggered whereas XOR denotes only one is triggered. Figure 7.5 shows an example dependency graph for the water tank scenario.

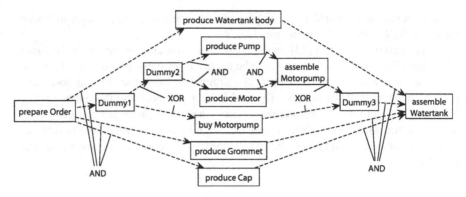

Fig. 7.5 Example dependency graph for water tank case

For example, Produce Pump and Produce Motor are to be carried out in parallel. The dummy activities are needed to express complex branching conditions, for example, an AND split followed by an XOR split [15, 16]. Note, however, that a dependency graph is not a process diagram, since the arrows indicate data flow, not control flow.

Dependencies can be automatically derived by analysing the local workflows for the data that they require from the outside world and the data they output to the outside world. However, the branching types need to be provided by the user, since these are domain specific. That is, depending on the specific problem domain, a branching type is either AND or XOR.

In the second phase, the composition module constructs a global workflow satisfying the data-flow dependencies. This global workflow is specified in eSML. Since eSML is a structured language, splits and joins need to be correctly balanced. However, the dependency graph is unstructured; split and join dependencies need not be balanced. For example, in Fig. 7.6 the XOR split following Dummy1 is not

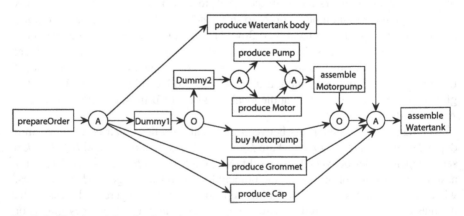

Fig. 7.6 Global workflow for dependency graph

followed by any XOR join. Thus, the balancing structure needs to be derived from an unbalanced input structure, which makes the translation far from straightforward. An algorithm detailing the translation can be found in [15, 16]. For the example dependency graph in Fig. 7.5 the constructed global workflow specified in eSML is graphically depicted in Fig. 7.6. A circle denotes a split or a join, where A indicates an AND, and O indicates an XOR.

Next, the constructed global workflow needs to be checked for correctness, both analytically and empirically, which is done in the workflow validation and prototyping phase.

7.3.2 Extensions

The black-box view on local workflows can be too coarse-grained in some situations. For example, partners may wish to see some internal details on the progress of a local workflow. However, the black-box view cannot disclose any internal details; for this, a white-box view is needed. With a white-box view, each local workflow is abstracted into an external-level workflow.

Adopting a white-box view on local workflows means the composition procedure has to be changed. Dependencies are now no longer between different local workflows, but rather between tasks of different local external-level workflows. The constructed global workflow has to satisfy all these dependencies, but must also keep the individual local workflow models intact. This can be done by propagating the dependencies from the task level to the workflow level, and next applying the composition approach as outlined for the black-box case.

7.4 Workflow Validation and Prototyping

The constructed global workflow may contain errors. Detecting and repairing such errors while the global workflow is being executed can be costly and time consuming, since for example, some production processes may need to be stopped or perhaps even be done anew. Therefore, it is vital that errors are detected before the global workflow is actually performed.

To spot errors in the constructed global workflow, it is checked both mechanically and manually. The mechanical check is done by a verification tool, which analyses all potential behaviours whereas the manual check is supported by a prototyping tool, which allows users to play execution scenarios in a laboratory setting, without actually performing the global workflow in practice.

7.4.1 Workflow Verification

To ensure that a composed global workflow contains no errors, it needs to be mechanically verified for correctness. While for black-box models the composed global workflow models are guaranteed to be free of errors, for white-box models this is no longer true and verification is needed to guarantee the absence of errors.

Woflan [29] is the tool used to verify the correctness of global workflows. It uses Petri net techniques to check for correctness. As explained in Section 7.3, the global workflow expressed in eSML/XRL can be translated to Petri nets using XML stylesheets. The feedback of Woflan is a text file that is interpreted by the workflow module. In case of errors, the workflow composition module can construct a new global workflow.

In addition, some simple quality-of-service global constraints regarding cost and time of the global workflow can be verified. For example, a global constraint could be that the maximal duration of the global workflow is 15 days. By calculating the critical path of the global workflow and taking the sum of the maximal durations of the local workflows on the critical path, such a constraint can be verified.

7.4.2 Workflow Prototyping

XRL/flower [29] is used as an evaluation tool in CrossWork for the in-house process of a service consumer and for the provider sphere of the service provider. The development of XRL and subsequently XRL/flower can be seen as a reaction to several XML-based standards for business process modelling that have emerged in recent years. Some examples of relevant present and past acronyms are BPEL4WS [11], BPML [10], WSFL [17], WSCI [8], XPDL [30], XLANG [28] and so forth. However, while their semantics and expressive power is suitable for technically composing Web Services, their satisfactory application in B2B collaboration poses a challenge. In contrast, XRL as a part of eSML is equipped with very clear Petri net semantics. Different to the mentioned XML-standards, one can determine *before* enactment whether an XRL-modelled workflow is sound or not. Such analysis power is crucial for avoiding the occurrence of abnormalities such as deadlocks during carrying out business transactions.

Since XRL is based on both XML for syntax and Petri nets for semantics, standard XML tools can be deployed to parse, check and handle XRL documents. The Petri net representation allows for a straightforward implementation of the workflow enactment engine. XRL constructs are automatically transformed to Petri net constructs. This allows for an efficient implementation. Next, the system is easy to extend by employing an XSL translator for mapping routing elements to PNML [9]. Thus, for supporting a new control-flow primitive, only a transformation to the Petri net format needs to be added and the engine itself does not need to be changed.

7.4.3 Architecture of XRL/Flower

Figure 7.7 presents the toolset architecture of XRL/flower where grey shaded elements have been implemented. Using both the control-flow data for the workflow

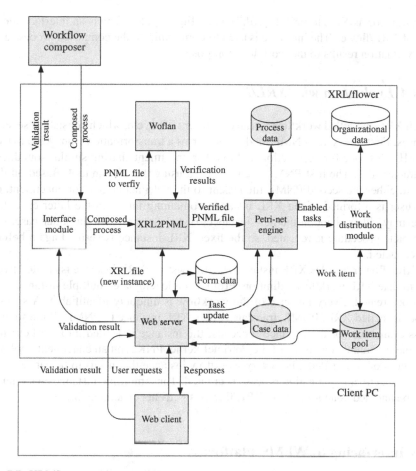

Fig. 7.7 XRL/flower architecture [29]

case and case-specific data, the Petri net engine computes the set of enabled tasks, that is, the set of work items that are ready. The engine sends this set to the work distribution module. Based on information of organizational roles and actors, the work distribution module fills the work item pool.

Resources that may carry out those ready worklist items can log into XRL/flower through the Web server. If the actor has registered beforehand, an online worklist manager displays the ready items in the Web client that are assigned by the work distribution module. By accepting a chosen worklist item, its content is displayed.

In order to enable an actor to perform an activity, the Web server fills the appropriate form template with case-specific data for the activity. The Web server stores updated case data and signals the Petri-net engine that the activity has been completed. The Petri net engine then recomputes a new set of work items that are ready. The actor can also start an XRL instance by sending the corresponding XRL file to the Web server. The Web server forwards the XRL file to the XRL2PNML module that transforms XRL to PNML [20]. Finally, Fig. 7.7 also depicts an interface module of XRL/flower. The interface is used to communicate the composed process and the validation results to the workflow composer.

7.4.4 Evaluation with XRL/Flower

Each XRL-modelled workflow has an enactment life cycle, which consists of several phases. First, the XRL2PNML module performs a transformation from XRL to two PNML files; one for verification and one for enactment sharing similar soundness characteristics. The first PNML file is verified using the Woflan tool. Based on the result, either the second PNML file is sent to the Petri net engine for enactment, or the user is informed of the XRL instance containing flaws. In the latter case, the user may either abandon the new instance, or fix the errors. In the latter case, the complete procedure is repeated, so the fixed XRL instance is verified again before it is enacted.

XRL/flower handles XRL instances as follows: An XRL instance is created from a template XRL workflow definition. From a single template, multiple instance files can be created. Every instance of the workflow is uniquely identifiable. A special module, called XRL2PNML, translates every XRL instance to PNML. If the soundness evaluation for the instance succeeds, the instance is loaded into the Petri net engine module that consists of the Petri net kernel PNK, and an enactment application built on top of PNK. For every workflow instance that needs to be carried out, a new enactment application process is created. Thus, multiple instance enactments can be handled concurrently by XRL/flower's Petri net enactment module.

7.5 Interfacing to WFMS Platforms

To execute a global workflow specified in eSML, it needs to be transformed first to languages processable by industrial state-of-the-art enactment tools. The industry language we have chosen for CrossWork is BPEL. Many industrial tools support the execution of BPEL specification. Adopting BPEL as an execution language leverages the use of CrossWork technology for the industry domain. However, adopting BPEL raises the problem of how to express the constructed global eSML workflow in BPEL. This section explains how eSML specifications can be mapped to BPEL specifications.

Both languages pursue different objectives, which impedes specifying a complete mapping from eSML to BPEL. BPEL is intended to orchestrate Web Services whereas eSML is intended for defining Sourcing configurations on an external layer. The primary goal of eSML is to provide a high level of suitability and expressiveness for modelling inter-organizational business processes. Practically, this means BPEL specifies the view of a single party, the orchestrator of a set of services, whereas eSML specifies the global view of an entire orchestra of services, including the orchestrator.

There are also more concrete differences between eSML and BPEL. For instance, eSML allows the specification of business rules, which is not possible in BPEL. eSML uses business rules for starting compensation processes, which is a mismatch to the compensation concept realized in BPEL, which uses fault and compensation handlers. As an eSML file is in essence an electronic contract, the definitions of collaborating parties need to be uniquely identifiable from a legal point of view and are therefore more elaborate than in BPEL. Finally, in eSML the data flow and resource perspectives are much more elaborate than in BPEL.

This brief comparison between eSML and BPEL makes it clear that mapping cannot be one to one. Instead, mapping is defined for the main perspectives that eSML and BPEL have in common, which is comprised of the control-flow perspective, the data-flow perspective and the resource perspective. This mapping is still powerful enough for execution, and is demonstrated in the following chapter.

The key part in mapping from eSML to BPEL is mapping the control-flow part of eSML, which is XRL, to BPEL. This can actually be carried out in a straightforward manner as both eSML/XRL and BPEL are block-structured languages that use if-then-else and while-do constructs. Moreover, both languages support the notion of *event*, which is used to specify interactions like receiving and sending. Furthermore, both eSML/XRL and BPEL support the notion of *link* to cross-synchronize parallel branches.

Regarding the data flow and resource perspective, for each eSML variable a BPEL variable is created in the translation. BPEL variables are mainly used as parameters for local services. Next, for each party (resource) a BPEL partner link is defined. Partner links define how the local services of the partners are linked to the global workflow, whilst the local services are defined in WSDL, the standard description language for Web Services.

Though much of the eSML information specified in the other perspectives are not expressed in BPEL, some of this information can be used to configure CrossWork-specific modules that can monitor and control the execution of the global workflow. For example, a partner offering a local workflow can decide to not only offer a black-box service but in addition a white-box view, which allows the caller to monitor (but not influence) the progress of the invoked local workflow, while from the BPEL execution point of view the local workflow is encapsulated in a black-box WSDL service.

The mapping has been implemented using XSLT, which is similar to the translation of PNML to XRL. The BPEL specification focuses on the coordinators view of the global VE workflow, whereas the eSML specification focuses on the global view of the entire workflow.

7.6 Related Work

As mentioned in Chapter 1, WISE and CrossFlow are the two approaches that most closely relate to CrossWork. We now examine how these approaches address the problem of business process composition.

WISE adopts a manual approach for composing global business processes. Local business processes are offered as black-box services in WISE. These services are published in a WWW catalogue. From this catalogue, a drag-and-drop interface is used to build a global business process. WISE uses a process-modelling tool that was considered the state-of-the-art in its time to specify the global business process. Each step in the global business process corresponds to a service offered by a partner in the VE. CrossWork adopts a semi-automated composition where dependencies and actual composition are derived automatically, although the user is still required to annotate dependencies with their branching types. As a consequence, the CrossWork business composition approach is less labour intensive than the WISE approach. However, in WISE, business process composition encompasses data flow, whereas CrossWork focuses on control flow. In contrast to WISE, CrossWork supports the validation of a global business process.

CrossFlow focuses on bilateral business collaborations, in which one organization called a service consumer outsources part of its business process to another organization, called a service provider. The outsourced process is specified within a contract. The internal provider process must comply with the contract but can contain some additional activities. A matchmaking infrastructure helps consumers and providers to find each other, where for a match to be successful a consumer process (request) has to match one-to-one with a provider process (offer). The process of finding and matching can be conducted on-the-fly at runtime while the consumer process is executing. Conceptually, the provider process is executed as a subprocess inside the overall consumer process. In CrossFlow, the actual business composition is already specified in the consumer process. The focus is on dynamically selecting a provider that offers exactly the requested process with the appropriate non-functional characteristics. This is in contrast to CrossWork, where providers are selected prior to the dynamic composition of their local business processes. Thus, the provider processes do not need to meet some prespecified process request. Furthermore, the structure of the global business process is composed dynamically, whereas the structure of CrossFlow is static as it is defined in the consumer process.

Next, there are several approaches from the literature that focus on composing services into processes [15], building on techniques from AI planning and program synthesis. We only discuss the two most relevant works; a more complete overview of related work can be found elsewhere [16]. The first work is by Duan et al. [13], who define a formal approach for synthesizing a BPEL skeleton from a set of services. As in the CrossWork approach, their composition algorithm is automated. But unlike the CrossWork approach, the services in their approach have to be formally specified with a pre- and post-condition. Note that such detailed information is not always available for services, as was the case in the industrial case studies of CrossWork. Therefore, for CrossWork an approach like [13] is not feasible. Moreover, the composition approach of [13] is less efficient than the composition approach outlined in CrossWork. Another related approach is by Liang et al. [22]. Here dependency graphs are used to construct a composition skeleton by translating each dependency directly into a control flow. However, this approach does not construct structured processes, and therefore does not always yield an output that is suitable for BPEL. The main difference of the CrossWork composition approach with [22] is therefore the use of the structured composition algorithm in CrossWork.

7.7 Summary

Once a team has been assembled through the team composition modules, the coordination of the team has to be arranged. Each team member has its own local business process, which defines its own optimal way of working. To coordinate the local business processes, a composite global process is constructed by the business process composition module. The global process specifies the global ordering of the local business processes and is used by the enactment infrastructure to perform the complete Business Network Process. Based on the theory of workflow patterns and electronic contracts, eSML is a modelling language that allows the definition of an inter-organizational workflow or business process from different angles, such as control flow, data flow and resource perspective.

The workflow composition module takes several partner services, which capture local business processes, and composes them into a global business process, expressed in eSML. To ensure that the composition does not contain any errors, it can either be mechanically verified or manually prototyped using dedicated tools. Finally, to allow the error-free composite global business process to be deployed using state of the art service technology, the constructed eSML model is mapped to a BPEL model. The next chapter explains how this constructed global business process is enacted and how it coordinates local business processes.

Once a VE team is assembled, we need to coordinate the work of the team members. For this, members are required to model work at both the individual company and cross-company levels.

Each member is likely to maintain pre-existing practices and processes. Are these compatible? Verification and validation follow the process composition to answer these questions. This is made possible by using a good modelling formalism to underpin our workflow models – Petri Nets.

The last stage of the composition work is to prepare results for deployment using service infrastructures.

References

1. Aalst, W. M. P. V., Hofstede, A. H. M., Kiepuszewski, B., Barros, A. P., Advanced Workflow Patterns, Proceedings of the 7th International Conference on Cooperative Information Systems (CoopIS), Lecture Notes in Computer Science, Vol. 1901, pp. 18–29, 2000.
2. Aalst, W. M. P. V., Verbeek, H. M. W., Kumar, A., XRL/Woflan: Verification of an XML/Petri-net Based Language for Interorganizational Workflows (Best paper award), Proceedings of

the 6th Conference on Information Systems and Technology (CIST), pp. 30–45, Informs, Linthicum, MD, 2001.

3. Aalst, W. M. P. V., Kumar, A., XML Based Schema Definition for Support of Inter-Organizational Workflow, Information Systems Research, Vol. 14(1), pp. 23–47, March, 2003.

4. Aalst, W. M. P. V., Verification of Workflow Nets, Application and Theory of Petri Nets 1997, Lecture Notes in Computer Science, Vol. 1248, pp. 407–426, Springer-Verlag, Berlin, 1997.

5. Aalst, W. M. P. V., The Application of Petri Nets to Workflow Management, The Journal of Circuits, Systems and Computers, Vol. 8(1), pp. 21–66, 1998.

6. Angelov., S., Foundations of B2B Electronic Contracting, Dissertation, Technology University Eindhoven, Faculty of Technology Management, Information Systems Department, 2006.

7. Basten, T., In Terms of Nets: System Design with Petri Nets and Process Algebra, PhD Thesis, Eindhoven University of Technology, Eindhoven, The Netherlands, 1998.

8. BEA Systems, Intalio, SAP AG, Sun Microsystems, Web Service Choreography Interface (WSCI) 1.0 Specification, http://wwws.sun.com/software/xml/developers/wsci/, 2003.

9. Billington, J., Christensen, S., Hee, K. V., Kindler, E., Kummer, O., Petrucci, L., Post, R., Stehno, C., Weber, M., The Petri Net Markup Language: Concepts, Technology, and Tools, Proceedings of the 24th International Conference on Applications and Theory of Petri Nets (ICATPN), pp. 483–505, Eindhoven, The Netherlands, June 23–27, 2003.

10. BPML.Org., Business Process Modeling Language (BPML), Version 1.0, Accessed August 2003 from www.bpmi.org, 2003.

11. Curbera, F., Goland, Y., Klein, J., Leymann, F., Roller, D., Thatte, S., Weerawarana, S., Business Process Execution Language for Web-Services 1.0. http://www-106.ibm.com/developerworks/library/ws-bpel/, 2003.

12. Dessler, G., Reinecke, J., Schoell, W., Introduction to Business – A Contemporary View, Allyn and Bacon, Boston, MA, 1989.

13. Duan, Z., Bernstein, A., Lewis, P., Lu, S., A Model for Abstract Process Specification, Verification and Composition, Proceedings of the 2nd International Conference on Service Oriented Computing (ICSOC), pp. 232–241, ACM Press, 2004.

14. Ellis, C.A., Nutt, G.J., Modelling and Enactment of Workflow Systems. Proceedings of the 14th International Conference on Applications and Theory of Petri Nets (ICATPN), Lecture Notes in Computer Science, Vol. 691, pp. 1–16. Springer-Verlag, Berlin, 1993.

15. Eshuis, R., Grefen, P., Till, S., Structured Service Composition, Proceedings of the 4th International Conference on Business Process Management (BPM), Lecture Notes in Computer Science, Vol. 4102, pp. 97–112, Springer, Berlin, 2006.

16. Eshuis, R., Grefen, P., Composing Services into Structured Processes, International Journal of Cooperative Information Systems, Vol. 18(2), World Scientific, 2009.

17. IBM, Web Service Flow Language (WSFL), Version 1.0, http://www-3.ibm.com/software/solutions/webservices/pdf/WSFL.pdf, 2003.

18. Kiepuszewski, B., Expressiveness and Suitability of Languages for Control Flow Modelling in Workflows, PhD Thesis, Queensland University of Technology, Brisbane, Australia, 2002.

19. Kiepuszewski, B., Hofstede, A. H. M., Aalst, W. M. P. V., Fundamentals of Control Flow in Workflows, Acta Informatica, Vol. 39(3), pp. 143–209, March, 2003.

20. Kindler, E., Billington, J., Christensen, S., The Petri Net Markup Language: Concepts, Technology, and Tools, Proceedings of the 24th International Conference ICATPN, Lecture Notes in Computer Science, Vol. 2679, pp. 483–505, Eindhoven, The Netherlands, Springer Verlag, Berlin, 2003.

21. Kindler, E., Weber, M., Petri Net Markup Language (PNML), Home Page. http://www.informatik.hu-berlin.de/top/pnml/, 2003.

22. Liang, Q., Chakarapani, L. N., Su, S., Chikkamagalur, R., Lam, H., A Semi-Automatic Approach to Composite Web Services Discovery, Description and Invocation, International Journal on Web Service Research, Vol. 1(4), pp. 64–89, 2004.

23. Norta, A., Exploring Dynamic Inter-Organizational Business Process Collaboration, PhD Thesis, Technology University Eindhoven, Department of Information Systems, 2007.
24. Norta, A., Grefen, P., Discovering Patterns for Inter-Organizational Business Collaboration, International Journal of Cooperative Information Systems, Vol. 16(3/4), pp. 507–544, 2007, URL http://dx.doi.org/10.1142/S0218843007001664
25. Russell, N., Hofstede, A. H. M., Edmond, D., Aalst, W. M. P. V. D., Workflow Data Patterns, QUT Technical Report, (FIT-TR-2004-01), 2004.
26. Russell, N., Hofstede, A. H. M., Edmond, D., Aalst, W. M. P. V. D., Workflow Resource Patterns, BETA Working Paper Series, WP 127, Eindhoven University of Technology, Eindhoven, 2004.
27. Soley, R., Unified Modelling Language, http://www.uml.org, 2004.
28. Thatte, S., XLANG: Web Service for Business Process Design, 2003.
29. Verbeek, H. M. V., Basten, T., Aalst, W. M. P. V., Diagnosing Workflow Processes Using Woflan, The Computer Journal, Vol. 44(4), pp. 246–279, 2001.
30. Workflow Management Coalition, XML Process Definition Language, http://www.wfmc.org/standards/docs/TC-1025_10_xpdl_102502.pdf, 2002.

Chapter 8
Business Process Enactment

Georgios Kouvas, Paul Grefen, and Ana Juan

In this chapter, we discuss the business process enactment environment of the CrossWork architecture, providing support for network business process enactment and legacy system integration. We first discuss the overall approach to enactment, which consists of global enactment and local enactment, supported by two modules as described in the architecture design (see Chapter 5). Details of the Global Enactment module are discussed in Section 8.2. The discussion of the Local Enactment module follows in Section 8.3. As described in the architecture, enactment is coupled to Legacy Integration. In Section 8.4, we therefore discuss the Legacy Integration module. We conclude this chapter in Section 8.5.

8.1 Overall Approach to Enactment

After a Business Network Process has been composed and verified, it is ready for enactment by an IVE. Enactment of a Business Network Process is based on a two-level mechanism, consisting of global process orchestration and local process execution. Both levels are designed such that they allow flexible enactment topologies through the use of remote workflow clients [6].

To assure interoperability with industry-standard process enactment platforms, the industry-standard Business Process Execution Language (BPEL) [2] is used for enactment. BPEL is an XML-based language, built on top of SOA and Web Services specifications. It is used to define and manage long-lived service orchestrations or processes. In BPEL, a business process is a large-grained Web Service, which executes a control flow to complete a business goal. The steps in this control flow execute activities that are centred on invoking partner services to perform tasks and return results to the process. The drivers for choosing BPEL in our approach are manifold. Firstly, enterprises are evolving their SOA implementations from simple, fine-grained services, to more complex, large-grained services. Secondly, enterprises are employing service-oriented architecture strategies for integration.

G. Kouvas (✉)
Exodus, Athens, Greece
e-mail: gkou@exodus.gr

N. Mehandjiev, P. Grefen (eds.), *Dynamic Business Process Formation for Instant Virtual Enterprises*, Advanced Information and Knowledge Processing, DOI 10.1007/978-1-84882-691-5_8, © Springer-Verlag London Limited 2010

Thirdly, in response to the first two items, vendors are creating integration and SOA infrastructure solutions that offer BPEL orchestration, and/or use BPEL for internal processing. Finally, the specification is maturing; BPEL 2.0, sponsored by the Organization for the Advancement of Structured Information Standards (OASIS), is now available.

Figure 8.1 depicts the CrossWork enactment architecture. The two levels of workflow enactment (global enactment and local enactment) are clearly identified in the enactment architecture. Next to this, we employ a monitoring user interface module.

Fig. 8.1 Enactment architecture

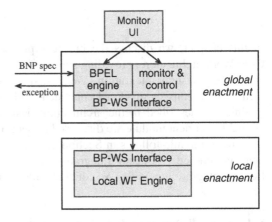

The Global Workflow Specifications (shown as Business Network Process Spec in Fig. 8.1) expressed in BPEL are obtained by automated translation of eSML process specifications. For this reason, an eSML2BPEL translation submodule is included in the global architecture. This submodule represents the bridge between the IVE formation and the enactment phase. For the real-time enactment of the Global Workflow, a standard BPEL engine is used. It reads BPEL process definitions (and other inputs such as WSDL files) and creates representations of BPEL processes. When an incoming message triggers a start activity, the engine creates a new process instance and starts it. The engine takes care of persistence, queues, alarms and many other execution details.

During the enactment of the global process and depending on the control flow, local partner Web Services (representing local business processes) are invoked either asynchronously or synchronously to perform their job. A precondition is that local partners have already exposed their business processes as Web Services and they have already exposed a WSDL interface. But this is not enough. In dynamic Business Network Process management, a Web Service that represents a business process, in contrast with a traditional Web Service, is often required to offer external visibility onto its internal process structure. For this purpose, we use the concept of BP-WS, introduced by [7], which includes a business process specification and business process state that can be accessed externally. Access to specification and state is provided through a number of dedicated Web Service interfaces. Grefen et al. [7] introduces four BP-WS classes following four control flow interface levels, which we use as a basis here. According to its internal business logic (or other initiatives) each local partner may decide to expose (or hide) details of its services by using the BP-WS classes. Local partners specify selected internals of their business processes (a projection of the business process specification) to the outside world by using eSML (for workflow composition) and BPEL (for monitoring and control purposes).

The concept of developing business process specifications (in BPEL) for the local Web Services enables the overall monitoring of the enactment at both local and global levels. For that, stateful global BPEL specification files need to be combined with stateful local specification files. In our approach, we expand the capabilities of the global Enactment Engine by adding monitoring and control functionalities; a Monitoring and Control engine. The purpose of this engine is twofold. Firstly, it is used to communicate with all specification and control ports of all local and global services in order to be aware of the combined status of execution. Secondly, it distributes all control messages to the appropriate local services through the control ports.

8.2 Global Workflow Enactment

In the previous chapter, we have seen how a global business process is composed and verified. This global business process is next enacted by the Global Enactment module, which interfaces to the Local Enactment modules, i.e. the local workflow management environments in each of the IVE member organizations. We first discuss the BPEL language used for the global business process representation and describe its process and activity structure. Then, we describe the BPEL engine selected for the actual implementation of the Global Enactment module. After having discussed these ingredients, we describe the architecture and realization of the Global Enactment module in detail.

8.2.1 BPEL Language

In the enactment phase, the language that we use for the representation of a Global Business Process is BPEL. While BPEL is not new – Version 1.1 of the specification was finalized in 2003 – enterprise uptake of BPEL is just recently gaining momentum. The specification is maturing; OASIS has announced the release of BPEL 2.0 as an accepted standard.

BPEL, also known as BPEL4WS and WSBPEL, is an XML-based language built on top of Web Service specifications, which is used to define and manage long-lived service orchestrations or processes. In BPEL [8], a business process is a large-grained stateful service, which executes steps to complete a business goal. That goal can be the completion of a business transaction, or fulfilling the job of a service. The steps in the BPEL process execute activities (represented by BPEL language elements) to accomplish work. Those activities are centred on invoking partner services (e.g. Web Services specified in WSDL) to perform tasks (their job) and return results to the process. The aggregate work, the collaboration of all the services, is a service orchestration.

If BPEL is used for orchestration, the primary service is a BPEL process, because BPEL processes are implemented as services. The BPEL process controls the overall sequence and invokes the collaborating services. To perform the orchestration, the BPEL process contains the logic (sequence, activities, invocations, assignments and case logic) to invoke other services (collaborators) to complete their combined job. The BPEL process may be asynchronous or synchronous. In an asynchronous model, the BPEL process is managing a long-lived flow of work; in other words, a process. In a synchronous mode, the BPEL process is more likely playing the (logical) role of another service type, such as request/reply, worker, agent or monitor.

BPEL's technology underpinnings are XML and Web Services. XML, as commonly known, is a standard, tag-based markup language used in document and message definition and processing. In addition, XML serves as the language base (format and syntax) for many special purpose languages such as WSDL (Web Services Description Language), and RSS (Really Simple Syndication).

BPEL follows this same model. The BPEL process description is encoded using XML language constructs. BPEL also incorporates XPATH to write expressions and queries. Web Services are important to BPEL in two ways. First, BPEL processes follow the WSDL service model, which is why BPEL processes are implemented as services. More specifically, BPEL processes have a WSDL definition, and are implemented as Web Services (usually compliant with WSDL, SOAP, and UDDI). Along with the basic functions of service definition, discovery and invocation, the Web Service implementation allows BPEL execution engines to leverage additional Web Service standards at runtime, such as WS-Addressing and WS-Coordination. Second, the collaborating services are also Web Services, described in WSDL. So, BPEL processes and collaborators are Web Services, and BPEL execution engines contain (and use) Web Services runtime components. Natively, the collaborating services (and the process service) are Web Services. However, BPELJ, an extension of BPEL, allows for a mix of Java Services and Web Services.

BPEL offers a good model to separate orchestration logic from the participating services, and process configuration using BPEL provides many advantages over hard coding of service interactions. However, there is a processing overhead and infrastructure expense, so BPEL might not be the best choice for simple orchestrations. As a rule of thumb, a simple orchestration is comprised of two to five services and has static interaction patterns. As a language to develop processes, BPEL is good at executing a series of activities, which occur over time, and interact with internal and external services. These processes may represent IT scenarios, such as integration, or business scenarios, such as information exchange, or flows of work.

As for its limitations, BPEL does not account for humans in a process, and as a result does not provide a traditional workflow management, as there are no concepts for roles, tasks and inboxes. In addition, BPEL does not support very complex business processes, those which evolve during their execution, branching out to incorporate new parties and activities. Lastly, BPEL does not have native support for Business Activity Monitoring (BAM). There is no data model for measurement and monitoring.

The BPEL environment is divided into five major parts (see Fig. 8.2), "Designer", "Server", "Server Host Environment", "Management Console" and "Process Database".

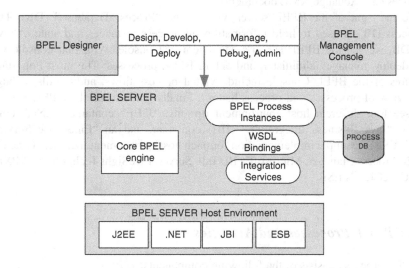

Fig. 8.2 Overview of BPEL processing

The "BPEL Designer" enables the user to design, develop and deploy BPEL processes. Here, we find the tools for business analysts and developers/integrators to describe processes (orchestrations) composed of steps (activities), associate services and add any special business or validation logic to the process flow. Additionally, partner links can be added and services located through the Universal Description, Discovery and Integration (UDDI) browser. We can also use function and copy wizards. These tools allow the user to perform these activities visually in a graphical environment without having to write BPEL code by hand. Most tools support a toggle between the graphical design view and the BPEL source code view. Changes made in one view should be reflected in the other. The Designer can deploy the developed processes directly to the BPEL Server. This eases the development and maintenance of BPEL processes considerably.

In the centre of the diagram is the "BPEL Server" (or BPEL execution environment). The "BPEL Server" contains the executing "BPEL process instances", the "WSDL bindings", the "integration services" and the "core BPEL execution engine". The "core BPEL engine" is the runtime environment where the BPEL processes are deployed and executed. It provides support for the process life cycle requirements (instantiation, communication, dehydration/hydration, correlation, transaction management, compensation and termination) as described in the specification. The "WSDL binding" framework is responsible for communication with the BPEL processes deployed on the server. This includes clients that would like to access a BPEL process and BPEL processes that would like to access other Web Services (partner links). The "Integration services" enable performing transformations of XML documents that go beyond the support of XPath. This is very useful especially if business processes described in BPEL communicate with Web Services and exchange XML documents.

To the right of the BPEL server, we see the "Process Database" (DB). The "Process DB" is used to hold information on process instances and state. Above the DB, we see the BPEL server's Management Console. With that console we can deploy, manage, administer, and debug BPEL processes. The most important features of the BPEL Console include visual process flows, audit trails, debugging view of processes and process history. Finally, underneath the BPEL Server, we see four different host environment options; "J2EE" container, ".Net" container, "Java Business Integration" (JBI) container, and an "Enterprise Service Bus" (ESB). Example implementation for each host environment includes; Oracle's BPEL Process Manager, Microsoft's BizTalk Server, FiveSight Technologies' PXE, and CapeClear's ESB.

8.2.2 BPEL Processes and Activities

A BPEL process consists of the following components:

- *Partner links*: relationships between two Web Services at the interface level;
- *Partners*: entities taking part in a Web Service transaction;
- *Variables*: containers for values;
- *Correlation sets*: sets of data that uniquely identify the business process; at different times in the process, different correlation sets may identify the process;
- *Fault handlers*: describe what to do when problems occur;
- *Compensation handlers*: describe how to reverse already-completed business processes;
- *Event handlers*: handle incoming messages and alarms;
- A *top-level activity*: a single BPEL activity, usually a container for other activities.

Activities are the building blocks of BPEL processes. Basic activities exhibit conceptually simple behaviour like receiving a message, invoking a Web Service and assigning values to variables. Structured activities are similar to conditional and looping constructs in programming languages. Special activities introduce variable scoping and handle abnormal activities such as process termination and compensation (explicitly undoing a process). Activities are joined by links, either explicit or implicit. The path taken through the activities and links is determined by many factors, including the values of variables and the evaluation of expressions. Every activity exists within a scope, which is a context for variables, fault handlers and compensation handlers. Scopes are conceptually similar to programming language blocks that introduce new variable scope and (depending upon the language and construct used) exception handling mechanisms. Some activities such as "scope" and "invoke" generate new scopes, whether implicitly or explicitly. Below, we list the activity types supported by BPEL.

Activity	Notes
Basic activities	
<receive>	Block and wait for a message from a partner
<reply>	Reply back to the partner that sent the message we received
<invoke>	Call some other Web Service, either one-way or request-response
<assign>	Assign or copy values to variables
<throw>	Generate a fault
<wait>	Wait for a given time period (time-out) or until a particular time has passed (alarm)
<empty>	A no-op
Structured activities	
<sequence>	Execute "child" elements in order
<switch>	Just like a "switch" or "case" statement
<while>	Repeat an activity while a condition is true
<pick>	Block and wait for a message, time-out, or alarm
<flow>	Children are executed concurrently; links can provide additional control structure
Special activities	
<scope>	Define a new scope for variables, fault handlers, and compensation handlers
<compensate>	Invoke compensation on an inner scope that has already completed normally
<terminate>	Immediately terminate a business process instance

Each activity has an associated state. The activities enter or exit these states based on the rules of BPEL. The activities also fire events to notify listeners of their changes in state. There are mechanisms in place for listening to these events. An activity must be in one of the following states (defined in AeBpelState):

8.2.3 BPEL Engine

A BPEL engine is a software module that reads BPEL process definitions (and other inputs such as WSDL files) and creates representations of BPEL processes. When an

State	Notes
INACTIVE	All BPEL activities are in the inactive state when the process starts
READY_TO_EXECUTE	Ready to execute. These activities have been queued by their parent and their join condition has evaluated to true
EXECUTING	Currently executing
FINISHED	Finished executing without a fault
FAULTED	Finished executing with a fault
DEAD_PATH	Removed from the execution path due to dead path elimination. When a parent activity's state becomes dead, that state is propagated to all of its children
QUEUED_BY_PARENT	Queued for execution by their parents
TERMINATED	Terminated
Unknown	The activity's state is null; when a parent activity's state becomes unknown, then the children's states change to INACTIVE

incoming message triggers a start activity, the engine creates a new process instance and starts its execution. The engine takes care of persistence, queues, alarms and many other execution details.

In CrossWork, we have used the ActiveBPEL open source software [1]. The ActiveBPEL engine is a commercial-grade open source implementation of the BPEL for Web Services Version 1.1 specification and is fully compliant with that specification. The ActiveBPEL engine is a robust runtime environment that is capable of executing process definitions created for the BPEL standard. The ActiveBPEL engine technology is developed and maintained by Active Endpoints, which also uses the same technology in its commercial products. Active Endpoints has created the ActiveBPEL open source project based on the belief that the open source model is an effective means through which to foster community interest, education and development around the BPEL standard. The ActiveBPEL engine runs in any standard servlet container such as Apache Tomcat.

Figure 8.3 shows the architecture of a BPEL engine. The "Database" elements on the right of this illustration represent generic persistent storage. The ActiveBPEL engine uses a pluggable architecture; different persistence managers may implement different storage mechanisms. The ActiveBPEL engine ships with a persistence manager that keeps everything in memory.

An engine factory manages the creation of an ActiveBPEL engine. Separation of responsibilities is achieved through the use of objects that handle services such as queue management, alarm and timer services and process deployment. Engine configuration is handled by an object that supplies default values and reads the aeEngineConfig.xml file. The engine is connected to a queue manager and a process state manager, and objects that are responsible for performing these services for the engine. The engine is highly configurable. aeEngineConfig.xml specifies not only values like cache sizes and logging state, but also determines the class of various factories, managers and handlers. A process deployment provider handles reading

Fig. 8.3 BPEL engine
architecture (adapted from
[1])

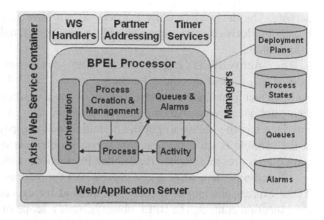

process deployment descriptor files, and a process deployment manager handles process creation. A work manager schedules asynchronous operations.

Each BPEL process must have at least one start activity. A new BPEL process is created when one of its start activities is triggered, either by an incoming message or by a Pick activity's alarm. The engine dispatches incoming messages to the correct process instance. If there is correlation of data, the engine tries to find the correct instance that matches the correlated data. If there is no correlation of data and the request matches a start activity, a new process instance is created. When the engine reads a BPEL process definition, it creates objects called activity definitions that model the process. Activity definitions contain all of the information required to instantiate a BPEL activity implementation object. In this regard, definitions are analogous to classes while the implementation objects are analogous to instances of those classes (objects). Both the engine and its event listeners have access to these definitions. The events contain an XPath value that indicates which activity in the process is triggering the event. These XPath values come from the activity definitions.

The engine creates its implementation objects by using a "Visitor" pattern to visit the activity definition object model, creating implementation objects from this model, as presented in Fig. 8.4. The ActiveBPEL engine encapsulates any implementation logic within this construction process. For example, an implicit scope within an invoke activity will generate an explicit scope with a single invoke child

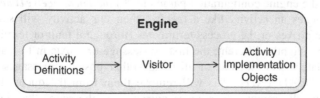

Fig. 8.4 The "visitor" pattern (adapted from [1])

activity. The designer or other listeners do not have to know about these implementation decisions since they are only aware of the definitions and their XPath
information.

The ActiveBPEL engine itself does not handle input and output.
Instead, protocol-specific handlers such as AeBpelRPCHandler and
AeBpelDocumentHandler translate data from a particular protocol to a message and vice versa. All variables implement the IAeVariable interface. This
interface has the ability to get the definition and the payload, which is different
if the variable is declared as a type versus an element or message. The message
payload requires an interface for detailed interactions with the part objects.

All activities and links allow expressions for various attributes of the object.
These expressions require a consistent method for execution and a description of
the execution context. The BPEL object is itself a scope (in the variable sense of the
word) and can be used to correctly retrieve the accessible variables of the expression
context. Evaluation allows all the XPath extensions which have been documented in
the BPEL specification (for example, bpws:getVariableData). During process execution, the ActiveBPEL engine fires events indicating its progress. When logging is
turned on, an instance of AEEngineLogger listens for engine events and writes them
to individual process log files. Once the process completes, the file will be closed.

Each BPEL process must have at least one start activity. A new BPEL process
gets created when one of its start activities is triggered, either by an incoming message or by a Pick activity's alarm. The engine dispatches incoming messages to
the correct process instance. If there is correlation between data, the engine tries
to find the correct instance that matches the correlated data. If there is no correlation of data and the request matches a start activity, a new process instance is
created.

The "receive queue" contains the currently executing receive activities across
all process instances. Receive activities include onMessage activities that are part
of a "pick" or an event handler. A "receive activity" is said to be executing when
it has been queued by its parent (for example, a scope, flow or sequence) but has
not yet received the message from the outside world that it is waiting for. The
"receive queue" also contains inbound messages from the outside world that did
not match a waiting "receive activity" already in the queue and were themselves
not capable of creating a "new process" instances. An unmatched receipt of data
like this is possible given the asynchronous nature of some Web Services. The
engine will accept these unmatched messages provided that they contain correlation
of data. These messages are queued until a time-out period passes. The period is
specified by the engine configuration parameter *UnmatchedReceiveTimeout*. When
a process queues an activity like a *receive*, then this activity will stay in there
until the data arrives or the process terminates (through a fault or terminate activity). Picks are slightly different; the first onMessage or onAlarm to match for the
pick immediately sets the state of all of the other possible messages/alarms for
that Pick to DEAD_PATH. This will remove them from the queue. Event handlers automatically remove their queue entries once the scope that defines them
completes.

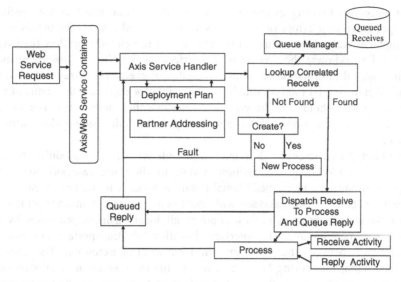

Fig. 8.5 BPEL request handling (adapted from [1])

8.2.4 Global Enactment Subsystem

The Global Enactment module is a runtime environment that is capable of executing process definitions created by the Workflow Composition module and expressed in BPEL 1.1 specifications. Moreover, the Global Enactment module is responsible for gathering and storing all monitoring information created during the execution of the process definitions. In more detail, this includes the following functions:

- Deploying of a process definition (for execution);
- Executing an instance of a process definition;
- Orchestrating the execution of all Local Business Processes;
- Gathering and storing all (global and local) monitoring details during execution;
- Informing the user of the status of execution (at global and local level);
- Analysing and passing any control orders from the user to the Local Business Processes.

The Global Enactment module uses two kinds of input. The first is a verified and validated global process definition expressed in a BPEL process file. The second is a WSDL interface (Web Service Interface) file which describes how the global process can be accessed by the outside world. The module also produces two kinds of output: SOAP messages for the invocation and orchestration of all Local Business Processes (Web Services) and XML files containing structured information regarding the status of the execution at both global and local level.

The Global Enactment module requires a user interface for two reasons. Firstly, it requires forms for the instantiation (and update, if necessary) of all global variables required during execution. Secondly, it needs an interface for feedback messages in case of errors or exceptions with proposed actions for the user. For the graphical view of the status of the execution of the global workflow (expanded with local workflows) there is no user interface in the Global Enactment module. Instead, all information regarding the status of execution is transferred to the Global Monitoring UI module which is responsible for depicting the status of execution. The same holds for the graphical interface that enables the user to start and intervene in execution, which is also incorporated in the Global Monitoring UI module.

The Global Enactment module interfaces with several other modules. It interfaces with the Workflow Composition module to allow the transportation of the composed, finalized and verified Global Business Process to the enactment engine that will execute it. The interface with the Local Enactment module allows the invocation and, in general, orchestration of all local business processes by the Global Enactment module. This interface also allows the transportation of all monitoring details between the global and the local level of execution. The interface with the Global Monitoring UI module allows the transportation of all structured monitoring information to the UI that will depict the current status of execution in a graphical way. Moreover, this interface is used for enabling the user to instantiate the execution of a global process definition as well as controlling the execution.

The Global Enactment module relies on the following technology for implementation:

- *Java Platform, Enterprise Edition (J2EE)*: This is a programming platform – part of the Java Platform – for developing and running distributed multi-tier architecture Java applications, based largely on modular software components running on an application server. J2EE includes several API specifications, such as JDBC, RMI, e-mail, JMS, Web Services, XML, and defines how to coordinate them. J2EE also features some specifications unique to J2EE for components. These include Enterprise Java Beans, servlets, portlets, JavaServer Pages and several Web Service technologies. This allows the developer to create an enterprise application that is portable between platforms and scalable, while integrating with legacy technologies.
- *ActiveBPEL*: The ActiveBPEL open source engine is a commercial-grade open source implementation of the Business Process Execution Language for Web Services Version 1.1 specification, and is fully compliant with that spec.
- *Web Services Protocol Stack*: According to the W3C, a Web Service is a software system designed to support interoperable machine-to-machine interaction over a network. It has an interface that is described in a machine-processable format such as WSDL. Other systems interact with the Web Service in a manner prescribed by its interface using messages, which may be enclosed in a SOAP envelope, or follow a RESTful approach. These messages are typically conveyed using HTTP, and normally comprise XML in conjunction with other Web-related standards.

Figure 8.6 shows the internal architecture of the Global Enactment module. The heart of the module is the "BPEL engine" discussed earlier. Coupled to it is the "Monitor and Control" submodule. This submodule extends the functionality of the "BPEL engine" with monitoring capabilities. This is required, as BPEL files are by definition stateless and most commercial BPEL engines do not keep track of the execution of a business process. In addition, the "Monitor and Control" submodule is responsible for monitoring and keeping track of all major events/activities that take place during the execution of a global process definition, at both a local and global level. The "BP-WS" interface provides the connection to the Local Enactment module, using the BP-WS paradigm discussed earlier.

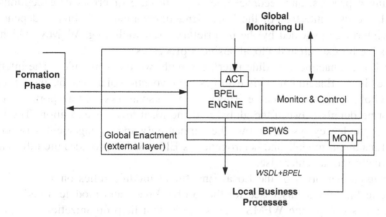

Fig. 8.6 Global enactment module internal architecture

8.3 Local Workflow Enactment

The Local Enactment module is a runtime environment that is capable of executing local business process definitions developed and managed by proprietary WorkFlow Management Systems (WFMS), or other tools, owned by the members of an IVE. Moreover, the Local Enactment module is responsible for informing the Global Enactment module about the status of the execution of the local process definitions. In more detail, this includes the following functions:

- Executing an instance of a local process definition;
- Informing the local supplier of the status of execution (at local level);
- Informing the Global Enactment module of the status of execution (at local level);
- Invoking local Legacy Systems where necessary (as described in the local business process).

The Local Enactment module uses a number of inputs. SOAP messages are used to trigger the execution of a local business process. SOAP messages allow an external party to request the specification/definition of a local business process. SOAP messages also allow an external party to issue control orders (stop, pause, resume) to a local business process being executed. XML documents are used to represent the legacy system (e.g. EIS) response to the execution of a requested operation by the local business process. The Local Enactment module produces three kinds of output; SOAP messages report the status of execution of a local business process, BPEL files are used to describe the specification/definition of a local business process and XML documents are used to represent a request to a legacy system (e.g. EIS)

Like the Global Enactment module, the Local Enactment module requires two user interfaces: forms for instantiation and update of local variables required while executing a process, and feedback messages in case of errors or exceptions. In general, the user interface of the Local Enactment module is highly dependable on the interfaces provided by the proprietary local tools (e.g. WFMS) which are responsible for executing the local business processes.

The Local Enactment module interfaces with two other modules. The interface with the Global Enactment module allows the invocation of a local business process by the Global Enactment module. This interface also allows the transportation of all monitoring details between the global and the local level of execution. The interface with the legacy systems allows the connectivity and management between the Local Enactment module and heterogeneous EISs, which provides the information infrastructure for an enterprise.

The implementation of the Local Enactment module relies on Java and Web Service technology as discussed for the Global Enactment module. In addition to this, it relies on specific WFMSs, i.e. systems that help organizations to specify, execute, monitor and coordinate the flow of work cases within a distributed office environment. In the CrossWork prototype implementation, the EXODUS i.Perform product has been used for this purpose. With i.Perform, a business can manage and monitor its processes with a view to maximizing profitability (for more information see www.exodus.gr).

As shown in Fig. 8.7, the internal architecture of a Local Enactment module consists of two submodules. A local WFMS is used as a runtime environment that is capable of executing local business process definitions. An example of such a system is EXODUS's i.Perform. The Local WFMS interfaces to the Global Enactment

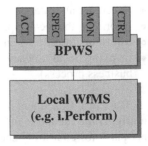

Fig. 8.7 Local enactment
module internal architecture

module through a BP-WS interface [7]. As discussed before, the approach of a BP-WS supports an internal business process specification that can be accessed externally through a number of dedicated Web Service interfaces. A BP-WS has the following interfaces (in order of typical use):

- *Invoke and reply interface*: These are not different from the situation where the BP-WS would have been a traditional, black-box Web Service. We cluster them in an activation (ACT) interface.
- *Interface to obtain the business process model*: Through the SPEC interface, a consumer can obtain a process specification of the business process service, e.g. in BPEL. The interface can be considered a reflection interface, as it provides information regarding the behaviour of a BP-WS.
- *Interface to monitor the execution of the internal process*: Through the MON information, a client can obtain status information about the execution of the local process.
- *Interface to control the execution of the internal process*: Through the CTRL interface, a consumer can issue control primitives to influence the execution of a service executed on its behalf; typical control primitives are *pause process*, *resume process* and *abort process*. Invocation of control primitives is typically based on information obtained through the MON interface.

8.4 Coupling to Legacy Systems

In order to complete the enactment process of an IVE, EISs and legacy systems of the IVE members have to be taken into account. EISs provide the information infrastructure critical to the business processes of an enterprise. EIS and legacy applications include relational database systems, enterprise resource planning systems and mainframe transaction processing systems. Legacy systems contain the business logic of an organization, and represent many years of coding, developments, enhancements and modifications. Nevertheless, they are often undocumented, tightly coupled, relatively inflexible and consequently, difficult to integrate into composite business processes. Because most companies have a significant investment in their legacy infrastructure, management is typically not open to replace those legacy systems. Rewriting or significantly modifying large portions of a legacy environment is neither practical nor realistically accomplishable with reasonable resources. The approach taken in the CrossWork architecture is the integration of the existing legacy systems and EIS by means of providing them with a uniform Web Service interface that can be integrated into Local Workflows.

The Legacy Integration module allows the creation of new value from existing enterprise systems by means of integrating them into new business processes, which can be exposed at local level as well as global level participating in IVEs business processes. CrossWork's Legacy Integration module offers to the Local Enactment module a unified interface to perform transactions into heterogeneous information systems, hiding the details of the operation in each concrete EIS. Solutions addressing the Legacy Integration such as the CrossWork Legacy Integration module have to consider the following aspects:

- *Heterogeneity and complexity of EIS*: Each EIS has a different programming model, increasing the complexity and the effort required to perform the integration.
- *Transactional access to EIS*: This is needed in order to preserve data integrity for critical enterprise information.
- *Secure access to EIS*: It is critical to assure data integrity in all access to EIS information – any loss of information or unauthorized access could be extremely costly to a company.
- *Scalability*: Companies exist in a very changing world – it is important to provide tools that can grow according to the needs of the enterprise.

The Legacy Integration module includes the following functions. It provides a Web Service interface allowing connecting and executing business processes into multiple and heterogeneous EIS and legacy systems. It validates requests to a concrete legacy system, avoiding unnecessary calls to this system. It transforms both requests and responses to the legacy system, to facilitate the integration with the Local Enactment module.

The Legacy Integration module takes as input SOAP messages describing the business process to execute. It specifies the EIS where to execute the operation, the business process to be executed, and an XML document with the request for this business process. As output, the Legacy Integration module produces SOAP messages representing the system's response to the execution of the requested business process.

As the module has interface functionality only, the Legacy Integration module does not have a user interface. The Legacy Integration module interfaces with the Local Enactment module. Local workflow enactment requests the legacy interface to execute operations on EISs.

The Legacy Integration module relies on the following technology for implementation:

- *JCA*: Employs Java-based technology solution for connecting application servers and EISs as part of enterprise application integration (EAI) solutions. Legacy Integration uses JCA resource adaptors to connect to several EIS.
- *Apache Axis*: Employs Java and XML-based Web Service framework consisting of an implementation of the SOAP server, and various utilities and API's for generating and deploying Web Service applications. Legacy Integration uses Axis in two ways; to provide a Web Service interface to the module, and to develop client classes to use Web Service connectors, mainly used to connect to .Net platforms.
- *EJB*: Employs server-side components that encapsulate the business logic of an application.

- *XSLT*: Employs XML-based language that is used for the transformation of XML documents. Within the Legacy Integration module it is used to transform the input and output messages.
- *XML Schema*: Employs the XML schema that is a description of a type of XML document. In the Legacy Integration module it is used to validate input messages.

As shown in Fig. 8.8, the internal architecture of the Legacy Integration module consists of the following submodules:

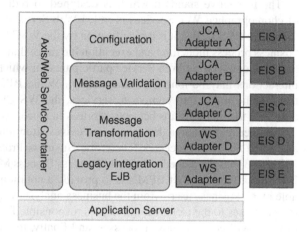

Fig. 8.8 Legacy integration module internal architecture

- *Legacy Integrator EJB*: It contains the business logic of the Legacy Integration module;
- *Configuration*: It stores EIS information, such as operations, users, passwords and servers;
- *Message Validation*: Input messages are validated to XML schemas defined for each EIS and each operation;
- *Message Transformation*: Messages can be transformed using an XSLT defined for each EIS and each operation.

8.5 Related Work

Besides the enactment approach followed in CrossWork, many different approaches exist today with regard to business process execution technologies, architectures, environments and languages. In this section we discuss some of the most important research and industrial efforts in this area.

In CrossWork, we use a Web Service orchestration standard (BPEL) for business connectivity. Although orchestration and its standard seem to be the most powerful tools for enterprise collaboration, there is another way of collaboration designed to reduce the inherent complexity of connecting Web Services together, called choreography. While with orchestration, the process is always controlled from the perspective of one of the business parties, choreography is more collaborative in nature. Each party involved in the process describes the part they play in the inter- action. Choreography tracks the sequence of messages that may involve multiple parties and multiple sources. It is associated with the public message exchanges that occur between multiple Web Services. The underlying intuition behind the notion of choreography can be summarized as "dancers dance following a global scenario without a single point of control".

The respective standard which is designed to reduce the inherent complexity of choreographed Web Services is called Web Services Choreography Description Language (WS-CDL). It is a specification by the W3C [10] defining an XML-based business process modelling and execution language that describes collaboration pro- tocols of cooperating Web Service participants, in which services act as peers, and interactions may be long-lived and stateful. While BPEL allows existing services to be orchestrated into composite services, the WS-CDL goes a step further and describes the relationships between services in a peer-to-peer scenario.

Another relevant area that currently receives attention is the area of semantically annotated business processes. There, the Business Process Management Initiative (BPMI) [3] has developed a standard Business Process Modelling Notation (BPMN) [4]. The primary goal of BPMN is to provide a notation that is readily understand- able by all business users, from the business analysts who create the initial drafts of the processes to the technical developers responsible for implementing the technol- ogy that will perform those processes, and finally, to the business people who will manage and monitor those processes. Thus, BPMN creates a standardized bridge for the gap between the business process design and process implementation. BPMN can be used in conjunction with BPEL, or can provide a process notation in its own right. The basic BPMN notation is very similar to that of UML Activity Diagrams. BPMN was developed with the support of many leading BP process modelling tool vendors and is well on the way to becoming the most popular notation among pro- cess modellers, although companies use so many different process notations that standardization will likely take quite a while.

With regard to the European funded projects, one of the most promising efforts is the ECOLEAD [5] project. ECOLEAD, among other issues, aims to propose new and strong mechanisms to support collaborative and distributed busi- ness process management. In that area, the challenge for ECOLEAD is to find and build approaches that support the management of virtual organizations (quite synonymous with virtual enterprises) from different aspects including enactment. For ECOLEAD, the Supply Chain Operations Reference (SCOR) [9] modelling approach including performance metrics is promising for further use. SCOR is a process reference model that has been developed and endorsed by the Supply Chain Council as the cross-industry-standard diagnostic tool for supply chain manage- ment, and describes the business activities associated with all phases of satisfying a customer's demand. SCOR uses graphical decomposition of processes from the Level 1 functions (PLAN-SOURCE-MAKE-DELIVER-RETURN) to Level 3 process elements. Modelling of inter-enterprise processes is undertaken by connecting one process element (i.e. SOURCE) from one supply chain member to the process element (i.e. DELIVER) of another member. Major benefit and reason for widespread acceptance of SCOR are the defined Key Performance Indicators (KPIs) used to measure and compare (benchmark) the performance of companies in their domains.

8.6 Coordinating Work Across the Instant Virtual Enterprise

In this chapter, we have described the CrossWork business process (workflow) enactment subsystem. This system consists of three main modules. The Global Enactment module is responsible for the execution of a global business process within an IVE, i.e. the workflow that links all the local workflows of members in that IVE. The Local Enactment module is responsible for the execution of local workflows within the boundaries of a single IVE member. The Legacy Integration module provides the interfaces to couple local workflow management to legacy systems residing within the boundaries of IVE members. The division of the subsystem into these main modules provides both the separation of concerns needed for a modular implementation and the flexibility to deal with extensions towards the future.

As we have shown in this chapter, the realization of the CrossWork enactment subsystem is heavily based on standardized and available technology. We use the BPEL process definition language, and a stable open source BPEL engine for global process enactment. We have used a specific local enactment engine for our prototype implementation, but it is shielded by well-specified interfaces and can thus be replaced by other choices. For Legacy Integration, we use a number of standard technologies.

Once the processes linking different partners are assembled, we need to deploy them on the existing service-based infrastructures of different members of the VE. A global workflow module is then responsible for coordinating the work access to different workflow engineers, driving the processes across the VE "in sync".

References

1. ActiveBPEL, Website: www.activebpel.org, 2008.
2. OASIS Web Services Business Process Execution Language (WSBPEL), Version 2.0, May 2007.
3. Business Process Management Initiative, www.bpmi.org, 2008.
4. Business Process Modeling Notation, Version 1.1, http://www.bpmn.org, 2008.

5. European Collaborative Networked Organisations Leadership Initiative, ECOLEAD Project, http://ecolead.vtt.fi/, 2008.
6. Grefen, P., CrossWork Global Architecture, CrossWork Project Deliverable D4.1, 2006.
7. Grefen, P., Ludwig, H., Dan, A., Angelov, S., An Analysis of Web Services Support for Dynamic Business Process Outsourcing, Information and Software Technology, Vol. 48(11), pp. 1115–1134, 2006.
8. Michelson, B., Business Process Execution Language (BPEL), Primer: Understanding an Important Component of SOA and Integration Strategies, 2006.
9. Supply Chain Operations Reference-model (SCOR), Supply Chain Council, http://www.supply-chain.org, 2008.
10. Web Services Choreography Description Language, Version 1.0, http://www.w3.org/TR/ws-cdl-10/, W3C, 2005.

Chapter 9
The User Perspective

Stefan Oppl, Peter Peherstorfer, and Christian Stary

In this chapter we argue for hybrid interaction system to support the formation, operation and evolution of an IVE. The main reason to have people involved is the complexity of the underlying information space, and the variety of procedures one may follow in establishing a VE.

9.1 Information and Interaction Needs of Virtual Enterprise Creators

Today's business environments tend to shorten product life cycles and increase product variability and complexity needs. These factors add to the growing importance of technologically mediated VEs, which assemble forces to address business opportunities [12]. Contemporary VEs and their processes are developed through tedious face-to-face negotiations although state-of-the-art technology would allow for time-saving automatic formation and coordination of such strategic tasks.

Currently, full automation of complex and dynamic tasks like process-development without any human intervention is still a future vision. Although automated systems are efficient, reliable, accurate and safe as long as they work, an entirely automated system is unfeasible due to a number of arguments from which the most important ones are summarized in [5, 11, 15] and discussed below.

CrossWork originally aimed at the fully automated formation of inter-organizational workflows. However, during project runtime, working with actual users has revealed some hindrances to that respect. Today, the original aims have to be considered as a future scenario. Full automation currently seems to be impractical both from a social as well as an infrastructural point of view.

In the light of these developments, the CrossWork system allows human intervention for special cases and on user demand. However, the basic system architecture still allows for fully automated workflow formation. In such cases, the user interface

S. Oppl (✉)
Johannes Kepler University Linz, Linz, Austria
e-mail: stefan.oppl@jku.at

N. Mehandjiev, P. Grefen (eds.), *Dynamic Business Process Formation for Instant Virtual Enterprises*, Advanced Information and Knowledge Processing,
DOI 10.1007/978-1-84882-691-5_9, © Springer-Verlag London Limited 2010

only informs the user. When intervening, the system allows input from users and get back in ambiguous or conflicting situations.

In two scenarios, (which were elaborated in cooperation with the user organizations Magna Intier and MAN, respectively), the CrossWork system guides users through the process of selecting a team to work on a certain problem and forming a workflow to orchestrate the individual activities. It however does not make all necessary decisions automatically, but checks back with the user, wherever it has been considered necessary (presenting itself to the user as some sort of decision support system). The points of necessary intervention differ between the scenarios. The CrossWork system is able to handle both cases. It is only a matter of configuration to adapt the system user control requirements.

The CrossWork system has been configured to the needs of the user for each scenario. After having tested these prototypes, the user organizations have identified significant improvements to the quality and reduction of time required for the formation of teams and workflows.

While fully manual workflow formation for complex systems (like the ones CrossWork aims at) is inefficient, error-prone or impossible to handle, fully automated formation has shown to be far ahead of its time in terms of availability and accessibility of necessary data as well as cultural issues. We therefore believe that it is necessary to provide a system which is flexible enough to handle different levels of automation and involvement of users. The CrossWork software suite has been designed to meet these requirements and has proven its feasibility through two different use cases, which are reviewed in Chapter 11.

9.2 Research in Balancing Automation with Human Intervention

On March 19th, 2007, the most deadly mining accident in Russian history at a mine in Siberia was caused by human intervention in the mine's automated methane-gas detection system, which led to an explosion, killing 110 people. Taking accidents like this into account, the need for differentiation between automatable tasks and non-automatable tasks arises.

Gebauer has identified three features that determine the costs associated with the build-up of a process infrastructure [4], which are; *complexity and up-front structuring*, *internal process conditions* and *uncertainty*, i.e. exceptions. Complexity and up-front structuring describes what we term as the differentiation between tasks that can be automated versus those that cannot be automated. We do this by distinguishing between routine, innovative and strategic tasks. Routine tasks do not have to respond to unforeseen events and hold a simple structure. As a result they can be fully automated (as in the methane-gas detection system, which has never been conducted manually, since this simple, yet critical task was fully automated from the beginning).

Strategic tasks require dynamic intervention capabilities. Advantages of computer-based, automated analytical tools in strategic decision making in terms of coping with complexity have already been publicized [1]. However, even though humans may leave decisions to the automated system, they have to accept them afterwards. This acceptance can be greatly enhanced by understanding the system and having the opportunity of interacting with the system at runtime. The necessity of providing the user with appropriate knowledge requires additional effort in order for automated concepts to become comprehensible, e.g. employing methods of visualization [7].

A number of measures to make automation more understandable/trustable have been outlined [9]:

- The system designer must consider the ways in which the human role is changed through automation (e.g. loss of authority), and determine for each function whether the human or the automated system or both should be given control;
- Show the past performance of the algorithms (logs);
- Reveal comprehensible intermediate results;
- Do not overwhelm the user with information;
- Show the purpose of the system in a manner that relates to goals of the user.

The first suggestion was incorporated into the CrossWork system through interviews with potential users. The next two recommendations have been considered and implemented through textual and graphical logs. The last point has been satisfied through the provision of documentation and training of future operators. Focusing on an increase in acceptance through the provision of system interaction, we have to recall the five different roles of humans in the human–machine system as identified by [5]:

- Acknowledge control system signals (no change to process);
- Acknowledge control system signals (make required changes);
- Record data and instrument readings and adjust as needed;
- Monitor system status and override as necessary;
- Monitor system status and report findings with no change.

During the development of the CrossWork system, potential users articulated the need to implement these five roles, which were then incorporated into the system. Demand for runtime human intervention exists particularly in the provision of data to the system, within decision making and exception handling.

At some stage, operators have to tell the system what it is supposed to do. In these cases the operator defines the basic data and desired actions and starts and stops the system. These tasks require some sort of user interface to allow for interaction. The situation gets more complicated when decision making is required. A variety of issues to that respect have been addressed by researchers, e.g. [3, 5, 8, 11]. The majority of these are concerned with aspects of freedom, the flexibility of the human operator, and the acceptance of automated decisions. Although most of these studies exemplify their findings within the aviation domain [5, 8, 15], we follow [6] and [11] in discussing problems relevant to WFMSs. Significant drawbacks of automated decision making for workflow formation are:

- It takes place in complex, dynamic environment and is affected by uncertain factors; so full automation is impossible;
- The mapping of the real world to workflows is prone to errors;
- Dealing with failures and exceptions at execution time in a manual fashion is inevitable.
- In order to overcome these drawbacks, several methods have been suggested by the aforementioned researchers:
- In the design phase, participatory design processes should actively involve the end-user to participate when explicating their mental model of work processes using concepts they are familiar with [13];
- The users should always be supported with appropriate information (info, status, possible recovery);
- The users should be given the freedom to choose from different execution paths if necessary and to undertake decisions;
- Characterize the problem by obtaining from the user the information necessary to classify an exception and hence be able to deal with it;
- Because the human operator would be needed for unexpected exceptions, the operator has to be kept aware of what's going on.

Particularly with novel technologies, as incorporated in the CrossWork system, users do not want to turn in their decision-making authority straight away – they may have faith but for sure they have doubts. In granting decisive privileges, the users are introduced step-by-step to the automated system.

In the course of the project we have learned from potential users that several metrics, e.g. for choosing the *best* team in the Team Formation module, only partially represent formal rules that could be part of an ontology. They are rather determined by strategic or even *soft*, personal factors, which finally require human intervention for an ultimate decision. The developed system reflects these insights involving users in a number of decision-making situations along the way.

Mourao and Antunes [11] have pointed out exceptions, i.e. situations not predicted during the design phase, which also require human involvement. This can be the redesign of workflows, ad hoc execution of affected modules/tasks, and the manipulation of the engine status. Predicting any possible cause of failure or exception during design is very difficult and often impossible. Being prepared to deal with failures and exceptions at execution time is a critical factor for the success of a WFMS.

Moving towards an entirely automated process will therefore not yield the desired performance [17]. The CrossWork system reflects this insight by including the end-user in several stages, although exception handling in the current version is limited to informing the user about a problem, allowing for rearrangement of certain parameters and restarting the module. Future versions will include opportunities for redefining the workflow, controlling single tasks and including case-based reasoning in exceptional problem solving for cross-organizational business processes [10].

9.3 Need for a Unified User Interface

The global architecture, as presented previously, shows the CrossWork system components from a functional, system-centric point of view. While this has been an important view to define functional modules and interfaces, the concepts of CrossWork from a users' point of view has to be communicated to the design team and potential customers. Thus, the architecture is redrawn in a user-centric way.

Figure 9.1 shows the CrossWork global architecture from a user interaction point of view. The main difference to the original version of the global architecture is the introduction of a "Unified CrossWork User Interface", which provides a common gateway to supervise and interact with the CrossWork software system. The concepts that the interface is built upon are elaborated in detail below.

Fig. 9.1 User-centric view
on the global architecture

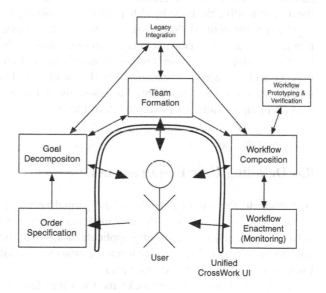

The directed links between the "User" and the CrossWork modules show direction and intensity of interaction from an abstract perspective. The actual use of the modules strongly depends on the scenario that CrossWork is deployed in. Once a module is used, the main direction of information flow can be considered as depicted.

As can be seen from the link directions, the main flow of information is towards the user (as originally intended for the full automation case). However, there are

situations which make human intervention necessary, e.g. to define the basic data
that the system should work on and to make final decisions.

The necessary data is basically defined in the "Order Specification" module
(which has been merged with "Goal Decomposition" in the implementation for reasons of comprehensibility and consistency). "Goal Decomposition" informs the user
of how the problem has been decomposed and only requires human intervention
whenever the underlying ontology does not contain substantial information to fully
complete the task.

"Team Formation" is the module with the highest level of user involvement.
While teams are formed automatically, most of the time there are several candidates
for a certain role or multiple possibilities to form the team itself. As the developers
have learned from the user organizations, the metrics to choose the *best* team or
team member can be represented in terms of rules, or as part of an ontology. They
are also determined by strategic or even *soft*, personal factors. The latter in the final
consequence require human intervention for final decisions.

"Workflow Composition", like "Goal Decomposition", works automatically
(with support of "Workflow Prototyping and Verification"), but needs human intervention whenever it encounters an irresolvable conflict within a workflow. The
module, however, is able to provide hints on the reasons for the conflict, but requires
the user to resolve the issue by either refining or modifying the affected workflow.

The module entitled "Workflow Enactment" here basically contains mainly the
monitoring features of enactment and thus only informs the user of the current state
of accomplishment. The user's possibilities of intervention are restricted to starting,
pausing and stopping the enactment of the workflow. However, on the operative
level (which is not depicted here), human–computer interaction is more intense, as
the enactment module has to keep track of the status of the workflow.

9.4 Detailing User Requirements

According to the building blocks of the global architecture defined above, there
are different requirements on the user interface. As a user interface bridges the gap
between users and the underlying application logic, requirements from both sides
have to be considered, especially when it comes to translating application data into
human-perceivable form and vice versa.

As the functional building blocks and their interfaces have been described in the
former sections of this part, they will not be reviewed in detail here.

9.4.1 Specification

This section covers the requirements of the functional blocks "Goal Decomposition"
and "Team Formation".

The following requirements have been derived from the industry partners' scenarios (Chapter 11) and from the CrossWork modules Goal Decomposition and Team Formation (Chapter 6):

- The UI has to support the visualization of the capabilities that an organizational entity provides. Furthermore it has to support the input and alteration of these capabilities;
- It has to provide means for specification of rules and constraints for team formation, going further than the capabilities required to accomplish tasks in principle, such as acceptable overall production time;
- It has to support different views on the process elements in order to provide intuitive intelligibility for stakeholders from different domains;
- It must be possible to specify general rules and constraints regarding resources, information and processes (process steps);
- The UI has to provide the possibility to specify goals;
- It has to support a structured way of specifying the automotive parts;
- Supplier capabilities must be linkable to the capabilities needed for a particular technology to produce an automotive part;
- The UI elements must allow various levels of abstraction.

9.4.2 Workflow Composition

This section presents the requirements of workflow composition to the user and provides the means for solving conflicts and custom changes.

The following requirements have been derived from the industry partners' scenarios (Chapter 11) and from the CrossWork module Business Process Composition (Chapter 7):

- The UI must be capable of displaying BPEL-compatible workflows, as it has to be considered as a minimal requirement to tune it with eSML;
- It must provide means for specifying construction rules and constraints as an input for agent-based workflow formation;
- It has to be flexible and extensible in order to allow the introduction of new types of constraints and rules and to display them;
- It has to include information, enabling user agents to support users when resolving workflow composition conflicts (e.g. whom to consult, involved roles);
- The UI elements must be able to allow various levels of abstraction;
- The graphical elements of this part must be clearly linked, or even be the same where possible with the elements used for the part described above;
- Views must provide interfaces for the different stakeholders.

9.5 Conceptual UI Design

The CrossWork UI concept has been designed to flexibly support the user in stepping through and supervising the CrossWork system's stages. The basic concept is to provide the user with a unified UI (Fig. 9.2).

Fig. 9.2 Conceptual overview of the CrossWork UI

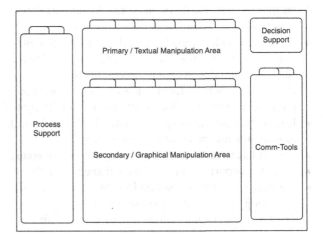

We have defined five UI areas, which can be configured for every module in terms of displaying relevant information. The areas are defined as follows:

- "Process Support" provides the user with the context that they are currently working in. This includes the currently active CrossWork module as well as the other (operational) processes that the CrossWork system accesses, influences or manipulates.
- "Primary/Textual Manipulation Area" is the main area for textual/structured input into the CrossWork system and is used for interaction with the currently active CrossWork module.
- "Secondary/Graphical Manipulation Area" supports the primary manipulation area with graphical display of parts, workflows, etc. and provides the user with additional information relevant to the currently active CrossWork module.
- "Decision Support" displays all unresolved issues that require user intervention. It is used by the system to check back with the users for cases which cannot be handled automatically.
- "Comm-Tools" is dedicated to communication with other users involved in the process. It displays possible relevant communication partners according to the current context (active module and concrete case).
- In this way, the UI allows supervision of a fully automated run of the CrossWork system as well as interaction between users and the system when necessary, which has turned out to be essential in the industry partners' scenarios.

9.6 The User Interface

The CrossWork UI has been implemented using the Eclipse Rich Client Platform (RCP) (Fig. 9.3). This allows rapid adaptation to changing requirements. It inherently provides the user with the opportunity to dynamically reconfigure the UI areas according to his/her needs (in terms of size and position of the areas). The RCP UI is only loosely coupled with the CrossWork backend agent system and communicates via a dedicated protocol. The latter basically allows the attachment of several UIs to a single CrossWork instance as well as exchanging the Rich Client with a Web Interface without changing the CrossWork system itself.

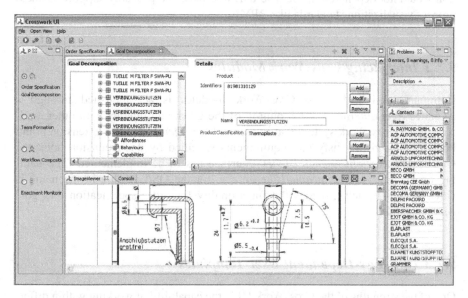

Fig. 9.3 Example of the CrossWork UI for the goal decomposition module

The CrossWork RCP UI is delivered as a self-contained package via Web download and does not set any requirements on system security policies (as it does not need to be installed). Eclipse RCP meets CrossWork's licensing policies as it is published under an open-source license that is compatible with the chosen dual licensing model.

9.7 Implementation Issues

This section summarizes the relevant aspects of the current status of implementation of the CrossWork UI. We revisit aspects of the Eclipse RCP, the interfaces to the other CrossWork modules, the ontology-dependent and dynamically evolving user templates and the BPEL visualization plug-in.

9.7.1 Eclipse RCP

The CrossWork UI has been implemented using the Eclipse *Rich Client Platform (RCP)*. The anticipated *minimal set of plug-ins* strategy did not hold for UI development, mainly due to incorporating the eclipse BPEL-plug-in. This plug-in depends on eclipse-specific plug-ins like the workspace resource model (*org.eclipse.core.resources*) and, of major importance, the generic workbench model (*org.elcipse.ui.ide*). All other plug-ins use the components as intentionally provided by the Eclipse RCP. However, replacing the BPEL-plug-in with a more sophisticated RCP-based plug-in would implement the *minimal set of plug-ins* strategy. This solution would not depend on the eclipse IDE internals, and probably support business process visualization standards like BPMN.

9.7.2 Interfacing CrossWork Modules

Communication with other CrossWork modules is accomplished through a so-called *AgentInteractor*. Each plug-in of the UI should interact with other modules of the CrossWork system that implement the *AgentInteractor* extension point. For any plug-in to satisfy the requirements specified by this extension point the *GUICommunicationChannelListener* interface has to be implemented. The naming convention is *[PluginName]Plugin*; e.g. for the OS/GD plug-in the name is *OSGDPlugin*, which provides the functionality for order specification and goal decomposition.

9.7.3 Ontology-Dependent User Templates

One of the strengths of the CrossWork UI is the capability of working within different domains. Different domains are modelled using specific ontologies (see Chapter 10). Using Protégé (http://protege.stanford.edu/) and the *beangenerator* plug-in Java code is generated from ontologies. The code can be visualized in a generic manner by the CrossWork components UI. Generic representations of ontology structures in terms of main building blocks as shown in Fig. 9.4 are:

- *SettableObject* class is the abstract super class of all other types and includes fields for the name, parent and type of the represented object.
- *TypeContainer* represents collections. There are basically two ways of handling *TypeContainer*s. They contain either a collection of *ComplexObject*s or a collection of *SimpleObject*s.
- *ComplexObject* represents any class structure that may consist of a collection of *ComplexObjects* and/or *SimpleObjects* and/or a collection of *TypeContainers*.
- *SimpleObject* represents any single basic data type (String, Boolean, Integer, Double, Byte, Short, Long, Floating-point number and Character).

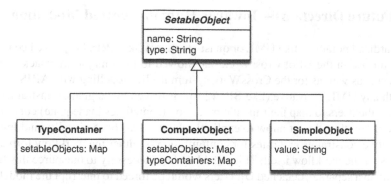

Fig. 9.4 Class diagram of the internal representation of ontological structures

The current implementation is designed for compatibility with the open-source ontology editor Protégé. However, using this editor is not a precondition as the ontology code generation facility has to follow particular rules in order to be interpreted by the CrossWork UI, which entails:

- Collections are identified through methods *add[object name]* and *remove[object name]*. Accordingly, a *TypeContainer* is generated;
- *ComplexObjects* are identified through methods *set[object name]* and *get[object name]* with the represented object being neither a collection nor a simple data type;
- *SimpleObjects* are identified through simple data types: String, Boolean, Integer, Double, Byte, Short, Long, Floating-point number and Character.

9.7.4 BPEL Visualization

A major requirement for the CrossWork User Interface (UI), as indicated in Section 9.4, is the capability of displaying BPEL-compatible workflows. For this reason, the eclipse BPEL-plug-in (www.eclipse.org/bpel) has been adapted to suit the needs of the CrossWork UI. This plug-in is designed to support the definition, authoring, editing, deploying, testing and debugging of WS-BPEL 2.0 processes. However, since the work on the eclipse BPEL-plug-in stalled during the development of the CrossWork UI, and due to the fact that the plug-in was still suffering from major bugs, our implementation only employed selected parts of the plug-in that were in working order at the time. Finally, the plug-in has been rewritten to support the visualization of BPEL-compatible files.

On top of that, the eclipse's BPEL-Designer supports WS-BPEL 2.0 compatible processes while the CrossWork system expects WS-BPEL 1.1 compatible workflows. Minor changes in the import module of the plug-in allowed its integration. In the course of future developments, visualization standards such as BPMN [2] should be considered, since corresponding eclipse-based plug-ins are under way.

9.8 Future Directions – Towards Human-Centred Modelling

Standardized notations like UML or quasi-standards like ARIS [14] have been evaluated for use in the UI of CrossWork but showed to have major drawbacks on the
user's side as well as for the CrossWork system itself. Modelling with ARIS as well
as with any UML derivative (like BILA [16]) is driven by language constraints and
requires the users to map their mental model on (sometimes inadequate) constructs.
Furthermore, they do not allow to explicitly define goals or to visually (and implicitly) define constraints and rules for configuration of either the workflow formation
process, or the workflow itself. This would make it necessary to outsource this functionality in a separate, detached UI. Users would be forced to interrupt the modelling
process or add another modelling cycle to define the respective constraints and rules
necessary for CrossWork.

In our interviews, it became obvious that for the acquisition of process models, the approach must be human-centred, not forcing users to model complex
relationships to represent their mental model, which is not very observable during
visualization (e.g. modelling the shamrock as a set of interconnected roles).

It is therefore necessary to decouple the *content* to be modelled from the limitations of visualization. The presentation of a process must include all the information
necessary for CrossWork and, at the same time, must not reduce the intelligibility
for stakeholders, as this is the case for ARIS and for UML.

A new visual mark-up language has been created in CrossWork, called SUNML.
The following sections discuss three classes of modelling elements this language
knows: Fundamental Modelling Elements, Relationship Elements and Contextual
information Types.

9.8.1 Fundamental SUNML Modelling Elements

The fundamental modelling elements are processes, goals, roles and data as well as
different types of relationships between them. They remain stable and are used for
modelling the respective processes with all their aspects, including roles and data as
well as their goals.

A *process* element represents a process step (which may also be part of a more
complex process). A process in general changes the state of the environment. It
contains a set of activities that initially are not further specified and may for example
contain work tasks of stakeholders or manipulation facilities of data. Processes are
the central parts of any model. In general, they have a defined start and end point
and can be set into temporal relation to other processes.

The possibility to model ancillary processes is provided through the same notation. An ancillary process is used for the specification of sub-tasks and can only be
connected to exactly one parent process, contributes to its goals and shares its roles
and data.

For the refinement of a process the same notation is also used. Sub-processes
are connected via a "part-of" relation to their more abstract "parent". In contrast to

ancillary processes, sub-processes may specify their own roles, data and goal but also inherit from their parent process since they contribute to its goals, have access to its data and its roles are also involved in the sub-process (Fig. 9.5).

Fig. 9.5 Fundamental modelling elements

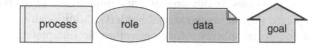

A *role* element represents a functional role within an organization. This role contains a set of rights and responsibilities and is assigned to a person, department or another kind of organizational unit. Roles can be assigned to a concrete position statically in advance, as well as dynamically, whenever the demand arises. This dynamical allocation will be used to model external entities involved in processes which are not defined in advance. In the latter case, the role's designator, which then is not assigned with an existing staff position, is put within quotation marks for a clearly visible distinction.

A role element has to be associated with each process. If a role is involved in more than one process, a respective role element may be inserted for each process for reasons of clarity. Processes always have exactly one process owner directly attached to them. Other roles can be directly attached to the process using connection modifiers, for example if one role is responsible for a process (i.e. owns it, explicitly denoted by *r* for responsibility) while the actual accomplishment is done by another role (denoted by *a* for activity). Downstream roles that have to be consulted or involved in the progression of a process are attached to the process owner, or the accomplishing role.

Data-elements represent the data involved in a process. They are created, used or modified by roles through a process. Inputs required by a process and its intended output are also modelled as data-elements. Data can be manifested within documents, files or oral information. Data can also be put into mutual relation to show dependencies explicitly (like *determines* or *is based on*). In a more generalized approach, data could be understood as a passive phenomenon (an *entity*) that would also include tools, hard- and software and physical and virtual containers (such as rooms or operating systems).

The explicit modelling of *goals* of a process was identified as being crucial for human-centred process representation schemes. Information types, such as performance and quality constraints for task accomplishment, allow the stakeholders involved in the elicitation process to experience the explicated knowledge in its context. Furthermore, the specification of goals in a structured form opens the possibility for CrossWork to derive constraints and rules for goal decomposition, team formation and workflow formation. Each goal is linked to a process.

All four fundamental elements are added to the capability to carry additional attributes to specify capabilities and constraints, which are needed throughout the entire CrossWork Global Architecture. These attributes for example include capabilities of roles, timely constraints for processes or formal constraints for data, as well as global optimization goals that need to be considered when evaluating the goals of a process.

Scopes provide the possibility to divide diagrams into a part that contains the modelled processes of the task at hand, and a part, which provides the context for those processes. In this way, external influences and interfaces to processes can be captured (e.g. at organizational borders). Additionally, scopes allow the definition of contextual spheres, which determine the interpretation of the respective model in terms of the rules and constraints to be applied. Scopes are visualized through a circumscribing dashed line.

9.8.2 SUNML Relationship Elements

Relationships mutually link process, role and data-elements. Their visualization can be modified to express different types of relations. The most generic type is *general link*. It associates two elements and is visualized through a direct line between them. The meaning of a *general link* is determined through the types of elements it connects (see Table 9.1); *responsible* links roles to processes, *involves/consults* links roles mutually. If a link is intended to represent other meanings than the standard type (e.g. *activity* between roles and processes), modellers have to provide an annotation that conveys the meaning of a general link.

Table 9.1 Generic meaning of general links

From/to	Process	Role	Data
Process	–	–	–
Role	Responsible	Involves/consults	–
Data	–	–	Are interdependent

As non-directed links are not sufficient to represent causal dependencies between elements, the second basic link type, *relation* was introduced and is visualized through an arrow. Again, if no annotation is defined, the particular meaning is determined by the respective source and destination elements (see Table 9.2); *before* links processes, *creates* links processes to data, *is Input* links data to processes.

In certain cases additional link types may be required to augment the intelligibility for the involved parties. SUNML therefore allows the definition of further link

Table 9.2 Generic meaning of relations

From/to	Process	Role	Data
Process	Strictly before	–	Creates
Role	–	–	
Data	Is Input	–	Determines

types, which will have to be determined via rules (e.g. a link type *information flow* will require the transmission of information from the starting point to the end point).

For CrossWork, it will be necessary to enable the modelling of splits and joins, so that options and concurrencies can be represented, which is necessary to model detailed activity diagrams as required for tuning with eSML. Therefore the standard UML activity diagram notation is used, providing *split* and *join* elements (indicated by bars) as well as a *decision* construct (indicated by a diamond), as shown in Fig. 9.6.

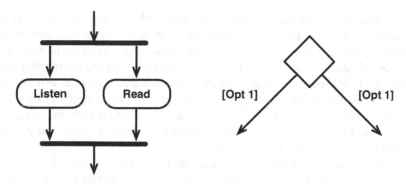

Fig. 9.6 Control flow constructs in SUNML

9.8.3 Contextual Information Types in SUNML

Contextual information types are intended to express knowledge about an organization's philosophy and basic concepts that lie behind any of its business processes. These concepts are in most cases tied to one of the fundamental modelling elements, but not sufficiently expressible through traditional elements. For this reason, we allow the definition of elements representing contextual information. It can be used to augment traditional process notation with additional knowledge. This way the communication among developers and stakeholders becomes context-sensitive.

Contextual information types thus can be used to specify rules and constraints for agents to search for a suitable team and to construct a valid workflow. They can also be used to provide information for user agents to enable them to support users in the construction process. The two contextual information types used in the MAN case (described in detail in the next chapter) and presented as an example here are the shamrock of involved departments, and the rhombus of goals, both shown in Fig. 9.7.

The *shamrock* of involved departments denotes an enterprise-wide philosophy of MAN, namely to involve those departments in every decision-making process. The five departments are (1) "procurement", (2) "logistics", (3) "quality assurance", (4) "engineering" and (5) "production". Each of them or rather a representative of them is consulted in all cases when changes of products or business processes are likely to occur.

Fig. 9.7 Contextual
information types

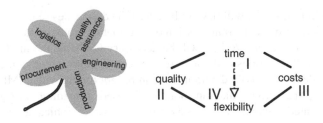

Modelling these five departments as separate roles is also possible, yet this representation does not convey the additional contextual information that the five departments have: to be consulted as a whole, which forms an essential part of the organization's decision-making culture. A successful layout preserving this is the overlay of any role-based diagram with the shamrock representation, which would show, for example, that the involvement of the MAN's engineering department in a Networked Business Process will necessitate consultation with the other four departments. This clearly signifies the consultative culture at MAN and provides an intuitive understanding of that culture.

The shamrock thus defines a rule, which can be used to configure the workflow formation process and its UI respectively. In this case, the relevant information for a department would have to be summarized with an appropriate view of the process, avoiding the display of unnecessary information (e.g. replenishment lead time of a part will be irrelevant for the engineering department, whereas stability measurements won't affect the logistic department's decision), and should then be displayed to the respective person, which can alter, comment on or agree with the proposed solution.

The *rhombus* of goals is the second example of a contextual information type that has been identified in the case study. It is used to arrange process goals according to global enterprise goals. Those goals are arranged in a rhombus to show their competitive nature. They denote the (1) (minimization of) "time", (2) (improvement of) "quality", (3) (minimization of) "costs" and (4) (improvement of) "flexibility". This depiction captures vague relations, e.g. that "flexibility" is "somehow" dependent on "time".

As the four global goals are of different relevance for particular processes, they were assigned roman numbers to represent priorities.

The rhombus of goals shadows each specification of goals for a single process with the relevant global goals marked. The marking represents how these *local* goals are perceived or interpreted in a global context. This concept was extended while modelling the showcase to the definition of predetermined or subsequent global goals of processes. Hereby, it becomes apparent that the specification of the global goals using the traditional goal notation would lack important aspects of enterprise-wide global goals, and the competitive nature of those goals. Furthermore, the process goals can be put into a global context and intuitively represent the relevant aspects (throughout the rhombus) of the respective process.

9.9 Conclusions

Forming and enacting processes in VEs takes place in a social environment within the context of traditional engineering practices. Fully automating the process formation and enactment activities is thus neither feasible nor desirable. For effective support users should be allowed to intervene and control these activities according to their needs. Thus they can take into account implicit knowledge, informal business considerations and social network factors. Consequently, design spaces for IVEs need to be broadened to include user constructs and hidden processes. This enables capturing the social reality within which the CrossWork system is to be used.

Customizing IVE developments to a particular industry, a set of companies or a single company should pay attention to the requirement specification activities. As the work with user organizations has revealed, implicit or hidden agendas may have significant influence to process formation and enactment. In particular, the representation of this knowledge requires novel techniques and flexible notations. It allows the design team to agree on which activities in the VE life cycle can be automated and which should be left to people.

User interface design for any instance of the CrossWork system has to be flexible not only in terms of the domain to be supported, but also in terms reflecting particularities of the organization utilizing the system. So far, human intervention plays a crucial role in decision making. This requires transparent process design and dedicated entry points into workflows, either built automatically or designed manually.

The target domain of the CrossWork shows clear requirements for user integration. Full automation in this domain is neither desirable nor possible, yet flexibility requires the creation of a generic user interface, which allows the automatic visualization of ontological structures without prior knowledge about them. The different software modules of CrossWork can thus interact with their users on the basis of their own domain model, encoded within a specific ontology. Further developments of the user interface should see the implementation of contextual information elements, as exemplified by SUNML. This aims to enable more human-centred modelling approach.

References

1. Bonabeau, E., Don't Trust Your Gut, Harvard Business Review, Prod. #: R0305J-PDF-ENG, Vol. 3604, May, 2003.
2. Business Process Modeling Notation, Version 1.1, http://www.bpmn.org, 2008.
3. Degani, A., Heymann, M., Formal Verification of Human-Automation Interaction, Human Factors, Vol. 44(1), pp. 28–43, 2002.

4. Gebauer, J.. Modeling the IT-Infrastructure of Inter-Organizational Processes – Automation vs. Flexibility, Proceedings of the Conference of the International Society for Decision Support Systems (ISDSS), 2007.
5. Haight, J. M., Kecojevic, V., Automation Vs. Human Intervention: What is the Best Fit for the Best Performance? Process Safety Progress, Vol. 24(1), pp. 45–51, 2005.
6. Heinl, P., Horn, S., Jablonski, S., Neeb, J., Stein, K., Teschke, M., A Comprehensive Approach to Flexibility in Workflow Management Systems, Proceedings of the International Joint Conference on Work Activities Coordination and Collaboration, pp. 79–88, 1999.
7. Hermann, T., Walter, T., Participatory Design and Cyclic Improvement of Business Processes with Workflow Management Systems, LS06 Informations system und Sicherheit, Information Retrieval, Informatik und Gesellschaft, 1998.
8. Hoc, J. M., From Human-Machine Interaction to Human-Machine Cooperation, Ergonomics, Vol. 43(7), pp. 833–843, 2000.
9. Lee, J. D., See, K. A., Trust in Automation: Designing for Appropriate Reliance, Human Factors, Vol. 46(1), pp. 50–80, 2004.
10. Luo, Z., Knowledge Sharing, Coordinated Exception Handling and Intelligent Problem Solving for Cross-organizational Business Processes, PhD Thesis, Computer Science Department, University of Georgia, 2001.
11. Mourao, H. R., Antunes, P., Supporting Direct User Interventions in Exception Handling in Workflow Management Systems, Workshop de Sistemas de Informacao Multimedia e Cooperativos, COOP-MEDIA, Portugal, 2003.
12. Mowshowitz, A., On the Theory of Virtual Organization, Systems Research and Behavioral Science, Vol. 14(6), pp. 373–384, 1997.
13. Oppl, S., Stary, C., Towards Human-Centered Design of Diagrammatic Representation Schemes, ACM International Conference Proceedings Series, Proceedings of the 4th International Workshop on Task Models and Diagrams (TAMODIA), Vol. 127, pp. 55–62, 2005.
14. Scheer, A. W., ARIS – Business Process Modeling, Springer, New York, 1998.
15. Skitka, L. J., Mosier, K. L., Burdick, M., Does Automation Bias Decision-Making? International Journal of Human-Computer Studies, Vol. 51, pp. 991–1006, 1999.
16. Stary, C., Stoiber, S.. Model-Based Electronic Performance Support. In Interactive Systems. Design, Specification, and Verification. LNCS, Vol. 2844, Springer, 2003.
17. Strong, D. M., Miller, S. M., Exceptions and Exception Handling in Computerized Information Processes, ACM Transactions on Information Systems (TOIS), Vol. 13(2), pp. 206–233, 1995.

Chapter 10
Domain Knowledge Integration

Iain Duncan Stalker, Martin Carpenter, Nikolay Mehandjiev, Ali Owrak, and Georg Weichhart

In this chapter we focus on the theoretical underpinning and enabling technologies which ensure that the knowledge about the domain embedded in the software system remains current and is understood by the members of the VE.

Our discussion focuses upon the distribution of expertise, the co-existence and co-evolution of multiple contexts and the need for a common understanding which evolves with the VE. We also discuss the approaches to achieving semantic alignment, noting that the most common approach is to converge upon a common agreed ontology. Finally, we review the knowledge integration choices made by CrossWork in regards to the prototype it developed.

10.1 Semantic Alignment in Virtual Enterprises

A fundamental aspect of any successful collaboration is successful communication. However, successful communication presupposes a shared understanding; a so-called *semantic alignment*. With the advent of the Semantic Web and related technologies, the path to semantic alignment is typically sought through ontology.

Informally, an *ontology* comprises of a set of concepts and a set of relations which describe and constrain how the concepts refer, interrelate and combine. Recent interest in ontologies has led to a number of definitions of the term "ontology", e.g. [17] or [10], but probably the most widely used definition of an ontology is that given by Gruber [9]: *an explicit specification of a conceptualization*. However, we prefer the definitionoffered by Guarino [11]: *an explicit, partial account of a conceptualization*, where a conceptualization identifies *a set of informal rules that constrain the structure of a piece of reality, which an agent uses in order to isolate and organize relevant objects and relevant relations.*

I.D. Stalker (✉)
University of Teesside, Middlesbrough, UK
e-mail: i.stalker@tees.ac.uk

N. Mehandjiev, P. Grefen (eds.), *Dynamic Business Process Formation for Instant Virtual Enterprises*, Advanced Information and Knowledge Processing, DOI 10.1007/978-1-84882-691-5_10, © Springer-Verlag London Limited 2010

Later in this chapter we review the issues arising when we attempt to achieve semantic alignment between members of a VE and propose an approach to addressing these issues but first we provide an overview of ontology standards, languages and tools.

10.1.1 Ontology Languages and Tools

The predominant use of ontology to foster semantic interoperability is reflected by the numerous research efforts, and software tool development and support in this area. In response to approaches to ontological modelling, such as those cited above, e.g. RDF, a number of tools for ontology editing, storage, querying and reasoning are now available. These include several semantic frameworks for accessing and manipulating documents in OWL, RDF and RDFS.

There are several RDF/RDFS-based reasoners and repositories available, including OWLIM, Sesame, Jena, Joseki, Kowari and 3store. While most of the repositories are based on triples, some of them additionally implement scalable inferencing for RDF/RDFS documents, or alternatively for OWL-Lite in SHIF(D) description logic. The most prominent semantic framework is Jena [12]. Current tableaux-based description logic reasoners include Racer, Pellet and Fact++. All implement various optimizations for tableau-based inferencing for SHOIQ(D) class of description logics. An alternative reasoner for the SHIQ(D) subset of OWLDL is KAON2 (kaon.semanticweb.org), which implements a novel resolution-based description logic reasoning.

Ontologies can be created using ontology editors, such as Protégé (protege.stanford.edu), an open source development environment for ontologies and knowledge-based systems which was developed at Stanford University (USA). OWL plug-ins for Protégé support the editing of OWL ontologies and the ongoing CO-ODE project (www.co-ode.org/) provides valuable support for user modelling in OWL. Many other ontology editors exist [5], including OntoEdit, which support translating the ontology from its own XML-based storage format to others, such as F-Logic and RDF; and OilEd, which allows the users to build ontologies using OWL and its precursor DAML+OIL. Finally, tools such as DUET (DAML UML Enhanced Tool) support visualization and management of ontologies, as indeed do a number of Web-based editors, such as OntoWiki or POWL (ontowiki.net).

10.1.2 Semantic Web

While the study of ontologies has deep roots within philosophical domains, the focus of much recent interest has been enabling the automatic comprehension of the semantic meaning of terms. The evolution of this field is comprehensively discussed by [20]. In recent times the related idea of the semantic Web, originally popularized by [1], has risen to prominence. The goal of this initiative is to place semantic annotations on elements within Web pages thus permitting their semantics to be machine interpretable. This will facilitate certain features such as intelligent Web searches.

Many proponents of the Semantic Web seek a universal medium for information exchange based upon XML syntax. This has given rise to such standards as the Resource Description Framework (RDF) and its elaboration in RDF Schema or the Web Ontology Language (OWL) and is also reflected in the vision of Semantic Web Services and related standards, namely, the Web Service Modelling Ontology (WSMO at www.wsmo.org), the Web Service Modelling Language (WSML) or OWL-S (www.w3.org/Submission/OWL-S).

A basic requirement for the realization of the semantic Web is that the documents within it must contain tags identifying the semantic meaning of their concepts. In the light of the enormous quantity of Web pages already in existence it is not feasible to expect their manual annotation, so the semi-automated annotation of Web documents is a key challenge for the realization of the Semantic Web. Several systems for performing such annotation through annotation protocols exist, including Annotea (annotea.org/), Rubby and RDF annotation. As discussed by Uren [26], annotation solutions can be manual, such as CREAM and Magpie, or semi-automatic based on Natural Language Processing (NLP), a document structure analysis or a learning approach (which requires training sets or supervision). Moreover, there exist pattern-based semi-automatic solutions, such as PANKOW and C-PANKOW [3], SemTag or pattern-based approach OnTeA [14].

10.1.3 Standards-Based Semantic Alignment

The conventional approach to semantic alignment between enterprises is to define standards governing both the structure of the information being exchanged and the manner in which this information should be processed. The semantics of any communication using such standards will then be fully understood. Indeed this approach underpins almost all practical solutions to semantic interoperability, e.g. RosettaNet (www.rosettanet.org) and ebXML (www.ebxml.org).

In general, this approach to providing semantic interoperability can be characterized as relying on mutual commitment to a single shared ontology. Such a commitment ensures that the terms used within communication have a shared meaning thus directly allowing for semantic interoperability.

The problems of using a common shared ontology for semantic alignment stem from the nature of VEs, and from the open nature of the environments which foster VEs. Indeed a VE stipulates interaction between a number of companies with different backgrounds and specialisms. The features of the environments within which VEs arise also suggests that there might be (a) a number of candidate ontologies for a given domain, and (b) a need for communication among parties from multiple backgrounds, each with its own particular vocabulary. Moreover, in such environments, ontologies tend to co-evolve with their communities of use [23]. These suggest that neither a fixed ontology nor a unique semantics is appropriate.

10.1.4 Ontology Sharing

The pragmatic solutions discussed above assume the existence of a single centralized ontology to which all parties involved in communication subscribe thus providing shared meaning. In practice however it is more likely that multiple differing ontologies will coexist. The existence of multiple standards is thus inevitable. The recognition that the use of a single ontology is untenable in a distributed environment has led to research in "ontology alignment". There are several techniques for aligning ontologies: an extensive survey can be found, e.g., within [13].

Two prominent techniques are the creation of local rules for translating concepts between the different ontologies and creating some "meta-structure" to relate the ontologies. In principle these techniques hold out the promise of enabling distributed ontology interactions: each document is defined according to the ontology used by its creator, the local rules of every receiver then map them into terms known by the reader of the document.

The major difficulty with this approach lies in the need to create the mapping rules. An obvious possibility is to support users in the manual creation of mapping rules between two ontologies, an approach used, for example, in the OntoMerge project [6]. A notable feature of such techniques is that in order to define such rules, complete descriptions of the two ontologies to be mapped between must be available. In addition a human expert is required to define the mapping rules. While this is reasonable for a pair of static ontologies, it may not be feasible for more dynamic situations, so the investigation of approaches for automatically deriving such rules was motivated.

However such approaches have tended to solely focus on identifying situations where concepts within two ontologies can be identified and, as noted in [13], typically still require some human input. This human input is required to solve perhaps the harder half of the problem, i.e. creating rules relating how the information within the attributes of the concepts of one ontology should be mapped into the attributes of the class identified as equivalent within the other ontology.

This problem is closely related to that of database schema integration. This has been well studied, e.g., by [19] who demonstrate that the formation of translation rules to deal with such syntactic matters represents a substantial problem.

Moreover a new company using an existing interoperability solution might bring new concepts with it which must then be inserted into the main centralized ontology. This might not only require substantial work on the centralized ontology itself but also requires the other companies using the same interoperability solution to learn the new concepts introduced.

Similar problems are encountered when considering approaches which use mapping rules – every time a new company started to use the interoperability solution, appropriate mapping rules or "meta-structures" for mapping from and to every other ontology within this solution to their local ontology would have to be created. This process would obviously be far from "zero-cost" and would indeed increase rapidly as more businesses started to use the interoperability system.

10.2 Devolved Ontology Model

Our approach to semantic alignment is informed by our work in *Devolved Ontology* [22–24]. Informally, a *Devolved Ontology Model* comprises a core ontology and a number of extensions of this into peripheral and inter-application domain ontologies. It is a structure to facilitate ontological and semantic alignment among communicating entities. To appreciate the devolved ontology approach, it is instructive to first consider typical uses of ontology.

In Computer Science, ontologies are typically used for one of two purposes: to formalize a domain of interest or to support communication through a controlled, unambiguous vocabulary. While it is possible and often instructive to view the second as a special case of the first – in that we formalize a domain of discourse – their respective, underlying motives are fundamentally different.

Formalizing a Domain: This is an exercise in (knowledge) engineering. We build an abstract model or construct a theory which ideally gives a precise and accurate account of the salient aspects of a domain of interest, which can be substantiated by practice or experiment. Thus, objectivity, i.e. independence of the account from the observer is of primary importance. Typically, defining a substantive concept within a given domain involves agreement at two levels; we must identify what objects exist in our (shared) conceptualization, and how these objects are characterized.

Implicit in our theory is an ontological commitment; by describing some phenomenon through the use of denoting symbols, we are committed to the existence of certain entities and relations among these. This echoes perhaps the most familiar theory of ontological commitment, that of Quine, which claims in essence that one is committed to an entity if one refers to it directly or indirectly [18].

Supporting Communication: Supporting communication is an exercise in pragmatics. Pragmatics is a subfield of linguistics which investigates the nature of communication in concrete situations. In particular, it distinguishes two intents within a given communicative act, usually verbal, but these apply in a wider sense, namely [15, 21] *informative intent,* or the (interpretive or referential) meaning of the sentence, and *communicative intent,* or the intended meaning of the speaker. Of special interest in supporting communication are the so-called *deictic* aspects, which, in a general sense, confirm that valid interpretation demands knowledge of the context in which the communication occurs. This suggests that we must assume the viewpoint of the agent responsible for a given communicative act to receive the communicative intent for the specific, concrete situation. On the other hand, to ensure that the communicative intent is conveyed, a communicating agent should not presuppose that its viewpoint prevails in a domain of discourse.

The nature of ontological commitment in supporting communication differs markedly from that arising when formalizing a domain; fewer concepts and relations are necessary, and importantly less structure is required. In our opinion, the failure to maintain this dichotomy is one significant cause of the delay in delivering on the promise of ontologies for communication, and frustrates much of the interaction between those active in the two different aspects. This is particularly evident when, as a first step to communication among partners from different domains, ontological alignment is sought in a manner which is tantamount to formalizing the domain of discourse. There is a perceived need to agree on precise concept definitions and much is made of the merging of ontologies to achieve this. Accordingly, independently of method, agreement is sought at two levels: the identification of what objects exist in the (shared) conceptualization and how these objects are structurally defined. Yet, for a given domain of discourse, we, as individuals acting upon the world, are capable of entertaining simultaneously a number of conceptualizations which may be inconsistent, even contradictory or at different levels of granularity. We choose the most appropriate to the task at hand; we select according to context. As such, it is neither convenient nor desirable to fix a unique characterization of the domain of discourse. Indeed, such a choice often proves to be an impediment. Thus, in a practical sense, maintaining the dichotomy means that we treat communication as a de facto exchange of a minimal set of essential tokens of information and we do not impose our ontology onto the communication.

The core ontology provides a common ground for understanding among partners and is central to the partnership. The concepts included within this are agreed through negotiation of all partners. As such, the responsibility for the evolution and maintenance of the core is shared by the partners. Each peripheral ontology represents an extension of the core ontology into an application domain. The responsibility for the evolution and maintenance of each peripheral ontology devolves upon the appropriate partner or partners. This includes the responsibility for extending the core into the particular context and ensuring that the peripheral ontology remains consistent with the core. Since two partners may share a number of concepts which are not part of the core, we recognize the existence of inter-application domains and ontologies. The responsibility for the initial extension of the core into the inter-application ontology devolves upon two agents jointly; for further extension into each, application ontology devolves onto the appropriate single agent.

Crucially, devolving responsibility upon the appropriate partner includes leaving the choice of appropriate syntactic structure to it (respectively them). Therefore, the first step in creating a formal devolved ontology model is the removal of syntactic aspects; structures are initially flattened. We propose that a given concept has a number of tokens, e.g. a set of attributes, associated with it. The tokens used to represent the concept (at a particular instant) are selected according to context, projecting away from those which are redundant to leave only an essential subset. We refer to the full set of tokens as the global (domain) concept; this may include inconsistencies. In the special case where the tokens are the same for each participant, we call this a common (domain) concept. To compensate for the removal of syntactic structure, it is imperative that we find some "natural" structure and allow this to emerge.

In the development of the model in this chapter, we use Formal Concept Analysis (FCA) [8], Closure Operators (see, for example, [4]) and Lattice Theory [2] to capture these ideas, and to provide sufficient rigor for systematic treatment. The selection of tokens as needed and the appeal to a "natural" structure allow our ontologies to be minimal and self-constructing.

10.3 Semantic Alignment in the Automotive Domain

This section focuses on the conceptual mechanisms proposed to ensure the alignment of ontologies within different partners under conditions of evolving partner knowledge and product structures, typical for open domains.

Indeed, open networks of entities which assemble opportunistically to fulfil a particular purpose such as VEs, Supply Chain Networks and eMarketplaces demand enabling software technologies which both capture the distribution of intelligence or expertise and facilitate meaningful communication. While multi-agent systems offer much to foster open networks, e.g., ad hoc interaction with new arrivals is supported through agent communication languages and interaction protocols [7, 27], and thus basing a substantial part of CrossWork on a multi-agent system gives us a good basis, there are limitations. In particular, communication within multi-agent systems presupposes a common ontology, which is typically fixed in both content and semantics.

We introduce an approach that implements concept evolution as a result of negotiation between VE partners. This approach is based on a particular instantiation of the devolved ontology model and uses utility functions and interaction protocols within a multi-agent system. The particular instantiation of the devolved ontology model combines FCA and partially shared views [16] which was first introduced in [22].

10.3.1 Concept Negotiation

We can assume that an agent is reluctant to alter its knowledge base unless there is some (positive) payoff. Moreover, once motivated to revise its knowledge base, it will seek to minimize the extent of any change. Accordingly, in any concept negotiation we have a natural focal point [25] for each agent, namely those essential details which must be conveyed to ensure that the transaction is appropriately informative. For the sender, this identifies a lower bound for the concept under negotiation, and any acceptable alternative will reside on a chain connecting it with the original concept. For the receiver, the closer he gets to this, the better, although, he may not know what this is, therefore it would be in his interest to strip away attributes at each stage.

We can use the notion of Partially Shared Views (PSV) to provide an appropriate structure to form the basis of such concept negotiation. In PSV a view is defined to be "a set of object types and their relations". A view V2 is subtype of V1, and some of the message types in V2 are specializations of ("children of") the message types in V1 (p.16) [16]. FCA provides use with an appropriate formalism through which to realize PSV.

Suppose that the structure of our domain (i.e. its ontology) is comprised of a common ontology and two (main) application ontologies, A and B. Each of the ontologies identified above is a correct subset of a (notional) global ontology which includes all concepts in the domain. Generalization identifies a sub-ontology relationship and so the common ontology is a correct subset of each of the application ontologies. In fact, the common ontology is a sub-context of the application ontologies [8]. We consider the context of the Table 10.1. As our common ontology, we consider the categorization of the planets solely according to their distance from the sun. As our application ontology A, we consider the categorization of the planets according to distance from the sun and the size. As our application ontology B, we consider the categorization of the planets according to distance from the sun and the presence of a satellite (moon).

Table 10.1 Planet context (taken from [4])

	Size			Distance from Sun		Moon	
	Small	Medium	Large	Near	Far	Yes	No
Mercury	X			X			X
Venus	X			X			X
Earth	X			X		X	
Mars	X			X		X	
Jupiter			X		X	X	
Saturn			X		X	X	
Uranus		X			X	X	
Neptune		X			X	X	
Pluto	X				X	X	

In each case, we enlarge the common ontology by (order) embedding the additional concepts from each augmented ontology into the common concept lattice, as illustrated in Fig. 10.1. The figure shows the common ontology (top), application ontology A (left) and application ontology B (right). In each application ontology, the common ontology is indicated by black nodes. The common concept lattice is a factor lattice of each application domain lattice cf. [8]. Moreover, the application domain lattices are factor lattices of the global domain lattice of Fig. 10.1 and provide an atlas decomposition of this [8]. Our intention here is to illustrate structure, thus for clarity in the diagram we omit the planets associated with each node. As such, the common ontology is a sub-lattice of each augmented ontology.

Figure 10.1 illustrates our (notional) global ontology and includes all of our concept lattices. The common ontology and each of the augmented ontologies is

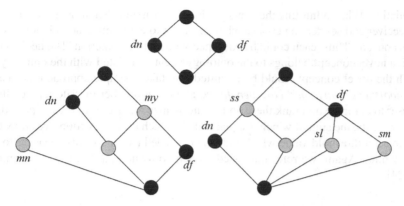

Fig. 10.1 Ontologies

sub-lattice of the notional global ontology. Borrowing the term *view* from [16] we consider the above ontologies as (defining) views of the planets in our solar system. *Common View*, V_C: the planets are categorized as near to the sun or far from the sun according to their positions inside of or outside of the asteroid belt. *Augmented View A*, V_A: is an augmented common view that includes a consideration of planet size. *Augmented View B*, V_B: is an augmentation of the common view to include a consideration of satellites (moons). *Global View*, V_G: is an all-encompassing view which we associate with the domain as a whole, essentially, a superset of V_A, V_B and V_C. Consider, Agent A sends a message, message = (...{size-medium, distance-far}...), which Agent B does not understand, as the concept does not exist in its view, V_B. Thus, if appropriate, we replace it with the closest super-concept in the common view, V_C: from Fig. 10.1 we see this is {distance-far}. We can use the partial order of our concept lattices to formalize notions such as closest super-concept, shared super-concepts, etc.; we refer interested readers to related papers, see for example [22–24].

10.3.2 Utility-Based Concept Negotiation

FCA provides a way to realize aspects of PSV and together these give rise to a particular instance of a devolved ontology model. While this is a model, it provides merely the *what* of concept negotiation for a set of interacting entities, leaving us to determine through other methods *when* and *why* these should seek to negotiate. This is the role of utility functions, and we need to equip our agents with these. We discuss this with simple examples in the current section. We assume that the decision to negotiate when faced with a novel concept depends, inter alia, on the *importance* of the third party(ies) involved, the *worth* of the (current) transaction, and the *cost–benefit* of admitting the concept. Moreover, the importance of each of these depends on the stage of negotiation. For example, the cost–benefit of admitting the concept is unknown in the initial stages and has little impact on the decision to proceed with negotiation. When admitting the concept, the cost–benefit is a dominant factor. Both the receiver and sender can choose whether or not to enter into a negotiation over a novel concept. Thus, each could be equipped with a utility function. The decision to admit a novel concept belongs to the ontology agent associated with the ontology to which the novel concept would be admitted. We take a simple approach. For each of, *importance, worth and cost–benefit* we identify a number of criteria, we allow the user to compare and rank these and we normalize the user rankings to provide a set of weights, the sum of which is equal to 1. For each utility function, we allow the user to set a threshold value which must be exceeded (for the utility measure to be worthwhile). Again, we refer interested readers to related papers, see for example [22–24].

10.3.3 Protocols for Semantic Alignment

Having presented the *what*, the *why* and the *when*, it remains to show the *how*. Negotiation protocols provide this. The manner in which an agent responds when faced with a potential case for (concept) negotiation is informed by the nature of the relationship with the third party(ies) involved. This includes considerations of trust, vested interests, the degree of acquaintance, and so forth. The intangible nature of these often proves an impediment to the construction of satisfactory models.[1] We consider this information beyond the more immediate, objective measures captured in (our) utility functions and thus provide a choice of protocol through which to negotiate. For example, if one implicitly trusts the third party, then one might comfortably seek his opinion of the usefulness of a concept in future communications, secure in the knowledge that a fair response is obtained. The choice of protocol can be derived from an agent's list of acquaintances, cf. [7], or from the values in the utility functions when deciding whether to negotiate, or a combination of both. We assume that the agents are equipped with appropriate utility functions. For simplicity, we also assume a single third party. We present an example protocol motivated by "future usefulness", which for historic reasons we refer to as "Protocol B" (Fig. 10.2).

Protocol B is driven by "future usefulness" judgement by the sender. As such a certain degree of trust is vested in the sender. The protocol begins once the two agents, Sender and Receiver, have agreed to negotiate over the novel concept in the message. The protocol takes place between the Ontology Agent of the Receiver and the Sender. If the Sender has an Ontology Agent on its platform, then this may also participate in the negotiation. The primary aim of the negotiation is to decide on the best way to treat the unknown concept, and it will produce one of the following three outcomes:

---

[1] Naturally, the same argument can be levelled at notions of importance and worth presented above, but we feel that a greater degree of objectivity obtains for these.

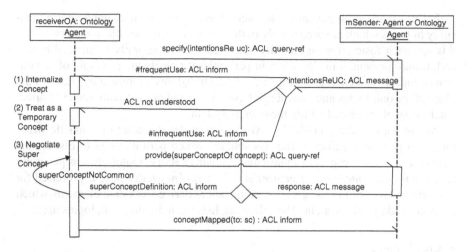

Fig. 10.2 Sequence diagram of protocol B

1. If the novel concept will be used by the Sender in future transactions, then it is internalized by (the Ontology Agent of) the Receiver.
2. If negotiation with the Sender is frustrated, for instance, the sender does not know the negotiation protocol, then the concept will be temporarily asserted, if necessary supporting constructs are available.
3. If the novel concept is to be used on an infrequent basis, then the negotiation will attempt to find an appropriate super-concept that is acceptable to both parties. Details of this aspect of the protocol are omitted. If an agreement cannot be reached, then we would revert to a temporary assertion.

10.4 Semantic Alignment in the Automotive Domain

In closely related domains there is typically a broad range of terms which are common and for which the meanings are generally understood and agreed. This is particularly the case in recognized subfields of well-established disciplines, such as engineering. Within the automotive domain and ancillary sectors, the application domain providing the initial case studies for CrossWork offers one such example; there exists a rich, widely used vocabulary. Naturally, in such cases, semantic alignment presents much less of a challenge. Typically, it reduces the identification or selection of an "essential" subset of terms to use; in the simplest of cases this is derived from a discussion of the use cases with intended end users. The technical aspect of semantic alignment then becomes one of ensuring that compatible representational structures are used to codify the terms. That is, it becomes a matter of *syntactic* alignment. This is a design decision based on economy, efficiency and influenced by the software architecture, and implementation strategy and tools.

In CrossWork, multiple ontologies were devised, each comprising a relevant category of terms which are used widely in the automotive and ancillary sectors. While this approach fostered manageability, the decision was strongly influenced by the architecture presented in Chapter 5 in particular it reflects the principle of separation of concerns taken. Indeed, Fig. 5.7 demonstrated this alignment by showing the place of the ontologies and knowledge bases (indicated as the traditional cylindrical database symbol) placed within the overall system.

An ontology in the (initial) CrossWork project denotes a set of syntactic structures that provide a sufficient rich vocabulary, which permits users to discuss the state of affairs with respect to a particular domain or scope. Ontology was generally reserved for the *conceptual structures* and the term *knowledge base* is preferred for concrete instances of ontologies. These instances derive from data elements which users entered into the system. The following lists the individual ontologies used:

- Core Ontology;
- Product and Service Ontology; and
- Market Ontology, which is further specialized into a Supplier Ontology and an Employee Ontology.

The *Core Ontology* was introduced as a number of concepts were shared among, i.e. common to, the different ontologies. The Product and Service Ontology (identified as 'Prod.' in Fig. 5.7) describes the goal for building a product (part) and allows the decomposition of that goal into sub-parts. The Employee Ontology is used for finding participants within an organization even when it is distributed across different manufacturing sites or subsidiaries, whilst the supplier ontology represents external organizations. Both are derived from the market ontology which holds the common concepts required for team formation. The Pattern and Infra (Infrastructure) repositories hold further information not captured within ontological structures.

10.5 CrossWork Ontologies

The technical requirements of the overall CrossWork system required that the ontologies and knowledge bases were usable from within the underpinning agent-based system platform. The JADE platform (jade.tilab.com) was chosen as the basic agent-based platform. JADE ontologies follow a frame-based structure. Ontologies were constructed using the Protégé Editor and the resulting class structures exported these for use by our agents, via the JADE Ontology Bean Generator plug-in for Protégé. In the following discussion we introduce the Core Ontology; we then detail some important concepts from the others.

The Core Ontology provides 78 classes and 113 properties (named slots in Protégé). It introduces the "Concept" class which is a common high-level concept from which the classes "Thing", "AgentAction" and "AID" (Agent Identifier) are derived. It is abstract and has no template slots. Going down, the specialization tree, "AgentAction" represents activities that an agent can do, and the "AID" concept is used by the Jade Agent System to address individual software agents distributed across a network. The third element specializing "Concept" is "Thing"; "Thing" is the top-level type of all concepts that represent subjects in the domain. For example, Fig. 10.3 shows the concept "AbstractOrganization" which is a "TeamMember" which in turn is a "Thing". A predicate (like "supplier of") can be used to relate two or more subjects. "Abstract Organization" is shown to contain information about its Products, Services, Capabilities and RolesPlayed.

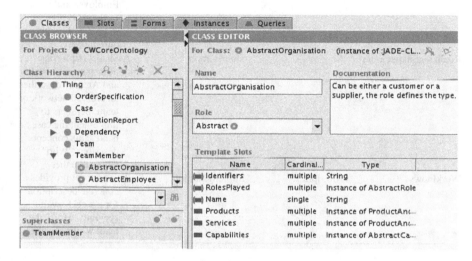

Fig. 10.3 The "abstract organization" concept in Protégé

To avoid having to pass a large volumes of data together with the passing of control between the CrossWork modules (e.g. Order Specification → Goal Decomposition from Fig. 5.7), CrossWork has introduced a central data storage facility termed a *Case File*. For each project, a central instance of *Case* is used to collect all information that is produced while the system runs through the individual stages. The structure of the Case concept is represented in Table 10.2.

Most of these entries are self-explanatory, with a case containing a problem definition, a set of team members and their workflows. "ShapeGraph" is an abstract representation of the manner in which team members will play the corresponding roles in the VE, highlighting the dependencies between the roles and tasks. Details of the structure are provided in Table 10.3 This is the output from the team formation module and is further used by the workflow composition module.

The Product and Service ontology describes 31 classes within a total of 45 properties. Not surprisingly (as the name suggests) it provides detailed concepts to describe products or services. These concepts are linked to the core ontology through the OrderSpecification concept appearing in Fig. 10.3.

Table 10.2 Case concept

Class Name: Case

Property name	Cardinality	Allowed type	Description
Identifier	Required single	String	Unique ID for the current Case
Problem	Single	ProblemDefinition	Used to configure the system's functionality
TeamMembers	Multiple	TeamMember	A team member may be an Organization or an Employee and is further specified in more detail in other ontologies
RealizingShapeGraph	Single	ShapeGraph	A ShapeGraph consists of instances of Node and Arc and describes an ordered network of team members to implement the case at hand. This concept describes "Who" works together
WorkFlows	Multiple	Implementation	This concept provides a concrete description for a workflow. It specifies "How" the team works together

Table 10.3 ShapeGraph Concept

Class Name: ShapeGraph

Property name	Cardinality	Allowed type	Description
Nodes	Multiple	Node	A node holds a Task List (multiple element of type AbstractTask). It also contains links to TeamMembers that might realize the tasks. A Node has also an idea
Arcs	Multiple	Arc	An Arc has a single input and output node. It holds also information about a Dependency which might be a ControlDependency, ResourceDependency or DataDependency

The Role concept provides an abstract placeholder for a member in a team, specifying *what* this member's contribution to the team will be. It is linked with the Capability concept, which specifies *how* this team member can contribute to the team. Behaviour is then defined to specify the concrete implementation of such a contribution by an individual member.

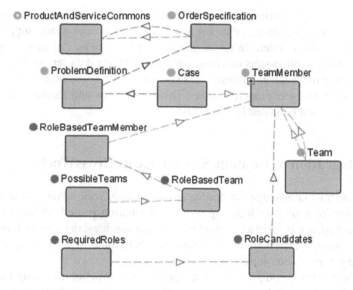

Fig. 10.4 Jumbalaya representation of a market ontology fragment

The *Market Ontology* is derived from the core and consists of 15 additional classes with 23 new defined properties. A fragment of it is shown in Fig. 10.4. It focuses on defining companies and facilities (sites) a company might own. The products produced and services offered are described for each. Multiple addresses may naturally be given. The capabilities and a profiling result may also be specified. A Profile is then defined as a measured performance of an individual organization. A top-level performance might be divided into a *logistics* view and a *quality* view. The logistics view might then be divided into an operative logistics view and an electronic data transmission view. A "leaf" view such as the operative logistics view would aggregate concrete ProfilingAndSkillData values, including values for Backlog in €, or a number of LateDeliveries, or a number of Failures.

10.6 Persistence of Data in CrossWork

The generic approach of CrossWork distributes knowledge structures across the overall system. This requires a database approach which is flexible and capable of remote access. To achieve this, CrossWork partners decided to use Hibernate, an object-relational mapping/persistence framework. Hibernate supports the implementation of a flexible data persistence layer.

The generic mechanism allows storing the ontological instances of a *case* (see above) without any prior knowledge about it and the included concept instances and concept classes. Java Reflection is used to analyses the objects and their properties. This is possible since the concepts described above have been exported into Java

Beans. Hence all properties are accessible through getter and setter methods. The implementation therefore accounts for a separation of concerns and supports evolution of the overall system in terms of allowing introduction of new concepts at runtime without requirements on changing the underlying data repository.

The storage mechanism analyses the class structures of the objects to be stored and recursively extracts property values. These properties and their associations to the objects are then persisted by Hibernate.

10.7 Integration of Domain Knowledge in CrossWork

The approach to knowledge integration used in CrossWork advocates abstracting from matters of syntax to focusing on the information passed within a concept. When a concept is passed to a recipient with a local ontology, the approach compares the atomic items of information within this concept to those within concepts existing within the receiver's ontology.

The results of this comparison can trigger a range of actions, starting from only retaining the subset of the concept's overall information which the recipient will understand, ending with a decision by the recipient to learn the complete new concept because of its future utility. This permits actors/trading partners to meaningfully communicate without the need for potentially expensive ontology agreement or alignment. A more complete account of this approach can be found, e.g. within [23].

> The mechanisms for integrating domain knowledge described here enable the work of the other modules in the system. These mechanisms can also be used to facilitate the automatic link to legacy systems, and to the automatic seeding of agent systems using a simple database of existing customers.

References

1. Berners-Lee, T., Hendler, J., Lassila, O., The Semantic Web, Scientific American, Vol. 284(5), pp. 34–43, 2001.
2. Birkhoff, G., Lattice Theory (3rd Edition), AMS Colloquium Publication, Providence, RI, 1967.
3. Cimiano, P., Ladwig, G., Staab, S., Gimme' the Context: Context-driven Automatic Semantic Annotation with C-PANKOW, Proceedings of the 14th International Conference on World Wide Web, pp. 332–341, Chiba, Japan, May 10–14, 2005.
4. Davey, B. A., Priestley, H. A., An Introduction to Lattices and Order (2nd Edition), Cambridge University Press, Cambridge, 2002.
5. Denny, M., Ontology Building: A Survey of Editing Tools, Retrieved October 2008 from www.xml.com/2002/11/06/ontology_editor_survey.html
6. Dou, D., McDermott, D., Qi, P., Ontology Translation on the Semantic Web, Journal on Data Semantics II, Published in Lecture Notes in Computer Science, Vol. 3360, pp. 35–57, 2005.

7. Ferber, J., Multi-Agent Systems, An Introduction to Distributed Artificial Intelligence, Addison-Wesley, New York, 1999.
8. Ganter, B., Wille, R., Formal Concept Analysis, Mathematical Foundations, Springer-Verlag, New York, 1999.
9. Gruber, T., A Translation Approach to Portable Ontology Specifications, Knowledge Acquisition, Vol. 5(2), pp. 199–220, 1993.
10. Gomez-Perez, A., Lopez, M., Corcho, O., Ontological Engineering (1st Edition), Springer, London, 2004.
11. Guarino, N., Giaretta, P., Ontologies and Knowledge Bases: Towards and Terminological Clarification, Towards Very Large Knowledge Bases: Knowledge Building and Knowledge Sharing, IOS Press, Amsterdam, 1995.
12. Jena – A Semantic Web Framework for Java, Retrieved October 14, 2008, from http://jena.sourceforge.net/
13. Kalfolglou, Y., Schorlemmer, M., Ontology Mapping: The State of the Art, The Knowledge Engineering Review, Vol. 18(1), pp. 1–31, Cambridge University Press, 2003.
14. Laclavik, M., Seleng, M., Gatial, E., Balogh, Z., Hluchy, L., Ontology Based Text Annotation – OnTeA; Information Modelling and Knowledge Bases XVIII, IOS Press, Amsterdam, Frontiers in Artificial Intelligence and Applications, Vol. 154, pp. 311–315, 2007.
15. Leech, G., Principles of Pragmatics, Longman, London, 1983.
16. Lee, J., Malone, T. W., Partially Shared Views: A Scheme for Communicating Among Groups that Use Different Type Hierarchies, ACM Transactions on Information Systems, Vol. 8(1), pp. 1–26, 1990.
17. Noy, N., Klein, M., Ontology Evolution: Not the Same as Schema Evolution, Knowledge and Information Systems, Vol. 6(4), pp. 428–440, 2004.
18. Quine, W. V. O., On What There Is, Review of Metaphysics, Vol. 2, pp. 21–38, 1948.
19. Rahm, E., Bernstein, P.A., A Survey of Approaches to Automatic Schema Matching, The VLDB Journal, Vol. 10(4), pp. 334–350, December, 2001.
20. Smith, B., Welty, C., FOIS introduction: Ontology – Towards a new synthesis, Proceedings of the International Conference on Formal Ontology in Information Systems, Vol. 2001, pp. 3–9, Maine, USA, 2001.
21. Sperber, D., Wilson, D., Relevance: Communication and Cognition, Blackwell, Oxford, 1986.
22. Stalker, I., Mehandjiev, N., Carpenter, M., Gledson, A., Dynamic Knowledge Management in Open Multiagent Systems, Proceedings of AMKM, Workshop of AAMAS, Utrectht, 2005.
23. Stalker, I., Mehandiev, N., A Devolved Ontology Model for the Pragmatic Web, Proceedings of the 1st International Pragmatic Web Conference (PragWeb), Lecture Notes in Informatics, Vol. 89, pp.38–52, 2006.
24. Stalker, I., Mehandjiev, N., Carpenter, M., Devolved Ontology for Smart Applications, Proceedings of the 15th International Conference on Conceptual Structures (ICCS), Lecture Notes in Artificial Intelligence, LNAI 4604, pp. 360–373, Springer, 2007.
25. Sugden, R., A Theory of Focal Points, The Economic Journal, Vol. 105(430), pp. 533–550, May, 1995.
26. Uren, V., Cimiano, P., Iria, J., Handschuh, S., Vargas-Vera, M., Motta, E., Ciravegna, F., Semantic Annotation for Knowledge Management: Requirements and a Survey of the State of the Art, Journal of Web Semantics: Science, Services and Agents on the World Wide Web, Vol. 4(1), pp. 14–28, 2005.
27. Wooldridge, M., An Introduction to Multiagent Systems, John Wiley & Sons, New York, 2002.

Part IV
Case Studies

Chapter 11
Automotive Industry Case Studies

Kurt Fessl, Martin Carpenter, Stefan Oppl, Peter Peherstorfer, Wolfgang Bittner, Ali Owrak, Nikolay Mehandjiev, and Christian Stary

This chapter provides integrated views of the BOAT levels, focused on specific business scenarios within the automotive industry. In particular, our discussion focuses upon three case studies that expand on the different aspects of these business scenarios and demonstrate their implementation through the application of the CrossWork prototype.

11.1 Automotive Associations

Chapter 3 discussed the major trends in the contemporary marketplaces, including the modularization of highly complex technology. In the automotive domain this is reflected by the trend where OEMs are modularizing vehicles into systems and modules to facilitate both concurrent development and flexible and scalable production. Automotive OEMs are thus able to manage the increased product complexity and number of variants for each make of automobile. The definition of systems and modules are driven by a set of technological, economic and inter-organizational objectives.

Technological objectives include the optimization of the product structure and quality, the improvement of product flexibility, allowing individual suppliers to focus on core competences and dealing with the technical complexity.

Economic objectives include the reduction of production costs whilst increasing the added value of additional features and customization facilities. Costs and cycle times for development and production are reduced, with cheaper quality management and logistics processes.

Inter-organizational objectives of system and module creation include the reduction of interfaces with suppliers and thus decreasing coordination and transaction costs for the OEM, tighter integration with selected suppliers and the establishment of clear responsibilities including authorizations.

K. Fessl (✉)
Automotive Solutions GmbH, Steyr-Gleink, Austria
e-mail: k.fessl@automotive-solutions.at

N. Mehandjiev, P. Grefen (eds.), *Dynamic Business Process Formation for Instant Virtual Enterprises*, Advanced Information and Knowledge Processing, DOI 10.1007/978-1-84882-691-5_11, © Springer-Verlag London Limited 2010

11.1.1 Requirements of Automotive Suppliers

The trend of modularization allows suppliers to improve their own value creation processes in terms of both development and production. This applies not just to technical implementation but also to coordinating work with other sub-suppliers. Tighter integration with the OEM is also considered to bring about strategic benefits. This is why automotive suppliers try to establish themselves as a system or module provider, offering product and process innovations.

The extreme manifestation of this trend is the maturity reached by the top 10 automotive suppliers, which are now able to become providers for complete solutions. Indeed, Magna already assembles a number of vehicles in its plant in Graz, Austria, including Mercedes M-Class and Jeep Grand Cherokee.[1] Following such a strategy requires a global sourcing approach, and companies reducing costs whilst observing strict quality standards. This strategy requires enormous investments in pre- and serial development.

To reach the coveted position of a system module supplier, suppliers need to invest in infrastructure and capabilities. The capabilities may be focused on a specific product, technology or a process. The levels of investment in infrastructure and skills are beyond the reach of ordinary automotive SMEs.

Instead of blanket capital investment, the solution highlighted in this book is for the SME to seek union with other SMEs offering complimentary competences, a union which is temporary and targeting a specific business opportunity, in other words a VE. Indeed, a stable and sustainable business development strategy should focus on well-defined core competences rather than seek excellence on a number of fronts.

Such a VE allows SMEs to seek different strategic positions in an automotive supply chain depending on the particular set of circumstances associated with a business opportunity. For some business opportunities it might be useful to act as a system or module provider which is tightly integrated with the OEM, thus improve the know-how with regards to a specific product. For other business opportunities it might be useful for an SME to act as a sub-supplier of specific parts, establishing a position of an expert in a process or a technology.

Helping SMEs to seek such temporary unions, or VEs, and to strategically position themselves depending on a particular business opportunity will have the long-term effect of improving the competitiveness of the said SMEs. Helping SMEs in a region by supporting collaborations between them is the approach of the Automotive Associations. They focus on dynamic formation of cooperative structures which focus on the individual core competences of SMEs.

---

[1] http://wardsauto.com/ar/magna_eye_chrysler/

11.1.2 Scenario

As discussed above, the scenario to be supported by automotive associations has to focus on dynamic formation of cooperative structures focusing on individual core competences. Automotive associations achieve this by registering at existing OEM platforms so that they can receive requests for quotations. Upon receiving such a request, a detailed quote has to be prepared and sent to the OEM within a deadline which is often set to 5 days. So the main challenge for this scenario is to select the best team available within strict timing constraints.

The Automotive Associations thus support local SMEs by allowing them to form a consortium with sufficient capabilities to respond to a request for a quote by an OEM. One SME will be acting as an integrator for the team and as a module provider to the OEM. This scenario represented a core motivation for the CrossWork project and grounding for the theoretical VE formation ideas. Hence it is of no surprise that the scenario of fast VE formation matches the drive of our approach towards "Instant" VEs, by automating the formation of a VE. Such a VE comprises complementary companies and experts according to the main product perspective, as well as experts according to key technology and manufacturing requirements. This scenario is illustrated in Fig. 11.1.

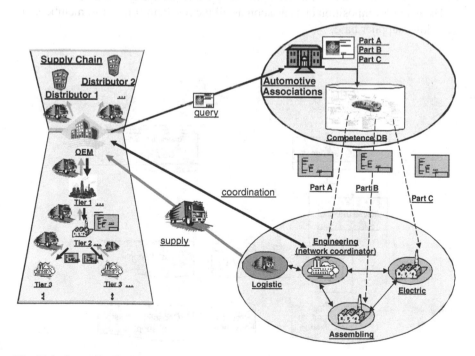

Fig. 11.1 Scenario of a VE

11.1.3 Goal Decomposition

We can conceptualize the processing of the OEM's request for quotation by the Automotive Association as analysis of a goal statement. Typically the core of the goal is a formal description of the product or service requested. Additional requirements might include quantities, preliminary lead time of delivery schedule and logistical issues of delivery (e.g. just in time or just in sequence).

The analysis of the goal statement leads to a goal breakdown structure, which enumerates the main roles in fulfilling the goal. CrossWork automates this analysis by implementing artificial intelligence style reasoning over knowledge structures, representing domain-specific knowledge about part-based or function-based decompositions within the automotive domain. Figure 11.2 illustrates the activities involved in arranging a quote workshop. For example, if a car door is requested, the CrossWork system will pull out of the knowledge structures repository the ontology of a car, where it is specified that a car door comprises a window, a door frame, a handle, hinges and an internal panel. It will then seek companies which can produce one or more of these key components, and can assemble and test them before delivering to the OEM. A functional specialization is also possible, for example our car door can be represented as implementing the functions of road safety, protection of wind, security, allowing entrance into the car and even acoustic box for the speakers. Retrieving the latter piece of explicit information will ensure that acoustic specialists are enrolled into the team providing the requested quotation.

The goal decomposition ends as soon as all the resultant roles fit to members of the exiting supplier base.

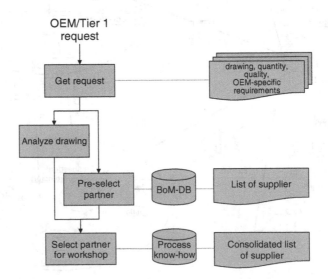

Fig. 11.2 Flowchart of automotive association activities to arrange a quote workshop

11.1.3.1 Team Formation

Once the goal is analysed into a set of roles, the Automotive Association attempts to identify possible combinations of suppliers which can play all the roles and thus fulfil the goal. The implementation of this activity within CrossWork is termed Team Formation (TF). Because of its automated nature, TF can afford to produce a large number of alternative teams and rank them according to certain criteria, offering only the "best" team to the CrossWork user.

The main objective of the Automotive Association is to form a team (a VE), and to pass the request for quotation to this team. For this the automotive association organizes a workshop with the potential suppliers, and appoints a "system integrator" organization to act as a workshop chair and VE leader. The main purpose for the workshop is to verify the social and legal aspects of the proposed collaborations between the team members. The following issues are of a particular relevance:

1. Is every potential collaboration partner willing to work in a network? This depends strongly on the stakeholders involved.

   - The OEM: Judgment is based on the team members' experiences and principles of the OEM's purchasing;
   - The members of the collaboration group: Do they trust each other sufficiently to reveal the level of know-how needed for work within the VE? Also relevant is the general match of individual companies' strategies, e.g. the willingness to invest.

2. Information regarding the target quantity of output, which involves balancing of capacities between different potential collaboration partners.
3. Verification of the availability of resources.

   - Quantity, qualification and development issues for human resources;
   - Clarification of requirements on technical resources;
   - Financial situation and check for the need involving investors (e.g. bank institutes).

4. Verification of regional capabilities in regards to the assembly activities and logistic processes such as just in sequence delivery.
5. Checking the strategic fit of partners' planned activities to avoid competition in specific countries and areas.
6. Discovering synergies regarding the direct investments required.

In addition to these compatibility criteria, the selection of partners to be identified by the CrossWork system should also observe the match to the formal criteria from the OEM, mainly concerning the technological capabilities of the suppliers. The OEM might impose fixed sub-suppliers and formulate a set of strict requirements regarding the legal aspects of the virtual supplier network.

When this is implemented in CrossWork, the constraints of the OEM should be complemented by soft parameters to be considered by the partner selection mechanism. These soft parameters can be implemented by creating skill profiles of potential collaboration partners. These profiles will introduce estimations about the effectiveness of collaboration, the flexibility of the partner and their capability for innovation. The selection procedure might be finalized by considering recent collaborative experiences of other partners.

Technical aspects and requirements for the selection of potential collaboration partners are mainly defined via the OEMs formal request for quotation. In addition, social competences on an organizational level are also important for fruitful cooperation. NoAE requires excellent technical competence of all partners at all levels. Strong cooperation reduces transaction and coordination costs in forming an NoAE. Therefore, the potential of collaboration value of potential partners can be characterized by the following typology and is illustrated in Fig. 11.3:

"Network player":   is a kind of network-champion that is able to combine cooperation competence and technical competence, and perform this expertise in a flexible manner.

"Specialist":   is a technically excellent partner which might be used for specific tasks and technologies required to fulfil the overall task. The greater the willingness to improve cooperation competence, the better the potential for collaboration will be (to be verified in the workshop).

"Libero":   is a technical competence commodity that might be used when a task requires high reactivity.

"Freeloader":   is a reference to the motivation needed to attain new orders or customers without participating in a network actively. This involvement might be necessary for technical reasons, but has to be eliminated as soon as it begins to endanger the balance within the network.

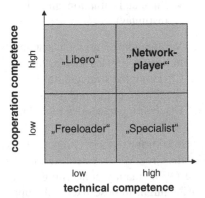

Fig. 11.3 Topology of collaboration value of potential partners

During the process of team formation, the selection of companies following an order is based on:

- What they produce;
- The processing capabilities they have; and
- Process engineering knowledge about quality, and tolerances linked to their processing capabilities.

Furthermore, the selection process includes a number of additional derivatives referred to as "quick checks", which include the gathering of business intelligence regarding companies' cashflow, their past and present projects and other internal matters that provide insight into the suitability and capability of a company to be selected for a given project. Companies which individually only fulfil part of the requirements outlined can be merged together to form a complete unit. This provides greater scope for selection, innovation and change, and serves to strengthen the composition and applicability of a VE.

Due its pivotal role, the scenario discussed in this section is of a generic framework, providing conceptual mapping to the CrossWork functionality discussed in previous modules. The following sections of this chapter present three case studies that have been used to expand on the different aspects of this scenario, and their implementation has been illustrated through a series of snapshots from the CrossWork prototype.

11.2 MAN

The MAN group is a large manufacturer of trucks and buses that uses a closely meshed network of subsidiaries and partners to provide an international service. The fundamental motivation for MAN's outsourcing of complete systems is the reduction of costs. Devolving responsibility for the delivery of a complete system to a Tier 1 supplier removes substantial administrative and managerial burdens from MAN which can lead to significant savings. Currently, MAN manages in the region of 1,200 suppliers across many tiers, but has established the intention to reduce this number to the order of 300 suppliers by 2010. To facilitate this transition MAN is interested in identifying suppliers which can be developed as single points of contact at Tier 1 and who will assume from MAN the responsibility for the delivery of an entire system. For convenience we refer to this as the *business process* in the sequel and summarize it in Fig. 11.4. The business process begins with the creation of a model of a system (cf. *Module*) to be outsourced, and concludes with an agreement with a Tier 1 supplier to assume full responsibility for delivery of the module or system. The individual activities are presented in more detail in the following sections.

11.2.1 Basic Requirements

As described above, MAN aims at using the CrossWork System for reducing the complexity of its relationships to suppliers. However, MAN focuses on the team

Fig. 11.4 MAN
"module-based" supplier
development (business
process)

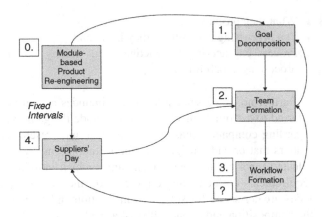

formation features of CrossWork for identifying the most suitable team of suppliers to assemble and deliver a part of a truck. Workflow formation here is considered as a supportive process to justify the feasibility of a certain team. Workflow Enactment has not been considered relevant at this stage of development of MAN's internal supplier management processes.

11.2.2 Scenario

We begin with the assumption that a module/system has been proposed. The proposal for a new module/system can derive from a number of sources, e.g. one of:

- Supplier;
- Management board;
- Purchasing management/department; or even
- An employee.

As our running examples we shall use a *Water Tank System* (*WTS*) and a *Wing* (in German: *Kotfluegel*). Once a module/system for outsourcing is identified, the following occurs:

1. A *Bill of Materials* (*BOMs*) for the particular module/system is obtained from the *Engineering Department*. All variants, i.e. all model variations and instances, of the initial system are identified and the BOM for each of these is obtained.
2. Ideally, the team formed and supplier developed will be responsible for all variants. Thus, the necessary capabilities must be considered from the start. Typically, there will be significant overlap in the BOMs, circa 80%.

3. In the case of the WTS, there are 6–8 variants. For cost reduction it is essential to outsource all variants immediately, because only then is it possible to eliminate the pre-assembly and logistics.
4. The current team(s), as coordinated by MAN is (are) identified and a unit cost for this team is determined. This is undertaken by the *Controller*.
5. This is *Team 1* and represents the *measure* with which other possible teams will be compared. Typically, the team with the cheapest unit cost is the preferred team, but this is not always the case: ultimately, the *Management Board* makes the choice accounting for strategic, political, etc. aspects.
6. Information about suppliers is obtained from appropriate databases; in particular, suppliers are organized according to *Material Group* and are evaluated using a *Scorecard* for each *Contract* with MAN.

11.2.2.1 Order Specification and Goal Decomposition

The Purchasing Department considers the BOMs for the proposed module/system and variants. These are used to identify all parts, to the detail of specific components, subcomponents, etc. Figure 11.5 shows the configuration of problem definition during the order specification phase. A BOM received from the Engineering Department may not directly correspond to the process through which the module/system is realized. An engineer compiling the BOM is often too familiar with the process and may omit components which are assumed to be there. As such, the BOM needs to be compared and cross-referenced with the working plan which corresponds to the process to ensure that a true (collated) BOM emerges. Figure 11.6 shows the order specification of the WTS following the configuration of the problem identification phase.

The CrossWork Goal Decomposition Module (GDM) provides the necessary functionalities to support the activities here. Specifically, each system/module is formalized using the concepts and structures from the product ontology. The resulting

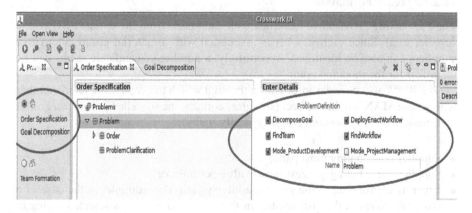

Fig. 11.5 Order specification 1: configuring problem definition in the MAN case

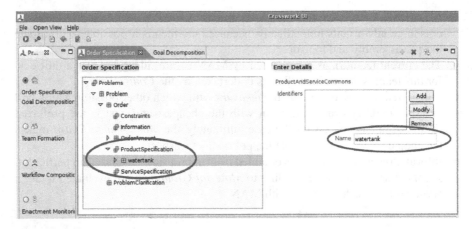

Fig. 11.6 Order specification 2: specifying module for outsourcing – watertank

formalization (called product descriptions) is maintained in a product database. By reasoning over these structures and descriptions, the GDM decomposes the appropriate variants into specific parts, identifying whether these parts are standard or bespoke. Figure 11.7 presents an example of the BOMs with its corresponding visual information area.

The GDM automatically identifies all the required components, subcomponents, etc. In many cases, knowledge regarding the module/system can be used to (partially) order the services needed to realize it. This information can be carried forward into Team Formation where it can be used to structure the team(s). The knowledge and information used can be formalized using a correspondence of Product–Process–Team. At a conceptual level, the information in the module/system is directly related to the information in the process(es) through which it is achieved. This avoids any mismatch of process and product.

11.2.2.2 Team Formation

The *Purchasing Department* identifies with each part (from the collated BOM) the supplier used. Since each supplier is associated with a material group, alternative suppliers can also be identified. Accordingly, a number of candidate teams can be identified for the module/system.

The BOM also provides information through which to propose the team member with whom MAN will have direct (singular) contact; the so-called *system integrator.*

Candidates for *system integrator* typically include:

- Supplier contributing most parts;
- Supplier contributing greatest (cost) value per unit; or
- Other as appropriate to the given module/system. For example, in the case of a *Wing* (*Kotfluegel*), the last supplier in the chain (*painter*) was selected owing to them selecting the appropriate variant.

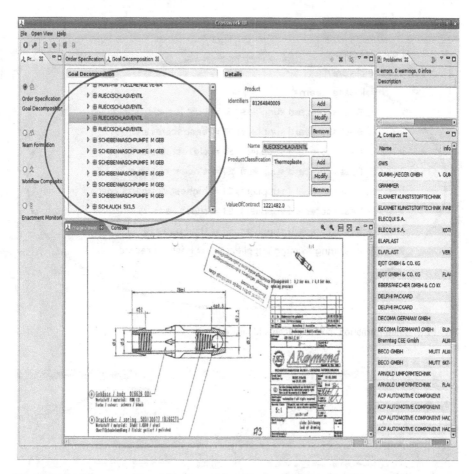

Fig. 11.7 Goal decomposition: bill of materials with visual information area

The same collection of suppliers may constitute two distinct candidate teams if two candidate *system* integrators are identified.

The *Management Board* considers the candidate teams constructed and chooses the most appropriate. This is typically based on lowest cost, but this is not mandatory; there may be strategic or political reasons for choosing the team. Figure 11.8 shows the identification process of team formation based on specific criteria. A closer examination of specific teams is shown in Fig. 11.9.

11.2.2.3 CrossWork Team Formation Module

The CrossWork Team Formation Module (TFM) provides the necessary functionality to support the activities here. In particular, the product decomposition and primary services from GDM are used to identify potential team members and

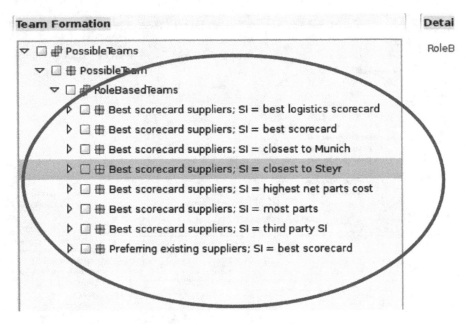

Fig. 11.8 Team formation: potential teams identified

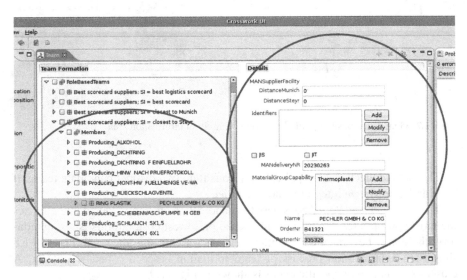

Fig. 11.9 Team formation: examining a particular team

to form candidate teams from these. Importantly, the structures from GDM can be refined and used to propose system integrators based on cost value of parts contributed, percentage of parts contributed and indeed interrelations of member activities. In the TFM, team formation is modelled as the following activities:

- Resource Identification: We identify the contacts, markets, databases, catalogues, libraries (cf. Yellow Pages) from which candidate team members can be selected. In this case, the stage of resource identification is directly supported by the databases suppliers maintained by MAN.
- Filtering of Suppliers: To ensure that we select only relevant suppliers, we make a simple, preliminary matchmaking of service providers to primary services and the provision of components. Appropriate, specifically devised conceptual structures are used. Here again, the MAN databases can be used, in particular the notion of Material Groups.
- Preselection of Candidates: Once the suppliers are filtered, we apply hard constraints. For example, we may only be interested in candidates having a certain EDI capability or located within a geographical radius, etc. In the MAN scenario, the scorecard is of direct relevance.
- Candidate Evaluation: Having reduced potential candidates to those meeting essential requirements, we can rank those remaining. We identify items of importance, e.g. geographical location, volume, spare capacity, experience, etc. In particular, we can consider soft constraints which we should prefer in a supplier, but the absence of which does not preclude a supplier, e.g. in-house logistics, etc.; and ranking criteria, which are objective quantifiable measures which can be compared from supplier to supplier. Again, the MAN scorecard is invaluable here.
- Team Evaluation: It does not necessarily follow that the best candidates in combination will give the best team. Moreover, in some cases the best supplier may depend upon the other members of a team. Thus, evaluation strictly comprises of two interdependent activities: candidate evaluation and team evaluation. The CrossWork TFM recognizes this by providing for each of these, allowing each to inform the other. In the MAN scenario, Team 1 can be used as a standard for comparison: potential replacements should better this in obvious aspects, e.g. cost, and/or perhaps other not so obvious aspects.

Since the Management Board makes the final decision, the goal of the TFM in CrossWork can be reduced to the creation of these alternative teams together with (semi-) automatic calculation of associated measures; perhaps, making recommendations based upon these.

11.2.2.4 Workflow Composition

Business process formation, in particular, for the purpose of generating workflows to be executed under direct control of workflow enactment systems, is not of immediate interest to the MAN scenario. Nor is the focus of the MAN scenario on operational aspects of supply chain management. Ultimately, the system integrator contracts to deliver the particular module/system according to agreed terms: for example, delivery within 10 days, or delivery three times a day, every 15 days, etc.

Explicit business process formation does, however, offer improved possibilities for better documentation of candidate teams, with respect to process structures implemented by these teams; and evaluation of teams formed, with respect to process characteristics of these teams, such as execution times.

For the above reason, process formation can provide an auxiliary step in the business process providing valuable feedback to the Team Formation step and in the longer term[2] providing input to the *Suppliers' Day* step.

The Workflow Formation Module (WFM) can provide valuable input to the TFM. In particular, this holds for quantitative aspects of processes implied by specific teams. The Workflow Evaluation Module (WFE) contains logic to evaluate these quantitative aspects. For example, if a requirement on a team is that it can produce a certain number of units within a specified number of days, then WFM can provide valuable information to TFM in the evaluation of candidate teams. Additionally, to accommodate the possibility of fluctuations in demand, e.g. seasonal variations or unforeseen increases, it is useful to establish some measure of spare capacity. Process/workflow evaluation can contribute to this information.

WFM can (semi-) automatically generate a number of alternative team processes with quantitative detail, once a team is formed. Specification of such alternatives can be used as input to the Suppliers' Days.[3] Moreover, the Workflow Prototyping Module (WFP) can be used to analyse dynamic characteristics of these processes without the need for an actual enactment environment.

11.2.2.5 Workflow Enactment and Monitoring

This stage has not been considered relevant by MAN for the current prototype, as their current interests focus on TF and draw enactment under consideration only partially or for future use, respectively.

11.2.3 Summary

The following points of human intervention can be identified for the MAN scenario:

- In Order Specification, the user has to define the part he wants to search a team for.
- Goal Decomposition is accomplished fully automatically based on the product ontology of MAN's truck parts prototypically defined within the project.
- Team Formation identifies the most suitable suppliers to form the required team based on supplier classification, supplier scorecard and other metrics defined within the project in a multi-stage process as described above. Human intervention is necessary to take the final decision upon the team and whenever no suitable

---

[2] The provision of analyses to inform a Suppliers' Day is something for which CrossWork provides the foundation, but which is strictly out of scope of the MAN Scenario developed above.

[3] Again, CrossWork provides a foundation for this, but it is strictly out of scope for the MAN Scenario developed above.

supplier is found to cover a necessary role. To leave the final decision to the user in this stage was a requirement of MAN, as this also incorporates strategic and "soft", personal factors, which in last consequence require human intervention for the final decision.

- Workflow Formation is again accomplished fully automatically and is only considered a supporting module in this scenario, which only checks whether a suggested team can basically work together based on their local workflows. It also checks the feasibility of the strict time constraints MAN imposes to its suppliers. Human intervention in this step is only necessary in the case of missing data at the moment; as a long-term perspective, optimization of workflows through human interaction in this step may provide valuable input for MAN's supplier development programs.

11.3 Magna Intier

Magna Intier, a division of the Magna group, is one of the largest automotive suppliers in the world. Magna Intier focuses on the provision of car interior components and contains several companies in addition to Intier Ebergassing. Each of these companies has considerable independence and, in particular, they are free to work with the best suppliers irrespective of whether they are also part of the Magna group.

Around the time of concluding the CrossWork experiments, the use of the CrossWork system at Magna Intier was strongly aligned with their internal project management practices which were based on the internal "Harmoney" manual, based on a DIN standard. CrossWork supports the accomplishment of the steps defined in Harmoney by suggesting the most suitable team members based on peoples' competences and checking the feasibility of the resulting workflows.

11.3.1 Basic Requirements

The prototype developed for the Magna Intier Use Case is intended to support the processes defined in the Harmoney Management Handbook. The scope of Harmoney is to define the management activities to be performed for an automotive product development project from identification of a business opportunity until the start of serial production (see Fig. 11.10). It defines all phases, processes within these phases, activities within this processes, roles and responsibilities within a development project.

Magna Intier provides an intra-organizational use-case for CrossWork. While the MagnaIntier Automotive Group consists of several largely independent facilities, Harmoney abstracts over these organizational entities and focuses on persons as the members of the project team. Therefore, distribution and collaboration has to be understood on a personal level with single team members interacting to fulfil a certain task.

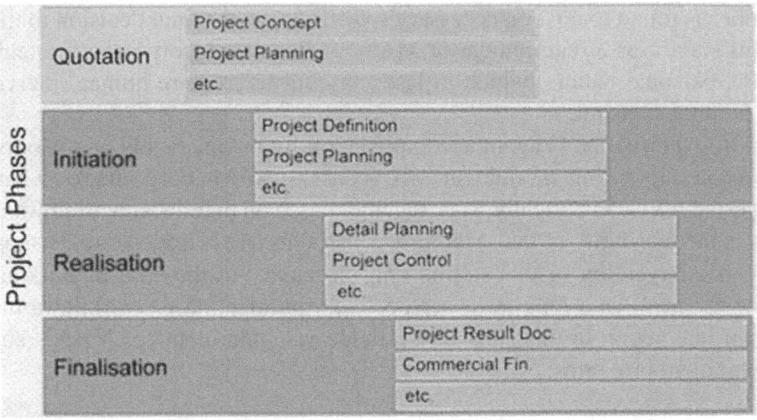

		Project Concept	
	Quotation	Project Planning	
		etc.	
	Initiation	Project Definition	
		Project Planning	
		etc.	
	Realisation	Detail Planning	
		Project Control	
		etc.	
	Finalisation	Project Result Doc.	
		Commercial Fin.	
		etc.	

Fig. 11.10 Overview of Harmoney phases

Harmoney defines the project team to be a set of roles. However, roles are defined on a management level. For each role (e.g. project manager, project financial controller and project team member), its responsibilities and global tasks are defined. Additionally, each role has a defined list of skills, which the person assigned to this role has to have (for an example Fig. 11.11). For each person employed at Magna Intier there is a table of skills available and therefore can be used to map role requirements and personal competences.

Fig. 11.11 Skill requirements for role project manager

Skill Requirements –including personal attribute requirement

- Structured thinking and acting
- Objective negotiation skills
- Competent leader
- Decision making capability
- Sales and customer oriented
- Able to manage stress
- Entrepreneurial approach to a project

However, it is important to recognize that Harmoney strictly stays on the management level. It therefore only defines that there has to be operative staff (project team members) and in later sections describes what activities have to be fulfilled by this staff, but does not define how the operative tasks (in terms of development) are implemented.

Each of the four main project phases is divided into processes. Again, only processes relevant on management level are specified (see Fig. 11.12). Operative (Product – Development-centric) processes are largely dependent on the project, and therefore are not addressed in Harmoney. In such cases Harmoney refers to the applicable organization manual of the responsible Magna Intier division (e.g. the Engineering Processes have a blank page in Harmoney).

Each management process is specified in the Harmoney manual (see Fig. 11.13 for an example), containing activities and activity relevant project roles and their

Fig. 11.12 "Project Realization" phase in Harmoney

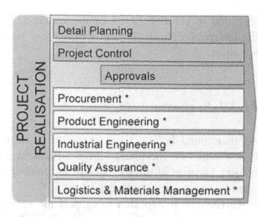

PROJECT REALISATION
Detail Planning
Project Control
Approvals
Procurement *
Product Engineering *
Industrial Engineering *
Quality Assurance *
Logistics & Materials Management *

Approvals Process

Process Start Condition:
This start of this process is the readiness of any deliverable that has been contractually agreed with the Customer as requiring their approval.

Activity	PJM	PTM	QP	SLS	CUS	Documents
Declaration of Readiness for Approval Submission	R/A	I	I	I	A	> Declaration of Approval Readiness
Submission for Approval	R	A	S		I	< Approval Plan > Test and Audit Protocols > Submission Protocol > Approval Protocol
Inspection and Testing for Approval	R	A	S		S	> Deviation List
Implementation of Corrective Action	R	A	S		I	<> Deviation List
Confirmation or Rejection of Approval	R/A	A	I	I	A	< Issue List (Deviations) > Completed Approval Protocol

Process End Condition:
This process ends when approval of the agreed deliverable is obtained from the Customer.

Legend

						Relevant Documents
CO	Controlling	PJM	Project Manager	R	Responsible	Declaration of Readiness for Submission
CUS	Customer	PTM	Project Team Member	A	Action	Approval Plan
EX	Executive Management	PUR	Purchasing	S	Support	Approval Protocol
GM	General Manager / VP OPs	QP	Quality Manager Program /	I	Information	Test and Audit Protocol
PB	Project Board		Project	C	Check	Submission Protocol
PC	Project Controller	SLS	Sales	( )	Depending on P.	Deviation Report / List
PD	Program Development	SUB	Sub Contractor		Classification	

Fig. 11.13 Detailed overview of the "Approvals Process"

responsibilities, and the documents required. A verbal description of what is expected to happen is provided for each activity.

For CrossWork, the activities are considered to be projections of local workflows to the global level. How an activity is actually performed is defined on a local level by a workflow involving the specified roles. These detailed workflows are not specified in Harmoney. So for the scenario, they were prototypically defined for the Harmoney phase "Project Realization" based on the verbal description of the activities.

11.3.2 Scenario

As mentioned before, the scenario to be supported by the Magna Intier prototype focuses on the phase "Project Realization" as specified in Harmoney. This phase comprises of three management processes specified in Harmoney and several operative processes left beside here.

CrossWork is expected to support the *setup and monitoring of a development project according to Harmoney.* The CrossWork system is therefore applied to the structure of Harmoney, supporting the selection of team members, setup of common workflows and monitoring of project progress.

Each Harmoney project has the same core structure on Harmoney Activity Level (i.e. no matter what type of project this is, the same activities have to be undertaken). However, the actual detailed structure depends on the size of the project (differentiated in A-, B- and C-projects), on the respective customer (OEM A requires some different activities and special attention milestones than OEM B), and the experience of the person taking over a particular role.

11.3.2.1 Order Specification

When setting up a new Harmoney project, the user starts the CrossWork system and is presented with the Order Specification User Interface (OSUI).

With the OSUI the user configures project-specific data like customer and project classification (see Fig. 11.14). Additionally the OSUI allows the Harmoney phases to be considered as well as the required level of solution, i.e. how far should the CrossWork system proceed (e.g. just a team is required, but no workflow composition).

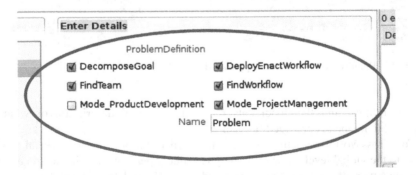

Fig. 11.14 Order specification: configuration of problem definition in the Magna Intier case

The OSUI template is generated automatically according to the structure of the used ontology. It therefore adapts to the respective application domain automatically. When the information is entered, Order Specification passes it on to Goal Decomposition.

11.3.2.2 Goal Decomposition

When the user has entered the data, they are presented with the Goal Decomposition view where the order (i.e. project) is decomposed into a set of tasks (following Harmoney) (see Fig. 11.15). Each task has a responsible role assigned and a number of roles that are required to execute the task, e.g. by providing input.

The Harmoney methodology prescribes the roles and activities needed for a Project Management Team. In particular, a role is characterized through necessary skills and these must be present in any candidate for that role.

Certain classes of project are identified (according to stage) with prescribed sets of roles and interrelations. Accordingly, the GDM determines the mode of the problem definition to be project management and then uses the project class

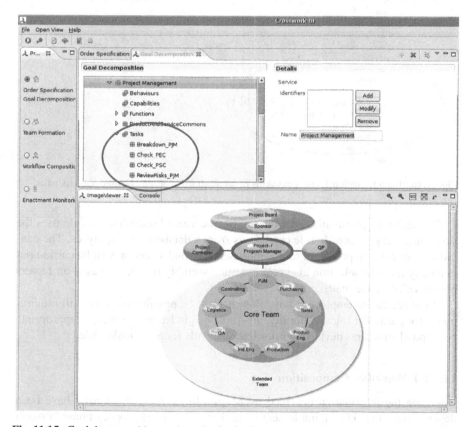

Fig. 11.15 Goal decomposition: tasks and roles in the project management showcase

information to retrieve the appropriate roles and activities. Since Harmoney is well established, these structures are necessarily already assembled. Accordingly, there is little reasoning needed for this Use Case. In a more general setting, the GDM would determine the project methodology according to user.

11.3.2.3 Team Formation

Magna Intier has provided a skill matrix describing the required skills of roles for the Harmoney project management. Each employee has for a particular skill a value of 0, 1, 2 or 3, where 3 means that they are good at a particular skill (see Fig. 11.16). For a particular type of project, the team members have to have particular strengths in some skills.

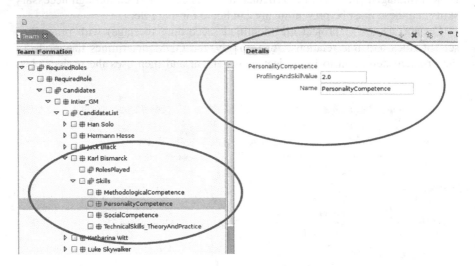

Fig. 11.16 Team formation 1: checking skills of an arbitrarily chosen potential team member

For each role communicated from GDM, the Team Formation Module uses the skills necessary to identify role candidates from a database of employees. The candidates per role are presented to the end-user; the final selection will be carried out manually as team selection also requires the assembly of a team based on factors not provided by the matrix.

If the search for employees fails, then it must be possible to relax skill requirements for particular roles. Naturally, this must be guided by the user; or appropriate conceptual structures devised to prioritize the skills for a particular role.

11.3.2.4 Workflow Composition

Based on the information provided by Magna Intier, local Workflows have been designed (see Fig. 11.17), implementing activities for the Harmoney phase "Project

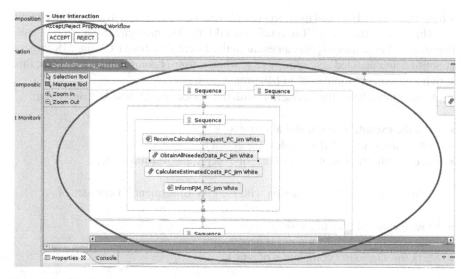

Fig. 11.17 Workflow composition: graphical representation and ability to accept or reject the proposed workflow

Realization". These local workflows are automatically combined to result in a global workflow which is consistent with Harmoney.

For the prototype we assume the following:

- The checks of the process start and end condition are explicitly assigned to tasks.
- The check of the start condition is the start task and the check of the end condition is the final task.
- Deciding whether two tasks are sequential or in parallel was based on the interpretation of the Harmoney text (in a way the user is as less restricted as possible).
- For some of the role-specific tasks several local workflow versions are available. These variations depend on the skills and the role of a person. Which variation of the local workflow is used in the composition depends on the participating person assigned to the role and the Order Specification.
- On the request of Magna Intier, the product engineering tasks that need to be done within the development process are not considered explicitly in the current scenario.

11.3.2.5 Workflow Enactment and Monitoring

In the enactment phase a previously composed workflow is being enacted from the Global Enactment UI from a manager who has the rights to follow and review the whole execution. The team members (employees) interact via their Local Enactment UI. The Local Enactment UI is synchronized with MS project/MS Sharepoint and, therefore, when a user triggers an event in the Local Enactment UI, the MS Project is notified and updated accordingly (e.g. when a user is completing an activity, this activity becomes "completed" in MS project as well).

At the global level, the interaction with the Global Enactment UI consists of:

- Start the execution of the global process;
- Enter values for global variables if necessary;
- Receive information (messages) about exceptions, warnings, etc.

At the local level, the interaction with the CW Enactment UI consists of

- Enter the actual start of a task;
- Enter values for local variables if necessary;
- Mark the *successful* completion of a task.

The CrossWork Workflow Enactment module receives and deploys the Harmoney Global Process. The user of the Enactment module is informed about all deployed processes. From the user interface they choose one (or maybe more) global process(es) to be executed in parallel and then start the execution.

In the Monitoring UI a task is shown in different colours depending on its state:

- No colour: task not started;
- Green: task ended successfully;
- Red: task should have started or is not successfully ended;
- Yellow: is set manually (overriding red or green).

At the same time, at the local level, the local employees have access through the iPerform portal to their local tasks so that they can report progress and completion of tasks. Based on the local processes, new local tasks are emerging. Each role of the employees can have access only to the tasks for which he/she is responsible. The task status information is synchronized between CrossWork and MS Project/Sharepoint.

11.3.2.6 Access to Legacy Systems

The legacy system infrastructure of Magna Intier consists of an MS Sharepoint portal (for storing the documents generated in Harmoney activities) and an MS project server (where each activity is mapped to a task in a Project).

- MS Project Server: There are Project files representing some Harmoney processes. The local workflow enactment tool will invoke the Legacy System integrator to update the Project Server. At each step of the local workflow the percentage of completion of each task (activity) in the Project (Process) will be updated.

- MS Sharepoint portal: The status of a project in Harmoney is stored in an Excel document. The Legacy System integrator will generate part of the information of this document which then is stored on the MS Sharepoint portal.

11.3.2.7 Summary

The following points of human intervention can be identified for the Magna Intier scenario:

- In Order Specification, the user has to define customer and project classification. According to these choices, different focal points and requirements are set in the problem space (which basically is the elaboration of a Harmoney instance). Furthermore, the required outputs have to be specified, as sometimes only a team but not a workflow is needed.
- Goal Decomposition is accomplished fully automatically according to the specifications of Harmoney.
- Team Formation identifies the most suitable persons to form the required team based on Magna Intier's internal skill matrix and current work load metrics. Human intervention is required to make the final selection from the set of possible candidates (this has been a requirement of Magna Intier)
- Workflow Formation is again accomplished fully automatically based on the local workflows, which have been derived from Harmoney.
- Workflow Enactment and Monitoring only requires human intervention when starting, stopping and finishing a task or the whole workflow. Interaction in the enactment phase is here routed through legacy system integration with Magna Intier's MS Sharepoint/Project infrastructure.

11.4 BMW Interior Design

This case study illustrates the potential for innovation inherent in the approach to team formation espoused by CrossWork. One particular aspect of this process, described in detail in Chapter 6 , allows companies to form consortia in a bottom-up fashion, but volunteering their contributions to shared noticeboards to provide partial solutions to business opportunities. The case study is inspired by a real life scenario, in which BMW contracted Intier Ebergassing to supply complete car interiors for a series of a car they were developing. This section examines how the processes of bottom-up team formation might have been used in this case. While the opportunities, companies and components are taken from actual data, the processes of team formation and the assignment of companies to components are purely illustrative.

11.4.1 General Approach

The process of forming a team to supply the complete module is initiated by Intier Ebergassing receiving the contract for the module from BMW. At this point Ebergassing has not chosen specific suppliers to work with on this project.

As an initial step, Intier Ebergassing decomposes the interior into three main submodules; the cockpit, door covering and overhead systems. Teams for each submodule can then be assembled independently.

Initially Intier Ebergassing decide if they wished to assemble the submodule. If they wish to do this they would need to work out which components would be required, thus creating a decomposition of the submodule into subcomponents. Depending on the level of knowledge Ebergassing possess about the submodule, the following scenarios can then unfold.

The first scenario occurs if Intier Ebergassing can fully specify the subcomponents required for the submodule. In this, team formation is instigated by Intier Ebergassing choosing the components they wish to supply, before assigning subsuppliers to the remaining components. This represents a pure form of top-down team formation.

The second scenario transpires if Intier Ebergassing lacks the detailed knowledge needed to decompose the submodule into subcomponents of a sufficiently small size in order to enable them to search for appropriate suppliers. Even in this case it is possible that Ebergassing will be able to identify suppliers for some, or indeed many, components. However they must seek input from the supplier agents regarding those subcomponents that they cannot decompose themselves. This relies on the fact that each company will typically possess local knowledge of which components are needed to produce certain components. This can be done by creating a noticeboard containing details of both the required module and of those components they have already identified suppliers for. This noticeboard catalyses the formation of potential teams for the complete submodule to be identified, the best of which is ultimately chosen by Intier Ebergassing. This combination of an initial, partial decomposition from Ebergassing with later bottom-up team formation represents a hybrid form of team formation.

The final case occurs when Intier Ebergassing are not sure if they wish to perform the final assembly of the submodules components. In this case it is inappropriate for them to mandate a specific decomposition. They therefore create a noticeboard stating simply that the module must be produced. This noticeboard then enables potential teams to form, from which Intier Ebergassing choose their preferred team. This case represents pure bottom-up team formation. Whilst this final case does not rely on an initial decomposition, it does not exclude the use of such knowledge. In particular if some company other than Intier Ebergassing wishes to assemble the submodule and knows which components it needs to do this, it can create a partial solution indicating which subcomponents it needs.

Finally, it is important to remember that before moving into production of the modules the teams produced here must co-design their components in detail, produce prototypes and finally design how they wish to mass produce the final submodule. As each of these stages is highly complex in their own right it isn't possible to ensure the teams will be able to complete them successfully and later changes may be required. To minimize this risk the requirements of these later stages are considered during team formation.

11.4.2 Detailed Case Study

We now focus on one of the modules from the interior, the overhead systems module, and a component list; windscreen wipers, sun visor shelf, sun roof and injection moulded caps. This list is provided to aid comprehension, and it is not provided to the companies as part of the process of team formation.

The following example of the overhead systems module illustrates pure bottom-up team formation driven by an external decomposition and how the system facilitates companies in only working with their preferred partners.

Throughout the following case study pictures from a demonstrator will be used. For the sake of clarity the case study will only show the formation of one team. However it should be remembered that many alternative teams would form.

11.4.3 Overhead Systems Module

As a preliminary to the case study it is assumed that a set of companies including Intier Ebergassing have formed a network supporting the formation of teams through bottom-up team formation within which they are each represented by capability provider agents.

In this case the assumption is that Intier Ebergassing are not interested in assembling the final overhead systems module. Since they are not planning to assemble the module they do not propose an initial decomposition but instead create a noticeboard with a minimal initial solution. In addition to this initial solution the noticeboard contains some utility information allowing the process provider agents to judge how attractive helping to supply the overhead module is to them. As this information is independent from the state information within each partial solution, it is kept in a separate area of the noticeboard. Here the information contains:

1. That the contract is likely to be for a substantial number of components;
2. That it is with BMW;
3. That the assembled component must be delivered to Intier Ebergassing.

The final element introduces logistical considerations, making companies near Ebergassing more likely to be interested. This noticeboard then stimulates the creation of several teams.

For the purposes of this case study it is assumed that Intier Straubing has expertise in the area of overhead systems. Their capability provider agent is thus programmed to contribute certain appropriate resources towards such opportunities.

However, on inspection of the noticeboard, the agent notices that this is an especially lucrative business opportunity. It thus notifies its human managers, who decide that they are, in context, also happy to assemble the final overhead systems module.

Since Straubing are also capable of producing the windscreen wipers, sun visor and have an existing supplier for injection moulded clasps, they do not look for external suppliers for these components. They therefore create a combined capability on the noticeboard saying that, given a sun roof and a shelf, they can provide the entire module (see Fig. 11.18).

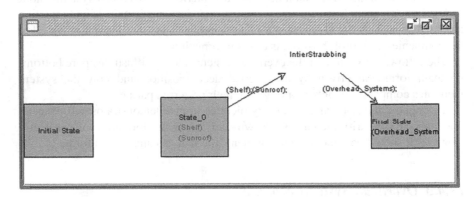

Fig. 11.18 A partial solution contributed

This partial solution makes the need for sun roof and shelf modules clear, and various companies, which are happy to work with Intier Straubing, propose to supply them. However the ability of Intier Straubing, as a company already present within the combined capability, to veto any such proposed extensions allows them to select promising alternatives as they develop.

As a result of this, several complete teams are formed. The teams consist of Intier Straubing together with sun roof and shelf suppliers. The best one is then chosen through negotiations between the potential teams and Intier Ebergassing. An example team is shown in Fig. 11.19.

This team would then go forward to negotiate the details of how they wish to work together, potentially using such elements as the workflow composition module offered within CrossWork. The above scenario clearly illustrates the most important feature of bottom-up team formation – the way in which it permits companies to reason about which processes they wish to offer in a manner dependent on their assessment of the project's worth. In this case this is exemplified by Intier Straubbing's willingness to assemble the final component.

11.5 Conclusions

The cases have demonstrated different instances of the BOAT approach, not only in terms of the organizations' particularities, but also in terms of the ways they use the frame of reference. As already indicated in Chapter 1 , the CrossWork application

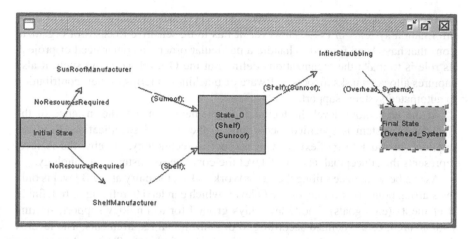

Fig. 11.19 Two alternative solutions assembled

differs from traditional information system development, since it is dynamically interwoven rather than progressing through a set linear sequence of steps from the business to the technology side.

The business level B still describes the business goals of e-business, or the economic model behind its existence. However, it evolves by designing organizational structures and negotiating commonly agreed processes. Hence, the question why a specific e-business scenario exists, or should exist, or what should be reached, is a matter of the negotiation and formation process. In CrossWork the topics are business opportunities or orders affecting the supply chain that are totally orientated towards customers requirements. The business level heavily relies on how things are done, although these details are not featured at this level.

As CrossWork deals with cross-organizational process development, based on team formation and leading to process enactments, the Organization (O) is of utmost importance. Based on an input at the B level, team formation and process design are triggered at the O level. Here, an organization of work is developed to achieve the goals and demands initially defined at the B level. It is achieved in an iterative way redefining or refining business goals and processes in mutual dependence. Figure 11.20 reflects this scenario.

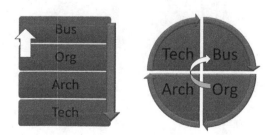

Fig. 11.20 Sailing with the CrossWork BOAT

The architecture level A still covers the conceptual structure (architecture) of information systems in IVEs. However, it has to be sensitive to cases of organizations that have been formed to handle a particular order, customer need or project. Its role is to make the organizations defined at the O level work. As such, it also captures allocated tasks to tools, software or machines in terms of their contribution to automated systems support.

At the technology level the technical implementation, i.e. the instance of the CrossWork system is specified, according to the A level specification. Both are required, in order to be flexible with respect to technology. Hereby, the A level represents the conceptual, and the T level the concrete (or instance) technology.

As can be seen, once sailing the CrossWork BOAT, the entry at the B level is only the starting point for working on the O level, which can lead to refining or redefining B elements (e.g., goals). The O level lays ground for technology support, starting with an architecture defined according to organizational requirements. The level A defines the requirements that must be eventually fulfilled at the T level. As such, the latter levels should be addressed only for agreed project or work organization, even when having to change the implementation platform.

The examples in this chapter illustrate the manner in which the technology developed by CrossWork can support a range of cases when VEs are formed in response to a business need. The examples highlight the flexible nature of the VE support processes and the scope for automating the VE formation activities in the pursuit of an IVE.

Chapter 12
Comparable Approaches to IVE

Nikolay Mehandjiev, Hamideh Afsarmanesh, Luis M. Camarinha-Matos, Lea Kutvonen, and Alex Norta

In this chapter we examine some approaches to VE formation and Business Network management which are comparable, at least in aspirations, to CrossWork. In each case, we present the principal ideas and main results and use these to distinguish the differences while highlighting the complementary aspects.

12.1 ECOLEAD Support for Agile Collaborative Networks

Hamideh Afsarmanesh and Luis M. Camarinha-Matos

ECOLEAD (1 April 2004–30 June 2008)[1] was a large EC-funded project that focused on establishing generic foundations for Collaborative Networks (CNs) and providing methodologies, mechanisms and systems for governance and support for the rapid formation and management of dynamic, goal-oriented consortia.

ECOLEAD begins from a belief that efficiency in the launch and operation of a Virtual Organization (VO)[2] requires "preparedness" in both the environment of the VO and in (potential) partners. Research and indeed practice have shown that long-term associations, or clusters, can greatly enhance the efficient creation of VOs, especially, in response to short-lived opportunities. Geographical proximity provides advantages for collaboration, such as a common local culture fostering trust through a "sense of community". The development of more effective communication infrastructures is gradually allowing such clusters to assemble beyond geographical regions to access new competences and new market opportunities. A paradigm of Virtual Organization Breeding Environments (VBEs) was introduced to capture the context such as "strategic" long-term alliances; ECOLEAD defines a VBE as

---

N. Mehandjiev (✉)
University of Manchester, Manchester, UK
e-mail: n.mehandjiev@manchester.ac.uk

[1] http://www.ve-forum.org/default.asp?P=284

[2] ECOLEAD focuses on Virtual Organizations, often understood as a wider concept than Virtual Enterprises, including ideas of open business and massively outsourced corporations. We shall therefore use Virtual Organization in the remainder of this section.

N. Mehandjiev, P. Grefen (eds.), *Dynamic Business Process Formation for Instant Virtual Enterprises*, Advanced Information and Knowledge Processing, DOI 10.1007/978-1-84882-691-5_12, © Springer-Verlag London Limited 2010

a "strategic" association/alliance of organizations and the related supporting institutions, adhering to a base long term cooperation agreement, and adoption of common operating principles and infrastructures, with the main goal of increasing their preparedness towards collaboration in potential Virtual Organizations.

ECOLEAD focused upon three main areas known as *ECOLEAD Pillars* and their interrelationships:

1. VO Breeding Environments;
2. Dynamic Virtual Organizations;
3. Professional Virtual Communities (PVC).

These primary areas are complemented by *horizontal ICT infrastructures* and *theoretical foundation* for CNs (Fig. 12.1).

Fig. 12.1 The ECOLEAD
focus areas

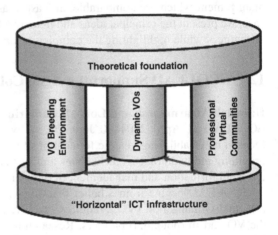

A fundamental assumption of ECOLEAD is that, to be successful, networked collaborative business ecosystems require a comprehensive, holistic approach. In particular, the complexity of the area, evinced by the multiple interdependencies of the participants and technological approaches, suggests that substantial progress will not be achieved through incremental innovation in isolated areas.

12.1.1 Virtual Breeding Environments (VBEs)

First steps towards the definition of a *Reference Framework* for VBEs were taken focusing on the fundamental elements. The initial framework was validated through empirical trials by a number of international industry-based VBE networks involved in the project, as well as a few others outside. Developments in this area include:

An extensive analysis of existing VBE cases together with the creation of *future scenarios* allowed the main elements of a VBE reference framework to be identified and modelled; see Fig. 12.2.

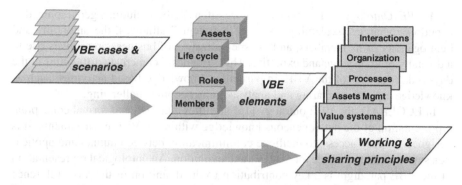

Fig. 12.2 Main elements in the VBE reference framework

The main elements of a VBE are

- VBE members: the organizations that are registered within the VBE, including:

  - *Businesses* providing products and services to the market, motivated to join a VE for profit;
  - *Non-profit institutions*, e.g. academic/research institutes, which get involved in the VOs for purposes other than fiscal advantage;
  - *Support institutions*, such as legal service providers, insurance companies, training institutes, ministries, sector associations, chambers of commerce, environmental organizations, etc.

- Roles: VBE actors may assume a number of roles; here, an actor denotes either a VBE member organization or an individual representing a VBE member organization. Examples of roles include inter alia: VBE administrator, opportunity-broker, planner or coordinator.
- Life cycle: representing all the stages that a VBE may go through, from its creation, to its operation, evolution and possible dissolution. In fact, as a VBE connotes a set of long-term alliances, its dissolution is unusual.
- Assets: representing all valuable things produced or collected during the life cycle of the VBE; these include processes, tools, information, knowledge, lessons learned, etc.

Working and sharing principles denote the organizational and governance principles of a VBE, which include elements such as

- *Main and auxiliary processes* that take place during the life cycle of the VBE;
- *Governance rules*, procedures and principles;
- *Organizational structures,* which are closely related to roles, interactions and governance principles;
- *Value systems*, which capture or guide the behaviour of a VBE.

A VBE Ontology – The typical nature of a VBE, including geographic distribution, dynamics, scalability issues of "strategic" alliances, the autonomy and heterogeneity of its members, and the specialization of business areas gives rise to a diversity of knowledge and expertise. This "richness" can create difficulties in the day-to-day running of the VBE, in particular, knowledge-based activities, such as knowledge collection, sharing and analysis, may become challenging.

In ECOLEAD, the VBE ontology [16] signifies a unified and formal conceptual representation of the heterogeneous knowledge within the VBE environments. It is designed for easy access, to facilitate communication between human and application systems and to provide for analysis and evolution. An ontological representation of the VBE paradigm is a key contribution to the definition of the VBE reference framework. The VBE ontology aims to support the following challenging tasks:

1. Establishment of a common semantic subspace for VBEs;
2. Instantiation of VBE knowledge repositories for VBEs from different domains or business areas;
3. Automated processing of knowledge (by software tools) in dynamic VBEs;
4. Enabling inter-organizational learning and co-working;
5. Integration of VBE knowledge with other existing standard ontologies.

The identified conceptual groups, each representing a sub-ontology of the VBE ontology, are shown in Fig. 12.3.

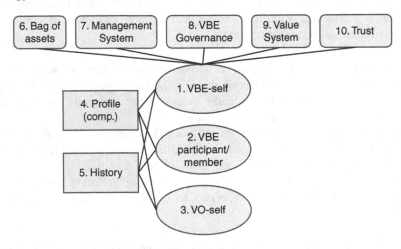

Fig. 12.3 Conceptual groups of the VBE knowledge

Profile and competency – A complete and correct classification of organizations' competences is challenging, owing to semantic and syntactic heterogeneity. Thus, one of the sub-ontologies within the VBE ontology is devoted to this aspect. To achieve the VBE's main goal, viz., preparing its member organizations for participation in VOs requires a record of information about its member organizations as related to the VBE. The concept *VBE member organization's profile* captures all relevant information and knowledge needed for each organization in the VBE. The concept *VBE member organizations' competences* is the fundamental concept in a profile: it is used to represent the qualifications of VBE members for collaboration within VOs. Additional concepts include *VBE entity*, which embraces all acting entities in the VBE, such as VBE member organizations, VBE support-providing organizations, VBE customers, etc.; *VBE profiles* and its main element *VBE competences*, which captures up-to-date information about capabilities and capacities of a VBE entity.

  VBE typologies – A systematic study of a wide variety of existing and emerging VBEs facilitated the modelling of structural, compositional, functional and behavioural aspects of a VBE and provided for the development of a base for reference modelling to classify VBEs. According, to the perspective taken, more than one typology can be defined for the VBEs. Three perspectives tend to be more prominent for the definition of a VBE typology, namely:

- Activity domain category perspective: (i) Stable products/services domain, (ii) Stable one-of-a-kind domain, (iii) Emerging domain, (iv) Innovation-driven domain;
- Main collaboration driver perspective: (i) Capacity achievement driven VBE, (ii) Customer-induced VBE, (iii) VBE oriented towards complementary competences, (iv) Regional ecosystem;
- Orientation/value system perspective: (i) Profit/market oriented, (ii) Social oriented, (iii) Hybrid market/social.

VBE instantiation and assessment of collaboration readiness – A generic set of processes, mechanisms and methodologies was devised. They support the instantiation of VBEs in different application contexts and replicability. Instantiation comprises five main steps: (1) VBE strategic planning, (2) VBE strategy implementation, (3) ICT set-up and governance establishment, (4) Membership population and (5) VBE launching. Migrating towards the VBE collaborative environment requires a new organizational orientation and infrastructure based on a *collaborative culture*, which implies qualities such as the *openness, commitment, leadership, trust-building, self-learning, continuous training, long-term and global vision, effective communication, knowledge sharing and innovation*. Assessment of these qualities can be used to reflect the "collaboration readiness" of the VBE members.

VBE value systems and metrics – Defining important theoretical concepts, like value systems, business models and governance rules, allowed for the development of a theoretical framework to analyse the business logic underpinning value creation within VBEs. VBE Value Systems refer to the ordering and prioritization of a set of values that a VBE (or its members) creates, holds or exchanges. Value Systems in a VBE must include inter alia economic, ethical and cultural values; values which are tangible (e.g. economic benefits, productivity related) and intangible (e.g. strategic and social values) [2]. Both qualitative and formal models for value systems are contributed by ECOLEAD.

Inter-organizational trust in VBEs – Trust creation (especially) within a medium to large-size VBE, whose members do not know each other well, is challenging.

To engender trust among organizations within VBEs, a rational (fact-based) approach was introduced [35]. The approach characterizes trust among the organizations as a multi-objective, multi-perspective and multi-criteria subject, where values for trust criteria derive from past/present performance and achievements of each organization. Formal mechanisms are used to calculate a "fact-based" trust level, promoting a rational reasoning based on (mathematical) equations.

VBE management system – For VBEs to operate smoothly a set of functionalities and services, some of which automated or semi-automated, supporting the activities and processes are needed: these constitute a VBE management system (VMS). ECOLEAD designed and developed a VMS [3] that includes services for supporting the management of the VBE ontology and specially the management of the organizations' competences, assessment and management of trust among the organizations, the structuring of VBE memberships, the management of VBE's Bag of assets and the processes related to decision making in VBE environment, as illustrated in Fig. 12.4.

In brief, the VMS includes: Membership Structure Management System (MSMS), Ontology Management System (ODMS), Profile and Competency Management System (PCMS), Trust Management System (TrustMan), Bag of Assets Management System (BAMS), and Decision Support System (DSS).

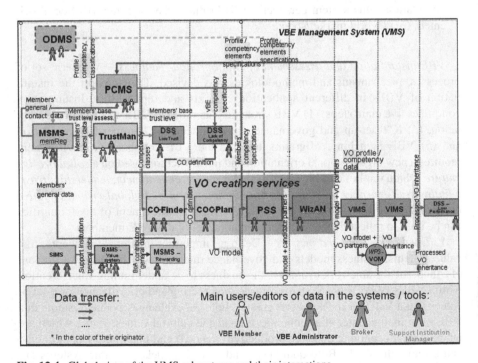

Fig. 12.4 Global view of the VMS subsystems and their interactions

12.1.2 VO Creation Framework

Rapid formation of a consortium triggered by and specially tailored to a business opportunity suggests agility. In ECOLEAD, a framework for VO creation was thus introduced and a set of assistance services designed and tools developed [10].

The main actors involved in the VO creation are the Opportunity-Broker and the VO Planner in the initial phases of the VO creation. Potential VO partners only participate in the last phase of the process. The Opportunity-Broker is responsible for finding the collaboration opportunity whereas the VO Planner is responsible for setting up the VO, i.e. for the characterization and planning of the Collaboration Opportunity (CO), finding the suitable partners and coordinating the process of reaching the final agreements between all parties involved. Figure 12.5 illustrates the main phases of the VO creation process for a given collaboration opportunity. In principle, any VBE member can act as a broker, but this depends on the adopted governance principles. Partners are primarily selected from the VBE members, nevertheless, in case there is lack of skills or capacity inside the VBE, other organizations can be recruited from outside the VBE boundaries.

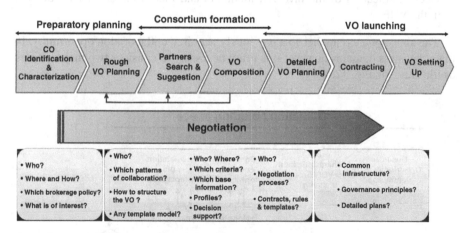

Fig. 12.5 VO creation process for a given collaboration opportunity

The *preparatory planning* phase includes:

- CO Identification and Characterization: A step that involves the identification and characterization of a new CO that triggers the formation of a new VO.
- Rough VO planning: Determination of a rough structure of the potential VO, identifying the required competences and capacities, structure of the task to be performed as well as the organizational form of the VO and corresponding roles.

The *consortia formation* phase includes:

- Partners' search and suggestion: The identification of potential partners, their assessment and selection.
- VO composition: The detailed organizational structure is defined and the assignment of roles to VO members is made.
- Negotiation: An iterative process to reach agreements and align needs with offers.

The *VO launching* phase includes:

- Detailed VO planning: This step addresses the refinement of the VO plan and its governance principles.
- Contracting: This involves the final formulation, and modelling of contracts and agreements, as well as the contract signing process itself, in other words, the conclusion of the negotiation process.
- VO set-up: The last phase of the VO creation process is concerned with the configuration of the ICT infrastructure, instantiation and orchestration of the collaboration spaces, selection of relevant performance indicators to be used, governance principles, assignment and set-up of resources, activation of services, notification of the involved members and manifestation of the new VO in the VBE.

The above process applies to a previously acquired collaboration opportunity. In many business domains however it is often necessary to consider two major phases as illustrated in Fig. 12.6.

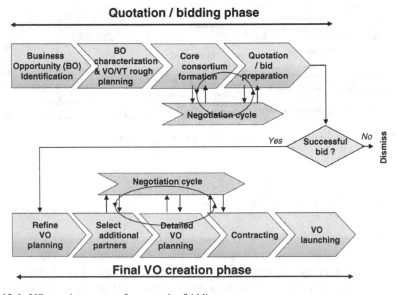

Fig. 12.6 VO creation process for quotation/bidding

Quotation/Bidding – When a collaboration opportunity is found it is necessary to prepare a bid/quotation in order to try to get a contract with the customer. For the preparation of this bid, it is necessary to make a rough plan of the foreseen VO and to also select the core partners. The bid is often prepared by this initial consortium. In case the bid is unsuccessful, the core consortium dissolves; otherwise it moves to the next phase.

Final VO creation – In case the bid is successful, the VO's rough plan needs to be revised, based on the specific conditions of the contract with the customer, new additional partners might be necessary and the VO will be finally detailed and launched.

As a result of the interactions with industry end-user networks and to support the two processes described above, four tools were designed and developed for the VO creation framework: collaboration opportunity Finder (coFinder); CO Characterization and rough Planning (COC-Plan); Partners Search and Suggestion (PSS); and Agreement Negotiation Wizard (WizAN) [9]. Although these tools attempt to assist and facilitate the entire process of the VO creation, the design assumption was that the decisions are always the responsibility of human actors.

Negotiation process – Through interaction with various end-user networks, various critical negotiation activities were identified:

- Reaching agreements concerning coordination aspects: for instance, deciding on who will be responsible for the VO;
- Reaching agreement concerning the sharing of risks among the involved partners. It also relates to the amount of impact that a problem in a task performed by one partner can cause in the whole VO. Moreover, agreement about the amount of budget retained to cope with possible problems is needed;
- Reaching agreements on the detailed activities and scheduling;
- Information exchange agreement, i.e. how should information be exchanged among partners, and also which kind of information should be exchanged. These agreements also have a close relationship with the detailed scheduling of activities;
- Detailed costs agreement, i.e. discuss and agree with each partner the value of the part that it will produce or the service it will perform;
- The contract should follow a basic set of standard templates: it is convenient to depart from common templates, selected for each kind of CO, and extend the selected template to cope with the detailed agreement specifications using "add-on" clauses.

In this process it is necessary to consider support for privacy of proposals, where only the involved partners have access to the information being negotiated. Having taken into account this list, it is evident that these types of agreements fundamentally require decision making by human actors rather than fully automated decision making.

12.1.3 VO Management

VO management addresses the organization, allocation and coordination of resources and their activities as well as their inter-organizational dependencies to achieve the objectives of the VO within the required time, costs and quality frame. Typical issues addressed in this area are the modelling and supervision of distributed collaborative (business) processes. Considerable work has been done in terms of process modelling languages, inter-organizational workflow and distributed process execution, and more recently Web Service composition and choreography. However, managing a VO is more than distributed process management. Although VO members come together to achieve a common goal, they have their own other objectives, internal processes, business culture and autonomous decision making. Therefore, VO management needs to be addressed under the assumption of: (i) having little or no power, because all partners are independent actors; (ii) relying on a collaborative atmosphere based on the promotion of trust; (iii) risk and benefits sharing; and (iv) having to make decisions based on incomplete and imprecise information.

VO management framework – ECOLEAD contributed governance principles, real-time management concept and requirements, critical issues and management styles [24]. As illustrated in Fig. 12.7, ECOLEAD identified and characterized the basic VO management processes. Those in darker grey are supported by existing tools, while others need further development.

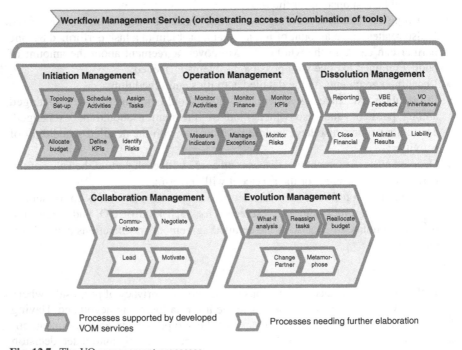

Fig. 12.7 The VO management processes

VO management support system – To support the VO management activities, an integrated platform combining a number of services was designed and developed, including: VO management workflow support, VO model development and management, VO indicators identification and definition, VO automatic integrated performance measurement, VO monitoring and exception management support, VO simulation and decision support and VO inheritance support [37]. The main functionalities of the platform are represented in the diagram of Fig. 12.8.

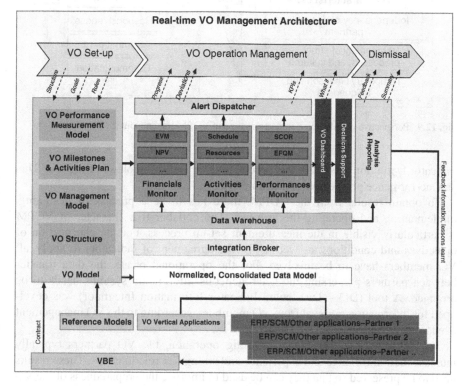

Fig. 12.8 VO management support platform architecture

VO performance measurement – Performance Measurement (PM) is an essential component of VO management. To be effective, PM has to take into account the specific characteristics of VOs and thus approaches that were developed for single organizations need adaptations and extensions to meet the requirement in collaborative networks. VOPM is defined as the systematic approach to planning for and conducting the collection of quantitative and qualitative data for performance indicators that assess the status of a VO. Most PM approaches developed previously focused on single enterprises and as such do not offer a concept of collaboration performance that fits the VO needs. ECOLEAD elaborated a list of KPIs particularly focused on the collaboration aspects, out of which the VO Manager can select the ones more adequate for each particular VO [50]. A software tool (SID – Supporting

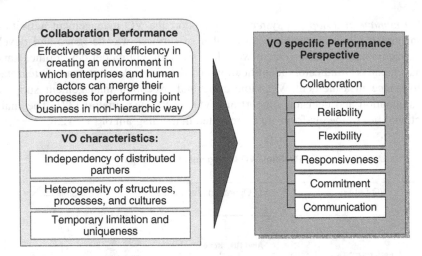

Fig. 12.9 Perspective of collaboration performance in VOPM (taken from [50])

Indicator Definition) assists in this process during the set-up phase of the VO. This new performance perspective is illustrated in Fig. 12.9.

To obtain results from the VOPM, there has to be a process of designing, implementing and operating this process. The collaborative character of VOPM is particularly visible in the measurement set-up process. For the clarification of objectives and conditions, as well as for the agreement of indicators to apply, all VO members have to be involved. For the operational phase, the data transfer between partners possessing the heterogeneous information systems needs to be arranged. A tool (DI3 – Distributed Indicator Information Integrator) was developed for information retrieval from VO members, according to the VO management needs.

VO inheritance management – During operation, the VO partners typically increase their knowledge and experience and strengthen relationships. These results need to be preserved so that they can be used to improve the preparedness of the VO breeding environment for future collaboration activities. Therefore, after the VO task has been fulfilled and the VO is dissolved, the increased knowledge, experience and other assets should be returned, "inherited" to the VBE, feeding the "VBE Bag of Assets". Further details can be found in [24].

12.1.4 Professional Virtual Communities

A *Professional Virtual Community* (PVC) may be viewed as a breeding environment focusing on human professionals (rather than organizations): it facilitates the creation of dynamic virtual teams (VT) in response to a collaboration opportunity. VOs are created within VBEs: VTs are created in a PVC. It can also be seen as a social network with business purpose. ECOLEAD provided a collaboration context in which it was possible to adapt most of the conceptual results from VBEs and VOs to PVCs and VTs. A major contribution of ECOLEAD in this area is related to the identification and characterization of different kinds of stakeholders and their roles, governance principles and structures, business strategy and model, and reference processes [43]. For instance, regarding the operational phase of the PVC, the following main processes are considered:

- Knowledge-related processes: Knowledge sharing, knowledge creation, research road-mapping;
- Business-related processes: Marketing, VT formation, VT operation;
- Social processes: Social networking, organization of events, community facilitation/social capital development.

Other contributions to the definition of a PVC framework include the definition of a set of business models from members' perspective and organizational perspective, as well as of principles and templates for a legal framework [15]. PVC management and VT creation and operation are supported by a collaboration platform [14] that extends the functionalities of traditional virtual community platforms, namely through the introduction of services for knowledge management and intellectual property handling, collaboration rewarding, VT creation and VT operation.

12.1.5 Support Infrastructure

ECOLEAD adopted a Service-Oriented approach for its ICT infrastructure (ICT-I), which includes the following services [43]: (i) Integrated CSCW services, (ii) Knowledge search services, (iii) Business Process Management services, (iv) Data Access services, (v) Registry and Discovery services, (vi) Stubless Invocation services, (vii) Billing services, (viii) Reporting services, (ix) Handler services, (x) Services composition and (xi) Security services. At a global level, ICT-I is designed to contribute to five macro problems faced by companies, mainly by SMEs:

- ICT-I is an *open and standard-based framework* where services can be implemented in different technologies (see Fig. 12.10);
- ICT-I is a *Web-based and SaaS infrastructure*, which facilitates customization, hides several interoperability problems, decreases training costs and reduces time to handle a collaborative infrastructure. This can speed up the process of companies' preparedness to become a member of a CN;
- ICT-I offers a Web-based *interactive BPM service* through which managers can model business processes and assign Web Services to them;
- ICT-I provides an embedded *security framework* helping in the management of the information access life cycle, granting access to the exact and required information for each business as long as transactions are being carried out, supported by AAA (Authorization, Authentication and Accounting) principles;

Fig. 12.10 ICT-I reference
framework (taken from [43])

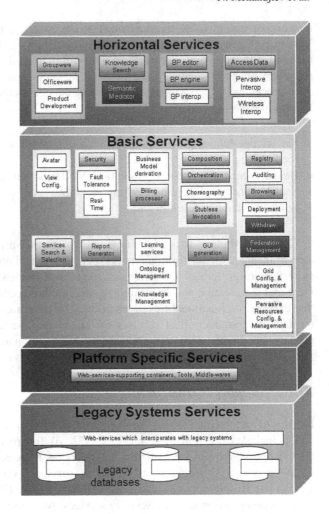

- ICT-I includes a *set of services* to aid companies in moving towards Web 2.0 and
  Enterprise 2.0 scenarios:

  - *CSCW* services integrating human communication in a Web environment;
  - *Knowledge Search* service enabling users to retrieve information and knowl-
    edge from CN's repositories, including some support for semantics and
    context definition;
  - *Data Access* service allowing some access to individual CN member's
    databases (representing their legacy systems);
  - *Stubless API* providing means to enlarge the collaboration among enterprises
    as their services can be seamlessly accessed, i.e. shared.

12.1.6 Theoretical Foundation and Reference Models

ECOLEAD sought to establish Collaborative Networks (CNs) as a new discipline [6, 11]. These efforts are summarized here. Particular emphasis is laid on modelling the multiple facets of CNs and establishing a comprehensive modelling framework. A reference model for CNs is introduced.

Modelling foundation – CNs are complex systems that can be described or modelled from multiple perspectives. In this context there is no single modelling formalism that can cover all perspectives of interest. Since CNs have a clear multidisciplinary nature, it is natural to look for applicable modelling tools and approaches that originated in other disciplines, such as Computer Science, Engineering and Management. ECOLEAD identified and assessed a large number of theories and modelling tools with potential applicability in collaborative networks. As a result a navigational map, as illustrated in Fig. 12.11, was elaborated.

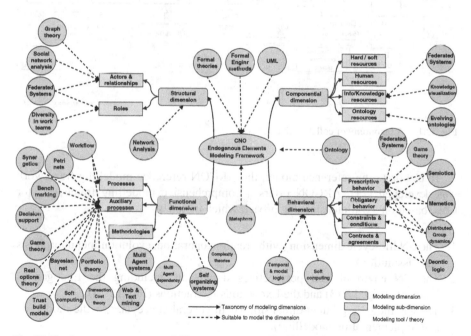

Fig. 12.11 An attempt to map modelling constructs applicable to CNs

Reference model – As a reference model for CNs provides a fundamental instrument, it is important to have a clear understanding of the reference modelling process and associated terminology. ECOLEAD sought to clarify basic concepts in CNs and their interrelationships [8], primarily through a taxonomy (with related definitions) of collaboration forms (see Fig. 12.12).

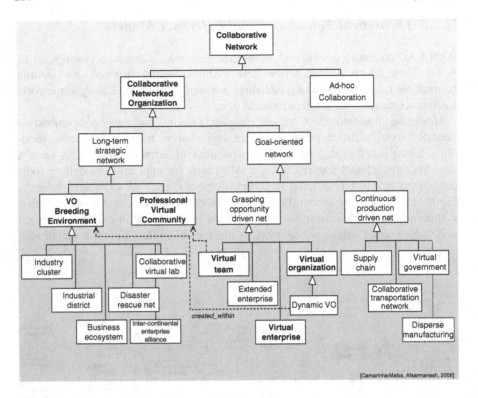

Fig. 12.12 A taxonomy of collaborative networks

To elaborate the reference model, the ARCON reference modelling framework was developed [11]. ARCON offers a comprehensive modelling framework for CNs, based on a 3-dimensional approach which includes

1. The CN life-cycle dimension (with creation, operation, evolution/metamorphosis and dissolution);
2. The CN environmental perspectives dimension, including the Endogenous Elements (Fig. 12.13) and the Exogenous Interactions (Fig. 12.14);
3. The CN modelling intent dimension (with general concepts, specific modelling and implementation modelling).

Using this framework, ECOLEAD organized the most common general concepts under the endogenous elements and exogenous interactions perspectives. The framework was first applied to the CN cases studied in ECOLEAD, namely VBEs, VOs and PVCs. An attempt to generalize from these cases was then made, trying to identify a common set of concepts and entities, which were discussed with a wide group of experts from different fields, leading to a first comprehensive reference model proposal. This is not a finished job but rather a starting basis.

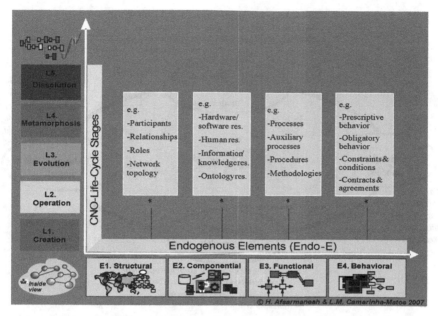

Fig. 12.13 Crossing CNO life cycle and the endogenous elements perspective

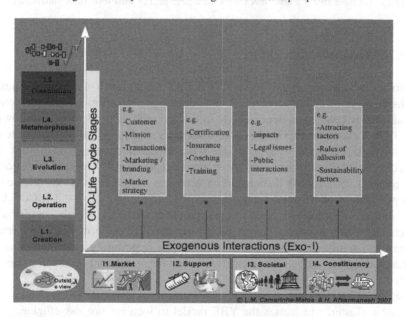

Fig. 12.14 Crossing CNO life cycle and exogenous interactions perspective

ECOLEAD developed an extensive number of cases for modelling different CN aspects where either the interoperability or the composition of several modelling tools or systems is applied. An example is illustrated in Fig. 12.15.

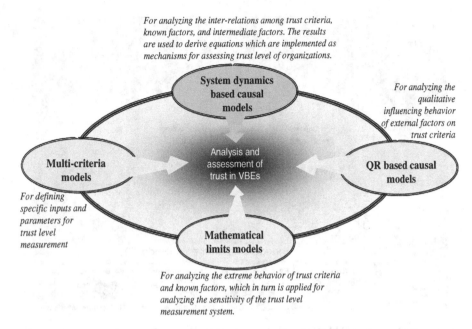

For analyzing the inter-relations among trust criteria, known factors, and intermediate factors. The results are used to derive equations which are implemented as mechanisms for assessing trust level of organizations.

For analyzing the qualitative influencing behavior of external factors on trust criteria

For defining specific inputs and parameters for trust level measurement

For analyzing the extreme behavior of trust criteria and known factors, which in turn is applied for analyzing the sensitivity of the trust level measurement system.

Fig. 12.15 Interoperability among models for the assessment of trust level of organizations

12.1.7 Demonstration Pilots

To provide a "field assessment" of the ECOLEAD results and to act as an instrument for dissemination and impact creation, nine demonstration pilots were implemented in real running business networks, eight in Europe and one in Mexico, as follows:

IECOS scenario – IECOS (Integration Engineering and Construction Systems) is a Mexican enterprise that uses the VBE model-integrating capabilities and competences of its partners (mainly in metals and plastics) to satisfy customer requirements. ECOLEAD demonstration activities within IECOS are oriented to the optimization of network management. The main end-user is the IECOS broker with the following objectives: improvement of the VBE member registration and characterization processes, formalization of the VBE performance management system, and semi-automation of the collaborative opportunity characterization to be matched against partners' competences, used for search and selection of best fit partners for VO configuration.

HELICE/CeBeNetwork demonstration scenario – HELICE is the Andalusian aeronautic cluster, which uses the VBE model to increase process efficiency and business opportunities. The CeBeNetwork is a supplier network, mainly located in Germany, in the aeronautical industry and a strategic supplier to the main customer Airbus. HELICE and CeBeNetwork have joined their efforts to coordinate a joint global VBE in the area of aeronautics, which applies ECOLEAD results to better manage the new network operation. Specific functionality applied by the joint Helice/CeBeNetwork is the dynamic management of the competences and trust levels of VBE members, organization of the VBE's Bag of Assets, performance-based decision support and the agreement negotiation wizard.

Swiss MicroTech scenario – Swiss MicroTech (SMT) is a regional collaborative network created in 2001 by SMEs of the mechanical subcontracting sector to explore new markets and develop new products beyond an individual SME. SMT has seven SME members. The emerging Chinese market led to the creation of DecoCHina in 2005, an international VBE combining two regional networks, namely the SMT and a new parent Chinese network in the Guangdong Province. ECOLEAD demonstration activities within SMT were oriented to the optimization of network management, which also impacts on its partners' (VBE members') performance.

Virtuelle Fabrik scenario – The Virtual Factory (VF) is a network of industrial SMEs (operating as a VBE) in Switzerland and Southern Germany. The network enables the SMEs to act in collaboration with other SMEs the same way as a very big industrial company. In ECOLEAD, the business case was part of the definition for a generic VO model. The application focused on VO modelling, performance measurement, monitoring and integrated VO management supported by simulation.

Supply Network Shannon scenario – SNS is an open network of companies in the Shannon region of Ireland. It provides a framework for companies to collaborate in joint marketing, training, development and collaborative quotation development for participation in outsourcing networks. SNS operates as a regional VBE with individual members creating sub-networks. The main application of ECOLEAD results was the introduction of structured VO management techniques to assist with the control and coordination of existing VOs in the network. This application includes the use of the VO Model to maintain structured information about the VO, particularly in relation to the work breakdown structure, the individual management styles used in the network and the structured measurement of VO performance indicators.

ORONA/OIN scenario – ORONA is the leading Spanish company in the lift industry and belongs to *MCC* – one of the leading business groups (made of 220 companies and entities) in Spain. The Orona Innovation Network (OIN), promoted by ORONA in 2002, is a research consortium supported by a network of experts (coming from universities, RTD Centres, companies in the sector, etc.) working in multidisciplinary and multi-company communities which organize their activity around: (a) the discovery of new technological opportunities and (b) the translation of these opportunities into innovative product ideas for short-distance transportation. In this scenario, OIN applied the ECOLEAD tools in two different cases, (a) Virtual Organizations for Technology Platform Development and (b) Virtual Organizations for New Product Development. Orona used the tools to (a) formalize the network procedures, (b) formalize and make easier the management of the network and (c) be prepared to increase the network with new external partners. All tools developed for VO management apply in this context.

AIESEC scenario – AIESEC is a non-profit, non-commercial, non-government global organization, run by students and recent graduates. AIESEC has offices in over 90 countries, with over 20,000 members globally. With the ECOLEAD pilot,

AIESEC aimed to build sustainable professional virtual communities for AIESEC alumni, leveraging existing social ties and harvesting their economic potential. This scenario focused on PVC creation and life-cycle management, PVC governance and virtual teams' creation.

EDINFORM/FEDERAZIONE demonstration scenario – Federazione Regionale Ordini Ingegneri Pugliesi is a regional Italian organization including all Apulian engineers (about 12,000). The objective for this scenario was to organize a pilot panel of professionals selected among all the community members and composed of 100 units whose task was to test the proposed methodologies and ICT tools available from ECOLEAD and to provide a feedback on the benefits.

Joensuu Science Park scenario – JSP is a technology park located in Eastern Finland. It is a regional development organization with a global vision towards the development of the third generation of science parks which can evolve towards a combination of VBEs and PVCs. The main focus of the scenario was in the area of new collaborative working environments, thus, PVC management and creation of virtual teams.

All these pilots were successful in demonstrating the usefulness of the various ECOLEAD results and also provided important feedback for future improvements and further research. Detailed descriptions of these experimental results are included in [4, 17, 18].

12.1.8 Differences Between ECOLEAD and CrossWork

There are naturally many differences between ECOLEAD and CrossWork, but the outcomes of the two projects are also complementary in a number of perspectives. Examples can be found, in particular, in terms of scope, application domain and theoretical background:

Scope – ECOLEAD had a broader scope, attempting to cover a large variety of CNs, including long-term and temporary networks, and addressing both networks of organizations and networks of people. CrossWork was more focused on VEs, and thus detailing more the process modelling and cross-organizational workflow aspects. When considered in ECOLEAD, these aspects did not form a primary focus. In this sense, the two initiatives are complementary.

Domain – CrossWork focused (initially) on the automotive industry and ancillary sectors and used these to derive case studies for demonstrators. ECOLEAD had broader domain coverage, aiming to develop generic solutions for industry and services which were evaluated through practical pilots in a number of domains including aeronautics, mechanical components and machinery, electronics, engineering and consultancy.

Theoretical background – The two projects made complementary contributions to the theoretical foundations of CNs. CrossWork made particular contributions to the formalization of workflow aspects and partner selection principles. ECOLEAD developed a generic modelling framework and reference models for various classes of CNs. The models of CrossWork fit well within the Endogenous Elements perspective (Functional dimension) of ARCON, especially, in the specific models intent.

12.2 Pilarcos Business Networks

Lea Kutvonen and Alex Norta

The goals of the Pilarcos architecture [29] are to support enterprises in the provision of business services on an open service market, dynamic eContracting and establishment of new business networks (like instant VEs in CrossWork), and enforcement of the governing eContract rules on the collaboration at operational time. The focus of the supporting infrastructure is on the distributed business network management functionality and interoperability management at technical, semantic and pragmatic (processes, policies) levels.

Traditionally, inter-enterprise collaboration has been supported by business process driven integration solutions that focus on the business functionality needs and the technology-homogenizing needs of the collaboration. This leads to situations where a change in the business processes induces large re-development projects. Furthermore, technology changes may cause domino effects cascading on the computing system of dependent collaborations.

The present goal is to narrow the gap between business management concepts and the computing solutions. It has become plausible to address the call for enterprise interoperability [40] and social networking [7, 42] with the rise of service-oriented computing [41] and Web Service technologies [5], model-driven engineering [48] and multi-agent techniques and contemporary work on business–IT alignment [13, 36, 47].

Here we consider the Pilarcos-federated approach to VEs and compare the architectural features to CrossWork.

12.2.1 Overview and Concepts

The Pilarcos architecture envisions an open, global ecosystem where new business networks can be established [27, 28]. In this global ecosystem, enterprises make available business services which are administered independently. Together with other enterprises they form task forces in which new kinds of business scenarios are developed; other enterprises collaborate to form business networks instantiating such business scenarios, using the available business services. Business networks are ad hoc, loosely coupled, eContract-governed collaborations.

The ecosystem relies on new infrastructure services (B2B middleware services) in the open network, such as business service discovery and selection, knowledge about existing business network models and ontologies related to service types. To participate in this ecosystem, enterprises have a private agent for supporting local decision making and running the joint B2B middleware protocols with other partners in the ecosystem. The protocols are involved with eContract negotiation, monitoring, breach management and reputation information distribution.

The key concept in the Pilarcos architecture is that of a *business service*. A business service is a software-based (distributed) service, administered by a single authority. The provider may have policies restricting its behaviour. The business service may in addition be governed by an eContract for each instance of provision, stipulating scope, functionality, properties and accessibility of the service. There is no guarantee that discrepancies between eContracts, enterprise polices and service capabilities will not arise. Instead, a breach detection mechanism through monitoring forms an essential part of the architecture.

Figure 12.16 illustrates the general architecture and functionality. Each enterprise can make tenders to the open marketplace by describing the (functional and non-functional) properties of its service; each enterprise can participate in the design of business network models which offer a template of rules for a forthcoming business network. These events of publishing meta-information are, however, not dependent on each other, but the models meet at population and negotiation time. For the necessary negotiation, control and management protocols between potential peers allow for each enterprise to be represented by a private agent. The automated negotiation process (with human intervention possibilities) results into the eContract

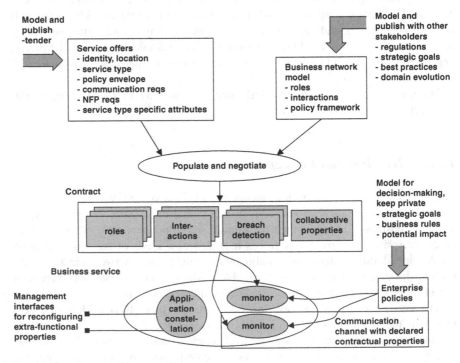

Fig. 12.16 Pilarcos architecture view

governing the business network membership, behaviour and breach management. For the operational time monitoring, the enterprise policies and eContract rules can be fed into local monitors guarding the business services. When a breach is detected as a monitor detects a message contradicting its rules, it sends a notification to the local agent, which in turn may request a breach recovery process to be started among the partners. Monitors can detect a reaching of processing milestones, and thus notify of significant state changes in the business network. As Fig. 12.16 illustrates, the technical properties of the business services are managed locally, taking into consideration the declarations of their properties in the eContract and enterprise policies. Thus, the properties of business services and the acceptability of a business process can be modified at operation time.

In the Pilarcos architecture, an eContract addresses multiple business services, and is negotiated among several enterprises. The eContract not only captures external business processes and selections made between alternative behaviours in it at the business level, but also complements this information with technical and semantic requirements for interoperability of the service-providing elements. However, the business services and enterprises involved in the business network preserve their privacy and autonomy. The reasons for agreeing or refusing to join a business network are not totally revealed. The business network establishment is a two-phase process: the first phase (*population*) utilizes public information, and the second phase (*refining negotiation*) utilizes private decision making for commitment or withdrawal from the negotiation. The method of implementing services is not revealed: the strong encapsulation of business services hides software implementations, local workflows, application platforms and other details, only making visible the external behaviour of the service (control exchange points, information exchange, quality and type of messaging services required for these).

Another property of the Pilarcos architecture is the use of clearly separated viewpoints of the managed business network. eContracts are used to capture all viewpoints. The viewpoints are closely related to those of the RMODP standards (Reference Model for Open Distributed Processing) [22, 23, 31]. The five Open Distributed Processing (ODP) viewpoints are addressed as follows:

- The enterprise viewpoint corresponds to the Pilarcos business network model expressed in terms of roles, interactions and governing policies. We have suggested the present RMODP amendment to include additional organizational concepts on top of the traditional concepts of federation (joint management of an aspect over the administrative domain boundaries) and community (in case of Pilarcos: business network).
- The information viewpoint specifies relevant information items, repositories and the rules for information modifications and invariants. These schemata are reflected in meta-information repository consistency rules.
- The computational viewpoint gives structures and interfaces for logical computation. For example, in Pilarcos, we consider different information exchange protocols as valid mappings for business network model requirement of passing a piece of information between parties.

- The engineering viewpoint specifies what kind of platform support is expected. This includes the Pilarcos facilities (populator, negotiation protocols, eContract management, monitoring, service offer repository, type repository, Business Network Model (BNM) repository) and various ways of realizing an abstract communication platform for exchanging messages with distribution transparency properties (transaction support, confidentiality, non-repudiation, access transparency, etc).
- The technology viewpoint specifies which concrete implementation or standards must be used. In Pilarcos, we have placed this viewpoint information as descriptive policy values in service offers or private decision-making information in negotiations.

The Pilarcos architecture is designed so that in each development process the designers need to consider only one aspect or abstraction layer; the infrastructure facilities carry the burden of keeping the aspects together. The approach is pragmatic, although steps in the overall process will address some of the same issues as more detailed work (e.g. utilizing logic, rule-based systems and semantic Web on ensuring hierarchy of normative systems to produce valid eContracts [19]).

The establishment and maintenance of business networks requires automation support at an infrastructure level. The Pilarcos Business-to-Business (B2B) middleware provides local agents (Business Network Agent) for each enterprise for their representatives in negotiations, maintaining eContract and progress information, and participating in renegotiations in breach situations or when any of the involved parties suggest changes to the eContract policies. For agents, a shared (current and evolving) vocabulary is essential; this vocabulary comes to existence through shared meta-information repositories.

12.2.2 Maintaining Interoperability Knowledge and Evolving the Ecosystem

The ecosystem for dynamic business networks is supported by a breeding environment for new business network instances and by generic agents and protocols for the federated maintenance of their governing eContracts. The necessary meta-information elements describe available business service offers, templates for eContracts to define the structure of the collaboration and reputation information about potential business partners' services for trust-based decision making. The Pilarcos architecture relies on the following meta-information repositories or flows:

- *Service offer repository* for storing tenders published by enterprises; the service offers identify the service interface and externally visible behaviour (exchange of information and control exchanges), declare the properties of the service (price, policies accepted, required communication channels, etc.) and publish expectations on the peers and their properties. This is the "open service market" from which business networks are built [25, 26, 32];

- *Business network model repository* for publishing potential business scenarios. The scenarios are expressed in terms of BNMs. A BNM is a set of (external) business processes (roles and interactions between them), declaration on how the roles of individual processes must be simultaneously played by the same business service provider (e.g. buyer of goods and receiver of invoice are the same), and policies with which the partners can agree to restrict the BNM alternatives. These models form structural templates for eContracts [28];
- *Service type repository* for publishing identified descriptions of service types together with the definition of required properties and their data types when publishing service offers [45]. The type repository is a key vocabulary-forming element in the architecture [26];
- *Flow of reputation information* from business network partners with experience on each other's trustworthiness to be used by those who contemplate on taking on a partner that they themselves have limited experience of [25]. This provides a basis for managing trust on business services dependability.

Together, these meta-information sources form the ecosystem knowledge base, breeding environment.

Traditionally, the establishment of business networks starts by the negotiation of joint objectives and goals, collaborative definition of the joint processes and definition of the methods of connecting individual computing elements to a coherent whole. This phase is supported by breeding environments where selection of partners, learning about their capabilities and designing the joint BNM takes place. In this process, the set of functionality is determined, as well as a set of business policies that must be adopted. Although all this is necessary for the business network establishment, it is not necessary to perform the whole process independently for each business network. Neither is it necessary to repeat the whole process when partners wish to make changes to the collaboration goals, processes, supporting applications or computing platforms.

We have separated the business network design phase from the network establishment phase. The BNMs can be collaboratively designed, verified and validated for their suitability. These models provide a common vocabulary for enterprises to match pragmatic interoperability (processes and policies) between partners. A separate vocabulary is necessary, as the services are independently developed and thus carry no inherent, implicit interoperability context information.

It is beneficial to create rather abstract behaviour groups when designing BNMs, to support evolution of collaboration styles. Each model can be further refined into alternative behaviours by choosing the guiding policy value at the eContract. The ability of dynamic policy management is a strong tool: selecting policy languages and targets suitably, most business management needs related to strategies and business rules can be modelled and transformed to rules that can be monitored at runtime. Effectively, the introduction of different types of policies allows mapping of business domain guidelines directly to B2B middleware facilities.

For defining the BNMs, a design tool and environment are needed. The BNMs comprise of business process models expressed in terms of roles (service requirements) and interactions between the roles [21].

The design of BNMs is a distributed activity. The BNMs are created in a unification process affected by all stakeholders, regulatory frameworks and best practices [39], and the resulting model should follow relevant regulations from the business domain or domains addressed. A common vocabulary is needed on-line for the designers to use, and strong guidance towards reuse of existing business process models is necessary. We use the type repository to provide a shared knowledge base for the modelling tools used in the enterprises.

The resulting models are published in an abstract (black box) [39] form, only revealing the obligated interactions, frameworks for non-functional property management and breach management rules. This view is then to be refined by other design and configuration phases. The BNMs are constructed by connecting together business processes that each have a single starting point, a single termination point and one functional goal, which is essential for verification purposes [1]. The processes can be connected by explicating which roles at each process model must collocate at a combined role. The new role inherits the service requirements from all these collocated roles. The business process models are annotated by criteria for assignment of business services and operational time criteria for not causing a breach. When the composite roles are created, annotations are added to restrict collocations, for example, to avoid legally invalid combinations of supervision relationships.

The non-functional properties of interest for business network management include modifiers of the functional interaction patterns between peer business services and negotiated declarations of business service or interaction qualities [30, 45]. For example, policies can be used to separate purchases with required prepayment and loyalty (program) credit payments. Further, a communication property declaration may require that all interactions between purchaser and seller are certified with a non-repudiation system involving a third-party notary not visible in the business level abstraction of the business scenario.

The rules determining breaches are explicit, as is the agreement on what recovery process to use. For this purpose, (a) multiple recovery business processes are defined and consistently viewed as a set of best practice definitions and (b) all BNMs should be analysed to determine their recoverability style; some networks are not able to recover from breaches but need to be terminated, while others may recover from the loss of some members, and further some require a set of compensation actions to take place before either continuing operation or terminating.

Before publication, the BNMs must be analysed and verified for properties like liveliness, fairness, privacy-preservation (data-flow sufficiency and minimality), termination of processes and recoverability. For this purpose, existing business process verification tools are applicable when each functional business network part is separately analysed.

12.2.3 Business Network Lifecycle

The main steps in the business network life cycle are (a) negotiation and eCon-tract establishment, (b) enactment and monitoring, and (c) breach and termination management.

12.2.3.1 Negotiation and Establishment

Negotiation of the business network structure and goals forms a separate step which results in an explicit, published model. Thus, eContract negotiation between enter-prises becomes more restricted in its scope. Effectively, negotiation must result in a situation where static validation can ensure or verify that interoperability at all levels exists between all parties, and that all parties are willing to participate in the collaboration.

The supporting facilities to be used here are as follows [27, 28]. First, the B2B middleware provides a population of the business network followed by a generic negotiation protocol between the enterprise agents. The population process ensures that, according to service offers, the business services of members joining the business network are interoperable at all levels. Then, the proposed eContract draft is sent to each enterprise to gather commitments of participation, or further refinements of the policies suggested. In the service offers, acceptable alternatives for policy values can be announced, but final decisions need to be made during negotiation. The negotiation cycle ensures privacy of decision making for each participant. In routine cases, it is possible for an enterprise's agent to provide an automated response to the collaboration proposals: an explicit meta-policy guides the agent to make routine rejections or commitments. Both for the automated deci-sion making and for the support of human intervention, we propose an expert system to gather the relevant knowledge and to feed governing policies into the enter-prise system [30]. The policies that guide the expert system decisions include the following:

- Meta-policies governing decision making: Some collaboration proposals or busi-ness interactions are clearly either to be accepted as routine cases of normal operation, or clearly to be rejected because the proposal is uninteresting or not trusted due to, for example, proposed partners or BNM [30];
- Decision-making policies with respect to reputation-based trust, risk and impor-tance tolerances [46];
- Privacy policy that may overrule any other decision-making reasoning in collabo-rative interactions; each service, information source and meta-information source must be protected [30];
- Constraints for granting use of services;
- The service type and business network models should include observable prop-erties that are relevant for the business process re-engineering needs. Such an observable property is, for example, the satisfaction of clients after completing a session on a business service.

The decision to join a collaboration must balance the risk of failure or loss of assets, as a consequence of participation, and the potential benefits of participation [46]. That is, the expert system should compute a three-value outcome (agree, disagree, call for human intervention) on whether a service or a collaboration is dependable and beneficial for the enterprise in a given context and situation [30]. A dependable service fulfils its business purpose and the use of the service does not involve intolerable risk of monetary loss or reputation loss, for example, caused by delivery failures or unacceptable delivery delays.

For the decision making, the system computes values for risk and risk tolerance, both of which are vectors over a set of assets, such as monetary assets, reputation, fulfilment of purpose and control of property [44]. For the risk values, the essential input comes from reputation information, i.e. positive and negative recommendations by members of earlier collaborations. For the risk tolerance, the essential input is from the perceived importance of the tasks or business network. The starting values for the importance and loss scenarios should be created by an extensive risk.

Once the agreement has been reached, the eContract data is formed to carry all relevant meta-information about the business network structure, behaviour, partners and policy values selected. In addition, a distributed eContract agent is established and replicated between the business network partners. At the business network startup phase each partner uses the eContract information for configuring its business services through its local service management interfaces. Likewise, the eContract includes policies declaring properties for the communication channels between business services and the local managements are expected to establish bindings using these requirements. The eContract also collects information about the progress of the activities at each partners' services. Furthermore, the monitoring system is able to notify the eContract of detected breaches. Because of these features, the eContract and the local service management facilities form a joint community-wide reflective system for the duration of the business network lifetime.

In relation to other work (e.g. survey [33], eNegotiation [13], OMNI [49], QAME [38]) and outsourcing management systems, we emphasize:

- The use of predefined contract templates that capture not only business level or technical level issues, but both;
- Running a multi-partner negotiation instead of bilateral negotiations;
- Support of contract template evolution through the facilities for creating new business network models and policy variations;
- Agility of business networks gained by operational time negotiations and renegotiations based on ontologies and abstract enough behaviour models created at design time;
- Privacy of decision making and using interoperability knowledge effectively for it;
- Potential to use multiple negotiation protocols for different types of collaborations (auctioning systems, simple commitment protocols).

12.2.3.2 Enactment and Monitoring

Once the eContract has been established, the business services are allowed to start their local processes. The services are expected to be *agents*, i.e. make initiative and respond to service requests, and internally follow local business process. In particular, no joint enactment platform is expected, in contrast with distributed workflow systems. One of the main design goals for Pilarcos was to encapsulate as much as possible, even the local computing platform. Besides the local agents and globally distributed services for meta-information and service discovery, the Pilarcos architecture requires little from the computing and communication platforms. Naturally, technical interoperability can only be achieved if the service offers utilized in peer roles can exchange messages over a shared communication protocol or can be supported in configuring a channel structure with mediators to reach connectivity. Elsewhere we discuss the relaxed matching and configuration support [32].

As the business services themselves are responsible for running the computations and initiating the exchanges of messages, the eContract and enterprise policies govern and restrict this behaviour. The processes in the BNM are split into tasks, vaguely similar to business transactions. For these, the same kind of trust-related decision making takes place, balancing between risk and risk tolerance.

During the operation of the business network, the monitors governing the business services can scan the messaging, reporting to enterprise level agents if the eContract is breached. *Proactive monitoring* holds the message until a decision has been made whether it is safe to send or receive it. *Active monitoring* lets the message pass but reports breaches thus potentially causing breach recovery or termination of the collaboration. *Passive monitoring* simply audits the events for later processing.

Breaches can mean failing to fulfil an obligation, or failing to provide the agreed quality level of the service; more formally, failing to provide the level of dependability expected. The concept of dependability, in terms of fulfilling the contracted aspects, can be conceptualized over two *fields*. There are general properties that can be set as service level expectations for any service, such as availability, timeliness and privacy-preservation, or interaction relationship, such as non-repudiation and immutability. In addition, there are properties which are relevant for individual service types, each requiring a definition of value domain and metrics for defining the service levels relevant for the property. For example, reputation information (recommendation) may have a credibility property associated to it, determining how completely a recommendation from that source is assumed truthful. Another example is the traditional Quality of Service (QoS) levels with different metrics for bandwidth and jitter in transfer.

The monitors receive rules from eContract and from their local policy repositories. These rules are not guaranteed to be non-conflicting, as they may address different issues and can be changed after eContract establishment. At detected breach situations, decisions are needed on whether the event is serious enough for terminating or leaving the business network. The same type of knowledge about the operational environment can be used, and again the expert system can make automated decisions or redirect the request for human intervention. Transformation rules are required to automatically map the various styles of monitoring rules captured in the eContract, to such monitoring rules or state machines that can be used to control the running service software. Despite the wide range of issues to address at business, semantic, pragmatic and technical levels, the analysis of the various monitoring needs shows that the required monitor techniques fall into a few simple cases:

- *Detectors* of denied values or value combinations in message fields;
- *Detectors* of non-acceptable ordering of messages, including failure to complete a task in time;
- *Detectors* of series of messages jointly exceeding the acceptable limits calculated from the messages as they pass the monitor; and
- *Authorizers* that hold the message while investigating whether the intended business transaction is to be trusted.

Using these techniques in various combinations in the application context, and utilizing the business semantics building from the messages, a rigorous set of constraints can be built; business semantics and social requirements can be encoded.

12.2.4 Comparison of CrossWork IVE and Pilarcos Business Networks

The goals of the CrossWork and Pilarcos projects were somewhat different, although the results complement each other. The projects share a vision of dynamic VEs and seek enabling technologies to reach that goal. The most immediate difference is that Pilarcos aims to automate routine formation of similar business networks and support the evolution of knowledge about useful type networks, whereas CrossWork is more focused upon ad hoc consortia.

Technical contributions from the projects differ. The technical contributions from Pilarcos include:

- Generic, commonly available services for maintaining knowledge about available services and their properties, interoperability qualities, reputation and business network models (i.e. predefined BN structures to choose from);
- Generic, local services to support eContract negotiation, monitoring, membership and transaction-involvement decisions based on trust;
- Facilitation for dynamic choices and changes during BN establishment and operation, including membership, policies and technical solutions;
- Automation support for BN establishment and maintenance in routine cases;
- Formation of IVEs (team formation: systematic discovery and matching of partners, selecting coordinator and supplying partners, creating bilateral contracts between parties where communication/service provision is needed);

- Global and local workflow enactment on standard workflow engines (each partner allows the coordinator to control its process partially, each partner informs the IVE and its members of local progress made);
- Framework for harmonizing local workflows of service provider and consumer (eSourcing) with business process composition and verification; and
- User interfaces that guide organizations trough the process of selecting a team and forming an inter-organizational business process to orchestrate individual activities.

The technical contributions from CrossWork include:

- Formation of IVEs (team formation: systematic discovery and matching of partners, selecting coordinator and supplying partners, creating bilateral contracts between parties where communication/service provision is needed);
- Global and local workflow enactment on standard workflow engines (each partner allows the coordinator to control its process partially, each partner informs the IVE and its members of local progress made);
- Framework for harmonizing local workflows of service provider and consumer (eSourcing) with business process composition and verification; and
- User interfaces guiding organizations through the process of selecting a team and forming an inter-organizational business process to orchestrate individual activities.

12.3 Collaborative Design of Supply Networks (SUDDEN)

Nikolay Mehandjiev

Empowering Instant VEs is also the focus of the EC-funded project SUDDEN (SMEs Undertaking Design of Dynamic Ecosystem Networks), which links real needs of four manufacturing SMEs with research in process coordination and agent-based team formation and management. The vision of SUDDEN is closely aligned with CrossWork; in particular, it includes the delivery of software to enable near-instantaneous formation of VEs, to bid for orders which would normally be handled by a bigger organization. Yet, SUDDEN extends this to cover co-optimization of the existing supply networks, allowing SMEs to leverage synergies within and across these, for example, to reduce (delivery) costs. This contrasts with current practice, where supply-network planning is largely manual and oriented to fixed and stable environments.

Where CrossWork codifies partner profiles, skill sets and workflow templates and uses these to inform planning and search algorithms, SUDDEN takes into account that codified skill sets often render (partner) search suboptimal, in the sense that it fails to recognize that partners may change their working processes or invest in training or capital expenditure for potentially lucrative opportunities. Moreover, SUDDEN supports IVE formation based on a closely knitted network of acquaintances, which work together to pursue a project idea, incrementally developing the details in a "situated", flexible manner. The SMEs targeted by SUDDEN go through intertwined processes of forming a VE, evolving their existing supply networks, learning from each bid and improving their qualifications for future bids by training, obtaining standards certifications, etc.

To accommodate these findings, SUDDEN is based on the following three main innovations:

1. A novel approach to multi-level supply network design and coordination, inspired by coordination theory and situated action;
2. A novel method for continuous and systematic evaluation and replacement of VO partners and their processes, which integrates three measures (i) the value of a partner to the network, (ii) the match between capability profiles and (iii) the degree of "coordination fit" between partner processes; and
3. A novel methodology integrating the processes of bidding and selection with on-the-job learning and development of actors and collaborations.

These three innovations are embedded in a conceptual "solution" which is mostly software but includes designs of the social structures and processes surrounding the use of this software.

Innovation 1 is the one most closely related to CrossWork. It proposes a novel approach to collaborative construction and evolution of a VE, which comprises:

1. A recursive VE model and
2. A set of model construction rules and operators to enable systematic collaborative construction of a VE model.

The following three principles underpin the SUDDEN approach:

1. *Iterative elaboration* of the model from an initial set of core partners to a fully operational VE which includes details of logistic processes.
2. *Devolved decision making* recognizes the autonomy of an actor charged with achieving a certain goal, leaving to him the choice of decomposition, outsourcing or operationalization (see below).
3. The *Situatedness* principle recognizes the need for actors to match their decisions to the execution context, refining and revising as appropriate.

The model achieves some of its flexibility and power by treating the following three categories of processes in a uniform manner:

- work processes across the VE;
- work coordination processes; and
- partner/supplier selection processes.

This allows the principles above to be extended to all three categories, allowing for example goal-driven and actor-specific coordination mechanisms.

Overall, the model and the construction rules serve as a framework within which we can plug a number of innovative mechanisms for VE analysis, construction and enactment. For example, the SUDDEN prototype is one instantiation of the proposed approach, within which we have included blackboard-based mechanisms for emergent team composition, process-aware evaluation of the set of proposed partners, and some other domain-specific evaluation and coordination mechanisms. We briefly survey some of the motives, results and theoretical underpinnings of SUDDEN. The detailed innovative mechanisms within SUDDEN are not in the focus here, with fuller descriptions elsewhere [20, 34].

12.3.1 SUDDEN and Supply Network Design

Synergetic potentials in business ecosystems concerning the bundling of service requirements and transportation needs in optimized supply network designs are currently not exploited. The prevalent approach is that each organization plans and runs its own supply network. Distribution centres are created and transport orders are placed individually, without reaping those benefits which may arise from cooperation with companies having complementary transport needs, such as offsetting densities, seasonal balancing and shared clients. The possibility of optimizing transportation networks is tentatively explored by 4th party logistics providers, with quoted savings averaging 15–20%, but their focus is often on a single big customer, and the scope limited to logistic activities such as transportation and warehousing.

The EC-funded project SUDDEN addresses the need for integrating effective network design and run-time flexibility by an overall approach bringing together advances in "Collaborative Planning", "Delayed Partner Recruitment" and "Systematic Evolution of Supply Networks". The SUDDEN approach is based on a decentralized mechanism for collaborative negotiation and planning, situated within a distributed architecture of software entities capable of automatic reasoning (intelligent agents). Figure 12.17 illustrates the operation of the SUDDEN approach.

In terms of "Collaborative Planning", SUDDEN takes an abstract perspective of supply networks, conceptualizing them as actors providing services (including the

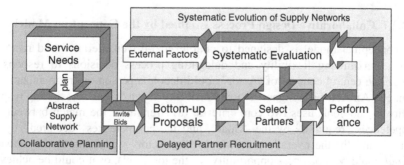

Fig. 12.17 The SUDDEN approach to integrating planning and execution

provision of goods). Service requirements are decoupled from the concrete actors chosen to fulfil them, allowing bundling of concurrent services (e.g. train personnel sorting mail onboard), or services sharing other similarities (e.g. deliveries to the same client).

This is complemented by the use of a "Delayed Partner Recruitment" mechanism to assign concrete satisfiers to the abstract service requirements. The timescales will be different for different services, ranging from appointing core partners on day one to routing a voice call through a particular telecom operator at the moment of placing the call. This allows flexibility in dealing with unforeseen events arising near to execution time. "Delayed Partner Recruitment" comprises two mechanisms: "Bottom-up Proposals" allows suppliers to form consortia which offer innovative combinations and bundling of activities, whilst "Select Partners" allows systematic selection. The latter is often informed by using the results of the "Systematic Evaluation" activity, thus closing the feedback loop in terms of "Performance" and reflecting "External Factors".

Within this context, work is focused on developing the knowledge structures and reasoning mechanisms to underpin software which can automate the stages of collaborative planning and delayed partner recruitment. Initial results in this area were reviewed by our end-users. The feedback triggered a number of enhancements to take into account the existing culture of close group collaboration and situated work, and this second set of results is reported here. As we show in the following, this second set of results fits the gradual nature of consortium building and the flexible and situated nature of work processes at our end-users.

12.3.2 The SUDDEN Approach

The EC project SUDDEN makes two primary contributions: a flexible conceptual model of the knowledge structures needed and a set of agent-oriented mechanisms to advise on optimal configurations based on information encoded in the model. The description here focuses on the conceptual model underpinning the approach. The "all-in-one" view of this conceptual model is shown in Fig. 12.18, the following sub-sections introduce it feature-by-feature.

12.3.2.1 Collaborative Design Process Enabled by the Conceptual Model

The conceptual model is designed to enable goal-driven, iterative and recursive design, maximizing flexibility and delegating process decisions to responsible actors. The central concept of "Actor" could denote a person or an organization, a team, etc. An Actor is assigned a "Responsibility" for a "Goal". Assigning responsibility to sub-goals uses two core criteria: (a) strength of the match between the competences "required" by the "Goal", and the competences "declared" by the "Actor", and (b) the overall value which this "Actor" will bring to the network. A *Goal* could be a business opportunity (at the top level), or it could be achieving something smaller. A "Goal" is defined as a desired state of the world, as measured

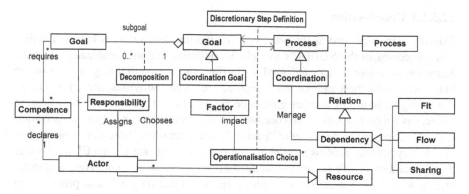

Fig. 12.18 Conceptual model of SUDDEN

by the values of a set of variables. An actor may (a) choose a "Decomposition" of this goal into a set of "sub-goals", or (b) make an "Operationalization Choice", choosing a "Process" for this goal. The technique is then repeated recursively at lower system levels, until all "sub-goals" are allocated to "Actors", who make the "Operationalization Choice" for this. A "Process" could be a short, one-step activity or a partially ordered set of process steps (sub-processes). A process step can be left underspecified, or even described only by a goal to be achieved by the actor who is responsible for this step. This "Discretionary Step Definition" closes the "design loop" and accommodates goal-driven behaviour. It is also aids if pre-specified process steps fail during process execution.

Instead of decomposing or operationalizing a goal, an actor may invite bids through a shared noticeboard; triggering a bottom-up mode of goal decomposition, where other actors bid to form consortia, each contributing its own sub-goals and negotiating feasible decompositions.

12.3.2.2 Inter-process Dependencies

A "Process" can be either atomic or a partially ordered set of process steps, linked by *Relations*. A particular type of relation is a "Dependency", which could be based on a "Resource" shared by two processes, for example, a machine may be shared by several processing tasks ("Sharing" dependency). A resource may be produced by one process and consumed by another, in which case we have a "Flow" dependency. Finally, different parts of a resource may derive from more than one process, in which case we have a "Fit" dependency. The set of these dependencies and the choices made by actors regarding how they wish to operationalize goals are the main inputs to our approach to collaborative design of a supply network. We also note that: (a) the "Operationalization Choice" is impacted by a number of "Factors" and (b) an "Actor" is also a "Resource", thus allowing us to optimize allocation of actors to processes.

12.3.2.3 Coordination

Coordination is defined as the process of managing dependencies between activities (processes in the SUDDEN model), to optimize certain organizational goals. Mapping onto our conceptual model clarifies the substantial degree of overlap between coordination and process design concepts and activities. Indeed, the coordination goal is simply another goal to be assigned to an "Actor"; the coordination process is another process. The coordination process is thus an "Operationalization Choice", impacted by a number of "Factors". The (meta-level) decision-making process is a systematic process for making the right "Operationalization Choice" under contextual factors. We use meta-management and switching to motivate a systematic review of (a) criteria for assigning responsibilities for goals and processes to actors, and (b) the choice of an appropriate coordination process.

"Resources", "Actors" and "Factors" are in general only known near execution time, so we say they provide execution context. Other elements are generally known at the time of designing the supply chain network.

12.3.3 Application

This section focuses on how the conceptual model of SUDEN can be used to support the formation of a VE in a flexible yet useful manner. An anonymous case study from the automotive manufacturing industry is used for this purpose.

Step 1: Establish Goals and Competences. The top-level goal[3] is derived from the business opportunity to produce and sell low-emission cars for city transport. This is shown as "G0" in Fig. 12.19, and the responsibility for it lies with the owner, AutoSystems Ltd. AutoSystems Ltd works closely with the manufacturing company ManSys GmbH, and they sit together to plan the overall project, allocating the responsibility for "G2" Engineering to AutoSystems Ltd and for "G3" and "G4" (set up and run production) to ManSys GmbH. "G1" (Marketing) and "G5" (Sales, not shown here) are left unallocated at present, until core issues of Engineering and Production are sorted out. ManSys GmbH is now the actor responsible for "G3". It decomposes this into sub-goals ("G3.1-3" and "G4.1-2" as shown in the figure), and seeks actors with the required skills (including themselves) to assign responsibility for these goals. "G3.3" and "G4.1" require competences which are not available in members of the consortium so far, so ManSys GmbH may offer this to open tender to other members of their ecosystem. A consultancy company TrainingUp places the best bid and is allocated responsibility for these.

This step illustrates the iteration enabled by our model, where planning goals and processes is separate yet intertwined with the definition of competences and making actors responsible for goals.

---

[3] Please note that the presence of many independent goals and different supply chains is presumed, which can be co-optimized using bundling mechanisms.

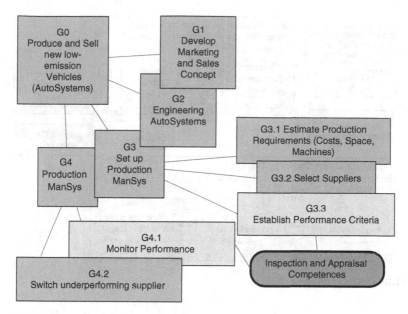

Fig. 12.19 Top-level decomposition and skills

Step 2: Make Operationalization Choices. An "Actor" allocated responsibility for a goal can either decompose it as shown in Fig. 12.19, or make an "Operationalization Choice" for the goal, and thus establish processes and their resources. The timing of the choice would be specific to the problem; for example, a telecom provider does not need to decide precise routing of a call until it is placed, whereas in our example the two processes must take place early in the project to enable subsequent stages. A key feature of the model is the ability to use "Discretionary Step Definitions" for "fuzzy" processes and process steps, creating the space for situated action. Consider, the details of the process step "Approach Supplier for a quote" may be left to the actor responsible for it; he can choose to ring, enquire by fax, visit in person or enquire when they meet at a trade fair.

In our example, ManSys GmbH and Training Up take responsibility for "G3.2" and "G3.3", and operationalize these as shown in Fig. 12.20. Dependencies between process steps are also defined and both processes have a (common) dependency, since each needs authorization by the Managing Director of ManSys GmbH. Note that Steps 1 and 2 are done collaboratively by all core partners in the network. In contrast, the next step is usually automated and done centrally, merging the collaborative input and bundling processes and satisfier requirements.

Step 3: Bundling and coordination. "Coordination" processes aim to optimize the overall supply network, including *goals, competences, actors, processes and dependencies derived so far,* according to the coordination goals *G*. For coordination processes we use the same model as for the work processes above. The difference is that the actors doing the *Engineering* process are likely to be humans

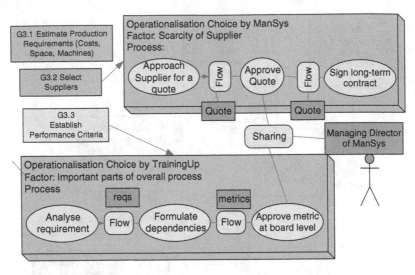

Fig. 12.20 Operationalization choices

supported by software agents, whilst here the likely actors are software agents operating mostly without human intervention. For example, for $G = \{minimize\ time,$
$maximize\ utilization\}$, we have following manipulations:

1. Consider the similarity of competences specified for the following goals:

   – Goals corresponding to consecutive processes;
   – Goals of parallel processes which follow from one process and lead to
     another;
   – Goals corresponding to independent processes with similar types of input or
     output resources (i.e. transporting in same direction, etc.);

   If the similarity of competences allows, integrate the goals and their processes
   in a single bundle, formulate this as a role thus allowing the recruitment of a single
   performer for this role at the next stage.

2. Consider re-ordering of processes to avoid competition for common non-
   shareable resources such as specialized machining centres, or the Managing
   Director above.
3. Consider the synchronization (push vs. pull) between consecutive processes and
   provide appropriate support.

Step 4: Delayed Partner Recruitment. The selection of some actors can be
postponed to the latest possible time depending on the specific features of the particular goal and its process. Following the virtually organizing approach, we allow
a number of systematic provider selection processes, e.g. centralized matchmaking of competences, call for proposals followed by selection from the received

bids, etc. For underspecified goal decompositions, we can use blackboard-based mechanism where actors volunteer partial solutions and thus allow (potentially) innovative solutions to ill-specified problems to emerge, for example, consortium bidding for the "design engine" sub-goal of the Engineering goal can propose a hybrid drive combining electricity and petrol engine. In addition, this approach allows further bundling. First, several providers can pool their capacities (e.g. transportation or manufacturing) to satisfy the volume requirement. Second, if a provider believes certain goals are best bundled (say carrying load for two customers to fill the two legs of a return trip), he can bid lower and get both jobs, effectively, passing savings on to the customers.

The abstract nature of process specifications used for "collaborative planning" stage of coordination prevents full consideration of actor-specific costs and timings at this early stage. However, at the stage of "delayed recruitment", this information is likely to be available, together with context-specific run-time factors, allowing a re-optimization of the network, if necessary.

Step 5: Systematic Evolution of Supply Networks. The SUDDEN theoretical model allows decisions about operationalization to be taken on an "as needed" basis, and treats the coordinating processes as another "work process". Facilities are provided to monitor the performance of actors and processes, and alert the appropriate actors when things no longer work within the threshold boundaries. The actors can then (a) revise their partner recruitment (subcontracting) decisions, and (b) revise their choice of processes to achieve the goals for which they are responsible given the most up-to-date context. As this mechanism includes coordination processes, (b) allows a re-coordination of work at runtime. For example, if a supplier takes too long to deliver their orders but the work is of excellent quality and reasonable price, ManSys GmbH can either replace the supplier, or consider a change from "just-in-time" to "deliver-to-stock". A coordination theory-based approach makes such changes easier by only considering dependencies which arise out of the nature of work at the level of resources needed to accomplish work, instead of operating with artificial design-time ordering of process steps typical for conventional workflow systems.

12.3.4 Differences Between SUDDEN and CrossWork

CrossWork supports the process of establishing Virtual Organizations, mostly focusing on product development, assembly and supply in the automotive and ancillary sectors. SUDDEN also targets the automotive domain, yet it targets the wider issues surrounding supply network coordination.

In terms of support, CrossWork aims to automate the formation of task teams and the design of the cross-organizational workflow necessary to coordinate their activities. It takes into account local rules and processes of collaborating partners whilst preserving their business autonomy and allowing information hiding regarding their business processes. Role-based enactment of business logic and security, formal specifications of processes and process patterns provide for an appropriate level of abstraction and ease of maintenance. These contributions provide a necessary complement of techniques for seamless collaboration and process integration within the target context of distributed and dynamic coordination of work.

In contrast, SUDDEN uses automation as means of supporting SMEs in their human-centric planning and management activities, integrating the benefits of early planning with last-minute adaptability. It uses goal decomposition and team formation mechanisms similar to those of CrossWork, yet these are controlled by a human-centred collaborative design component.

Importantly, the targeted end-user community has changed. CrossWork focuses on OEMs (e.g. MAN) and large first-tier suppliers (e.g. Magna Intier), while SUDDEN focuses on the SMEs. While MAN does select suppliers they do not further develop them but use an external consultancy. In this respect, the results of SUDDEN and CrossWork are complementary. In addition, SUDDEN aims to construct innovative bundles of services and components by using agent-based reasoning and task negotiation mechanisms. Each participant will be able to review its knowledge base of active collaborations and services, and offer better terms for services which reuse existing activities and resources.

Overall, SUDDEN builds on the innovative mechanisms of goal decomposition and team formation of CrossWork, and puts these within a theoretical framework, which uses the principles of meta-management and coordination theory to ensure separation between planning and allocation, and systematic feedback into allocation mechanisms and evaluation criteria.

12.4 Conclusions

This chapter describes three research efforts in the domain of supporting collaboration between organizations in pursuit of business opportunities. At a first sight, they seem to present alternative approaches to the one taken by CrossWork. Yet, upon closer examination, we find that these are more complementary than comparable.

Notions of network development and preservation, partner selection, trust, service compatibility and infrastructure interoperability arise as common goals. This is to be expected with current economic climates, industry trends and market volatilities conspiring to make collaboration not only an attractive way in which to improve opportunities, but in many cases the only path to ensure a sustainable growth.

The three research projects described here thus offer complementary approaches to CrossWork to the issues involved in supporting the formation of collaborative organizations (IVEs). We therefore find that rather than exploring the portability or transferability of results from one project to another, it is perhaps more fruitful to explore further the mutual strengthening to be derived from a deeper exploration of the complementary nature of these projects.

References

1. Aslst, W. M. P. V., Verbeek, H. M. W., Kumar, A., XRL/Wo An: Verification of an XML/Petri-net Based Language for Interorganizational Workflows (Best paper award), Proceedings of the 6th Conference on Information Systems and Technology (CIST), pp 30–45, Informs, Linthicum, MD, 2001.
2. Abreu, A., Camarinha-Matos, L. M., On the Role of Value Systems to Promote the Sustainability of Collaborative Environments, International Journal of Production Research, Vol. 46(5), pp. 1207–1229, 2008.
3. Afsarmanesh, H., Msanjila, S. S., Ermilova, E., Wiesner, S., Woelfel, W., Seifert, M., VBE Management System in Methods and Tools for Collaborative Networked Organizations, Springer, New York, pp. 119–154, 2008.
4. Arana, J., Berasategi, L., Aranburu, I., Bollhalter, S., Landau, B., Oswald, M., Heavey, C., O'Reagan, E., Liston, P., Byrne, P., VO Management Pilot Cases in Methods and Tools for Collaborative Networked Organizations, Springer, New York, pp. 431–462, 2008.
5. Booth, D., Haas, H., McCabe, F., Newcomer, E., Champion, M., Ferris, C., Orchard, D., Web Services Architecture, Technical Report, W3C, http://www.w3.org/TR/2004/NOTE-wsarch-20040211/, 2004.
6. Camarinha-Matos, L. M., Afsarmanesh, H., Collaborative Networks: A New Scientific Discipline, Journal of Intelligent Manufacturing, Vol. 16(4–5), pp. 439–452, 2005.
7. Camarinha-Matos, L. M., Afsarmanesh, H., Modeling Framework for Collaborative Networked Organizations, Network-Centric Collaboration and Supporting Frameworks, International Federation for Information Processing (IFIP), pp. 3–14, Springer, Boston, 2006.
8. Camarinha-Matos, L. M., Afsarmanesh, H., A Comprehensive Modeling Framework for Collaborative Networked Organizations, Journal of Intelligent Manufacturing, Vol. 18(5), pp. 527–615, 2007.
9. Camarinha-Matos, L. M., Oliveira, A. I., Contract Negotiation Wizard for VO Creation, In Digital Enterprise Technology, Springer, New York,, pp. 333–342, 2007.
10. Camarinha-Matos, L. M., Oliveira, A. I., Ratti, R., Baldo, F., Jarimo, T., A Computer-Assisted VO Creation Framework, Establishing the Foundation of Collaborative Networks, Vol. 243, pp. 165–178, 2007.
11. Camarinha-Matos, L. M., Afsarmanesh, H., Collaborative Networks: Reference Modeling, Springer, New York, 2008.
12. Chen, H. M., SOA Enterprise Architecture and Business-IT Alignment: An Integrated Framework, In: H. R. Arabnia, H. Reza (eds.), Software Engineering Research and Practice, CSREA Press, Las Vegas, NV, pp. 566–573, 2007.
13. Chiu, D. K. W., Cheung, S. C., Hung, P. C. K., Chiu, S. Y. Y., Chung, A. K. K., Developing e-Negotiation Support with a Meta-modeling Approach in a Web Services Environment, Decision Support Systems, Vol. 40, pp. 51–69, 2004.
14. Conconi, A., Gusmeroli, S., Ratti, R., A Collaboration Platform for PVC, Methods and Tools for Collaborative Networked Organizations, Springer, New York, pp. 307–334, 2008.
15. Crave, S., Vorobey, V., Business Models for PVC: Challenges and Perspectives, Methods and Tools for Collaborative Networked Organizations, Springer, New York, pp. 293–306, 2008.
16. Ermilova, E., Afsarmanesh, A., Modeling and Management of Profiles and competencies in VBEs, International Journal of Intelligent Manufacturing, Vol. 18(5), pp. 561–586, 2007.
17. Ermilova, E., Afsarmanesh, H., A Unified Ontology for VO Breeding Environments, Proceedings of Distributed Human-Machine Systems Conference (DHMS), Athens, Greece, March 9–12, 2008.
18. Galeano, N., Molina, A., Beeler, J., Monnier, F., Pouly, M., Aguilera, C., Olmo, A., Laessig, D., Tiefensee, B., VBE Pilot Demonstrators, Methods and Tools for Collaborative Networked Organizations, Springer, New York, pp. 405–430, 2008.
19. Gelati, J., Rotolo, A., Sartor, G., Governatori, G., Normative Autonomy and Normative Co-ordination: Declarative Power, Representation and Mandate, Artificial Intelligence and Law, Vol. 12, pp. 53–81, 2004.

20. Hosking, J., Mehandjiev, N., Grundy, J., A Domain Specific Visual Language for Design and Coordination of Supply Networks, Proceedings of the 2008 IEEE Symposium on Visual Languages and Human-Centric Computing, 16–20 Sept, Herrsching am Ammersee, Germany, IEEE Press, 2008.
21. ISO/IEC JTC1/SC7: Information Technology, Open Distributed Processing Reference Model, Enterprise Language, 2004.
22. ISO/IEC JTC1: Information Technology, Open Systems Interconnection, Data Management and Open Distributed Processing, Reference Model of Open Distributed Processing, Part 2: Foundations, IS10746-2, 1996.
23. ISO/IEC JTC1: Information Technology, Open Systems Interconnection, Data Management and Open Distributed Processing, Reference Model of Open Distributed Processing, Part 3: Architecture, IS10746-3, 1996.
24. Jansson, K., Karvonen, I., Ollus, M., Negretto, U., Governance and Management of Virtual Organizations, Methods and Tools for Collaborative Networked Organizations, Springer, New York, pp. 221–238, 2008.
25. Kutvonen, L., Metso, J., Ruohomaa, S., From Trading to eCommunity Population: Responding to Social and Contractual Challenges, Proceedings of the 10th IEEE International EDOC Conference, pp. 199–210, Hong Kong, China, 2006.
26. Kutvonen, L., Building B2B Middleware – Interoperability Knowledge Management Issues, Enterprise Interoperability II – New Challenges and Approaches, Springer, Funchal, Portugal, pp. 629–632, 2007.
27. Kutvonen, L., Metso, J., Ruohomaa, S., From Trading to eCommunity Management: Respond-ing to Social and Contractual Challenges, Information Systems Frontiers (ISF), Vol. 9(2–3), 181–194, 2007, Special Issue on Enterprise Services Computing: Evolution and Challenges, URL http://dx.doi.org/10.1007/s10796-007-9031-x
28. Kutvonen, L., Ruokolainen, T., Metso, J., Interoperability Middleware for Federated Business Services in Web-Pilarcos, International Journal of Enterprise Information Systems, Special issue on Interoperability of Enterprise Systems and Applications, Vol. 3(1), pp. 1–21, 2007.
29. Kutvonen, L., Ruokolainen, T., Ruohomaa, S., Metso, J., Service-Oriented Middleware for Managing Inter-Enterprise Collaborations, Global Implications of Modern Enterprise Information Systems, Technologies and Applications, 2008.
30. Kutvonen, L., Tools and Infrastructure Facilities for Controlling Non-Functional Properties in Inter-Enterprise in Collaborations, Workshop on ODP for Enterprise Computing (WODPEC), Munich, Germany, 15th September, 2008.
31. Kutvonen, L., Architectures for distributed systems: Open distributed processing reference model. In: HeCSE Workshop on Emerging Technologies in Distributed Systems (1998).
32. Kutvonen, L., Trading Services in Open Distributed Environments, Ph.D. Thesis, 1998.
33. Medjahed, B., Benatallah, B., Bouguettaya, A., Ngu, A. H. H., Elmagarming, A. K., Business-to-Business Interactions: Issues and Enabling Technologies, The VLDB Journal, Vol. 12, pp. 59–85, 2003.
34. Mehandjiev, N., Stalker, I., Carpenter, M., Recursive Construction and Evolution of Collaborative Business Processes, Proceedings of the 2nd International Workshop on Collaborative Business Processes, Milan, 2008.
35. Msanjila, S. S., Afsarmanesh, H., FETR: A Framework to Establish Trust Relationships Among Organizations in VBEs, Journal of Intelligent Manufacturing, DOI 10.1007/s10845-008-0178-1, 2009.
36. Nayak, N., Nigam, A., Sanz, J., Marston, D., Flaxer, D., Concepts for Service-Oriented Business Thinking, IEEE International Conference on Service Computing (SCC), pp. 357–364, 2006.
37. Negretto, U., Hodik, J., Kral, L., Mulder, W., Ollus, M., Pondrelli, L., Westphal, I., VO Management Solutions, Methods and Tools for Collaborative Networked Organizations, Springer, New York, pp. 257–274, 2008.

38. Neisse, R., Pereira, E. D. V., Granville, L. Z., Almeida, M. J. B., Tarouco, L. M. R., A Hierarchical Policy-Based Architecture for Integrated Management of Grids and Networks, Proceedings of the 5th IEEE International Workshop on Policies for Distributed Systems and Networks, pp. 103–106, 2004.
39. Norta, A., Exploring Dynamic Inter-Organizational Business Process Collaboration, PhD Thesis, Technology University Eindhoven, Department of Information Systems, 2007.
40. Panetto, H., Scannapieco, M., Zelm, M., INTEROP NoE: Interoperability Research for Networked Enterprises Applications and Software, On the Move to Meaningful Internet Systems Workshop, pp. 866–882, 2004.
41. Papazoglou, M. P., Traverso, P., Dustdar, S., Leymann, F., Krämer, B. J., Service-Oriented Com-puting: A Research Roadmap. In: F. Cubera, B. J. Krämer, M. P. Papazoglou (eds.) Service Oriented Computing (SOC), no. 05462 in Dagstuhl Seminar Proceedings. Internationales Begegnungs-und Forschungszentrum fuer Informatik (IBFI), Schloss Dagstuhl, Dagstuhl, Germany (2006). URL http://drops.dagstuhl.de/opus/volltexte/2006/524/
42. Rabelo, R. J., Gusmeroli, S., Arana, C., Nagellen, T., The Ecolead ICT Infrastructure For Collaborative Networked Organizations, Network-Centric Collaboration and Supporting Frameworks, Vol. 224, Springer, New York, pp. 451–460, 2006.
43. Rabelo, R., Advanced Collaborative Business ICT Infrastructures, Methods and Tools for Collaborative Networked Organizations, Springer, New York, pp. 337–370, 2008.
44. Ruohomaa, S., Viljanen, L., Kutvonen, L., Guarding Enterprise Collaborations with Trust decisions – the TuBE Approach, Interoperability for Enterprise Software and Applications, Proceedings of the Workshops and the Doctoral Symposium of the Second IFAC/IFIP I-ESA International Conference, pp. 237–248, ISTE Ltd, 2006.
45. Ruokolainen, T., Kutvonen, L., Managing Non-Functional Properties of Inter-Enterprise Business Service Delivery, Proceedings of the 5th International Conference on Service Oriented Computing (ICSOC), The Non-Functional Properties and Service Level Agreements in Service Oriented Computing Workshop (NFPSLA-SOC), Vienna, Austria, 2007.
46. Ruohomaa, S., Kutvonen, L., Making Multi-Dimensional Trust Decisions on Inter-Enterprise Collaborations, Proceedings of the Third International Conference on Availability, Security and Reliability, pp. 873–880, IEEE Computer Society, Barcelona, Spain, 2008.
47. Sauve, J., Moura, A., Sampaio, M., Jornada, J., Radziuk, E., An Introductory Overview and Survey of Business-Driven IT management, 1st IEEE/IFIP International Workshop On Business-Driven IT Management, pp. 1–10, IEEE Communications Society, Barcelona, Spain, 2006.
48. Schmidt, D., Model-Driven Engineering, IEEE Computer, Vol. 39(2), pp. 25–31, 2006.
49. Vaquez-Salceda, J., Dignum, V., Dignum, F., Organizing Multiagent Systems, Autonomous Agents and Multi-Agent Systems, Vol. 11, pp. 307–360, 2005.
50. Westphal, W., Mulder, W., Seifert, M., Supervision of Collaborative Processes in VOs, Methods and Tools for Collaborative Networked Organizations, Springer, New York, pp. 239–256, 2008.

Part V
Conclusion

Chapter 13
Conclusion

Paul Grefen, Nikolay Mehandjiev, Georg Weichhart, and Kurt Fessl

In this chapter, we draw the main conclusions from the work in this book. We first summarize the analysis of the state of the art in the field. Then, we look at the potential impact from a business perspective of the CrossWork results as described in this book. Finally, we look at the benefits of using the instant virtual enterprise concept. In the next chapter, we further conclude the book by taking a look into the future starting from the contents of the previous chapters.

13.1 Analysis of the State of Art

In Section 2.4 of Chapter 2, we have compared the goals of the CrossWork project to the results of a number of other research efforts. In this section, we perform an analysis of the state of the art by comparing the results of the CrossWork project to the results of the other research projects. As a basis for the comparison, we use six main topics and group the other projects into two perspectives, as indicated in the table below. The table also summarizes the analysis that follows below.

13.1.1 *Workflow Perspective: WISE and CrossFlow*

The WISE [1] and CrossFlow [7, 8] projects have been described in Section 2.4 as related workflow-oriented projects. We compare them here to CrossWork using the six topics from Table 13.1.

Dynamic formation of teams is not supported by the run-time environment of the WISE system. The CrossFlow system supports dynamic formation of teams through its matchmaking functionality. Teams are, however, limited to two parties only (as CrossFlow uses a bilateral service outsourcing paradigm) and matchmaking is performed on the basis of standardized contract templates. The Goal Decomposition

P. Grefen (✉)
Eindhoven University of Technology, Eindhoven, The Netherlands
e-mail: p.w.p.j.grefen@tue.nl

N. Mehandjiev, P. Grefen (eds.), *Dynamic Business Process Formation for Instant Virtual Enterprises*, Advanced Information and Knowledge Processing, DOI 10.1007/978-1-84882-691-5_13, © Springer-Verlag London Limited 2010

Table 13.1 Comparison of project results

	Workflow	Distributed work	CrossWork
Contract management	√	√	
Dynamic formation of teams	(√)	√	√
Dynamic composition of processes	√	(√)	√
Validation of processes	–	–	√
Workflow management	√	–	√
Service-enabled legacy integration	–	√	√

and Team Formation modules of the CrossWork system go considerably further, as they allow teams of arbitrary complexity and partner matching in a much more flexible context.

Contract management is not supported by WISE. The CrossFlow approach pays very explicit attention to contract management [8, 10]. It includes a dedicated contract specification language, explicit contract establishment and contract-based setup and operation of the VE infrastructure. The CrossWork approach does not include contract management. This is an area that does merit extension of the approach.

Composition of workflow processes in WISE is performed statically, i.e. at workflow design time. Both CrossFlow and CrossWork support dynamic process composition. In CrossFlow, however, composition is limited to the bilateral service outsourcing paradigm again. This means that composition is actually reduced to "inserting" a service provider process at the reserved location in the service consumer process. CrossWork supports much more flexible service composition, leading to process networks that can in principle have arbitrary complexity.

Validation of processes is not explicitly addressed in WISE or CrossFlow. The CrossWork approach does provide explicit attention to process validation in the process composition phase.

Obviously, workflow management is supported by all three approaches, as they are all workflow-oriented approaches. The WISE approach relies on a centralized workflow engine. CrossFlow relies on coupling pairs of workflow engines in a peer-to-peer fashion by means of dynamically generated VE infrastructures. CrossWork uses a more complex hub-and-spoke topology, in which one workflow engine executes the global workflow process and synchronizes a number of other workflow engines that execute local workflow processes. The CrossWork approach is therefore the most flexible of the three.

Both WISE and CrossWork concentrate on pure workflow management environments. CrossWork includes explicit support for coupling the workflow environment to existing legacy systems residing at the partners in an instant virtual enterprise. In this respect, CrossWork goes a considerable step further towards usage of the approach in an industrial environment where legacy systems form a back-end infrastructure that has to be dealt with.

13.1.2 Distributed Work Perspective: MaBE and TRUSTCOM

The body of research in Distributed Work focuses on the requirements and techniques facilitating the distribution of goals and tasks amongst sets of collaborating actors (organizations or software agents). One cluster of research activity focuses on the use of Multi-agent Systems (MAS) for planning and/or execution of business processes exist. In approaches like ADEPT and CONOISE [9, 12], software agents implement business services. Each service is essentially a task to be executed by the agent as part of a cross-organization business process. Buhler and Vidal [2, 14] add to this the ability to work with a BPEL workflow specification, and assign individual tasks to software agents, using a bridge technology [5, 13].

These systems are but a small selection of the work in this area. Here we focus on the research aspects of two projects which we consider closest to CrossWork: MaBE/IntLogProd and TrustCoM. They have been described in Section 2.4, here we analyse their capabilities in reference to Table 13.1. Note that MaBE and IntLogProd are very similar in terms of the results listed in Table 13.1, with IntLogProd focusing on initial exploration of the problem space, whilst MaBE focuses on the infrastructure support for these issues. We therefore use only "MaBE" to refer to both in this section.

Contract Management is targeted by TrustCoM, which used technology to establish documented and transparent contractual relationships. These relationships are used to determine what all parties in a VE should do, and drive monitoring of process execution within a Service-Oriented Architecture. In contrast to this, MaBE considers contract aspects to be handled within the general framework of MAS, and has not focused on delivering specific technologies in the area.

Both TrustCoM and MaBE aim to support the dynamic formation of VEs. TrustCoM focuses on explicit representations of the capabilities of the different participants as a basis for selecting the right teams, whilst MaBE is also concerned with co-optimizing the selection of team members against transport costs between their sites and the final destination.

Coverage of dynamic composition of processes was only focused on the issues involved in balancing production availability and logistic costs, and did not deliver any formal composition techniques. Validation of processes was hence also not included. Workflow management was only found to a limited extent in TrustCoM, where contract information is used for monitoring of process execution within a service-oriented infrastructure.

Both MaBE and TrustCoM focused on infrastructural issues, and on using service-oriented concepts to facilitate the integration of legacy systems into their results. TrustCoM in particular sees infrastructure integration as fundamental, together with ensuring stability of support infrastructures and transparency of contract-driven relationships.

In contrast to these systems, CrossWork integrates dynamic team formation and legacy systems integration with a stronger results "in the middle of the life cycle", by supporting formal process composition and validation, and linking these phases with a service-enabled support infrastructure.

13.2 CrossWork – Potential Impact

Often discussed industry trends such as "globalization" and "outsourcing", highlight more and more products that are a result of a collaborative effort. Especially in the automotive industry (the prime target business sector of CrossWork), these trends have been highly visible for decades and continue to grow as Fig. 13.1 shows. The top part shows the percentage of Original Equipment Manufacturers (OEMs) in value creation throughout the different phases of automotive production in 2002. The bottom part shows the same for 2015. As can be realized, in the intermediate future, the OEMs will continue to outsource tasks, and suppliers will be able to realize a larger portion of the value creation process. Business models like system cooperations, production cooperations, engineering service providers and made-to-order production drastically change the modes of collaboration in the automotive sector, resulting in an increased total added value of 250 billion Euros until 2015. The results of CrossWork can contribute to facilitating this development.

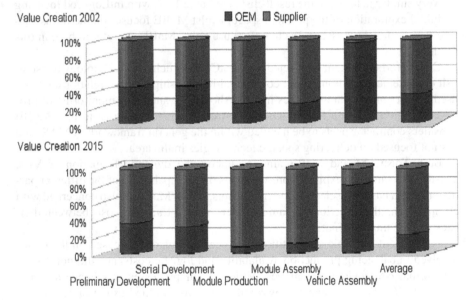

Fig. 13.1 Difference of OEM's value creation between 2002 and 2015 (adapted from [11])

Empirical studies show that international collaborations indeed have a positive impact on the business performance of enterprises [4]. This is to a great extent driven by the need to promote business efficiencies across the value chain, minimize overall costs, attain access to new and larger markets and access to know-how and technology. The same report identifies that the potentials for cooperation are not yet fully utilized. Collaboration support tools (e.g. CrossWork), which enable efficient and effective collaboration, find a growing market. According to Gartner [6] by 2008, users will seek the business process platform as a means of orchestrating custom business processes to meet the demands of dynamic business models and processes. While collaboration is found to result in overall cost and time-to-market benefits, achieving an efficient engineering collaboration still remains a challenge. Participating organizations are globally distributed and there is an intense need to communicate, coordinate and exchange rich information on a continual basis. Supporting ICT in order to meet the required dynamics in an engineering collaboration needs to enable contract management, asynchronously and synchronously (product) information exchange, partner search functionality, provide means for a partner to autonomously define its own processes (in order to account for local particularities), provide data security, manage workflows that span multiple organizations and control and audit the data-flows. Various products available in the market today address these requirements in part but fail to provide a complete solution.

The opportunities in this business area seem very promising. The integrated collaboration market is in an embryonic stage, but is clearly emerging. The revenue is small ($100 million in 2004), yet steadily growing [3]. There is an increasing business demand for an integrated set of products for efficient and effective corporate collaboration before this market can be considered as durable. During the next 3–5 years, as this market continues to grow, Gartner [6] expects leaders with broad and deep offerings to emerge, together with a corresponding market consolidation.

13.3 Benefits from Enrolling into the IVE Club

The use of the CrossWork approach enables business organizations to start using the IVE concept, or in other words "enrol into the IVE club". The latter can be interpreted as being able to join an IVE-enabled business market or to actually join an IVE being formed in such a market. Enrolling into the IVE club brings a number of business benefits, which we briefly discuss below. We first quote actual observations from the automotive industry (as the CrossWork prototype application domain). Then we discuss benefits more generally.

Potential end-users from the automotive industry have evaluated the CrossWork software with respect to their expected benefits. From a task perspective, users felt supported by the prototype system. With respect to support for forming a new team during the (re-)engineering phase of an automotive module, one of the end-users highlighted that with CrossWork, team formation can be performed more effectively and efficiently. All the different aspects concerning price, quality, key performance indicators can be considered in the first phases of the formation process. The CrossWork software enables this user to realize time savings by making the formation process more effective (in terms of making more information available and manageable) and efficient (in terms of time savings that can be realized when using it). This user underlined that using CrossWork could realize savings of 58% during the analysis phase, 70% during the definition phase and 7% during the planning phase.

The list below highlights the identified potential benefits that can be realized through the application of the CrossWork approach and software:

Increased Effectiveness:

- Fosters work effectiveness explicitly;
- Provides more efficient information feeds;
- Reduces the impact of re-allocation to eastern countries; and
- Provides simple overview of complex processes.

Increased Quality:

- Increases process definition quality;
- Improves quality of supply (technical and logistical);
- Reduces error rates in process definition; and
- Reduces error rates in inter-organizational synchronization.

Reduction in Costs:

- Reduces the coordination effort in VE setup; and
- Reduces the coordination effort in VE enactment.

Reduction in Time:

- Supports faster team creation for a specific project;
- Supports faster process engineering;
- Reduces the need for coordination- and monitoring meetings; and
- Supports faster preparation of meetings between VE members.

Overall, we believe that the use of the CrossWork approach will result in increased effectiveness and quality of VE composition because of the explicit process representation and the provision for systematic team selection and process validation. It will also help VEs reduce coordination costs involved in their setup and enactment, and shorten the time for team creation and work coordination.

References

1. Alonso, G., Fiedler, U., Hagen, C., Lazcano, A., Schuldt, H., Weiler, N., WISE: Business to Business E-Commerce, Proceedings of the 9th International Workshop on Research Issues on Data Engineering, Sydney, Australia, pp. 132–139, 1999.
2. Buhler, P., Vidal, J. M., Enacting BPEL4WS Specified Workflows with Multiagent Systems, Proceedings Workshop on Web Services and Agent-Based Engineering, New York City, USA, 2004.

3. Burton, B., Drakos, N., Smith, D. M., Austin, T., Cain, M. W., Understand the Opportunities of the Emerging Integrated Collaboration Market, Gartner Research, ID Number: G00126560, April, 2005.
4. Consortium, E. N. S. R., Observatory of European SMEs – Part 8: Highlights from the 2003 Observatory, European Network for SME Research (ENSR), European Communities, 2004.
5. FIPA – Foundation for Intelligent Physical Agents, http://www.fipa.org, 2007.
6. Genovese, Y., Hayward, S., Phifer, G., Plummer, D. C., Comport, J., Smith, D. M., Flexibility Drives the Emergency of the Business Process Platform, Gartner Research, ID Number: G00126854, April, 2005.
7. Grefen, P., Aberer, K., Hoffner, Y., Ludwig, H., CrossFlow: Cross-Organizational Workflow Management in Dynamic Virtual Enterprises, International Journal of Computer Systems Science and Engineering, Vol. 15(5), pp. 277–290, 2000.
8. Hoffner, Y., Field, S., Grefen, P., Ludwig, H., Contract Driven Creation and Operation of Virtual Enterprises, Computer Networks, Vol. 37(2), pp. 111–136, 2001.
9. Jennings, N. R., Faratin, P., Norman, T. J., O'Brien, P., Odgers, B., Alty, J. L., Implementing a Business Process Management System using ADEPT: A Real-World Case Study, International Journal of Applied Artificial Intelligence, Vol. 14(5), pp. 421–463, 2000.
10. Koetsier, M., Grefen, P., Vonk, J., Contracts for Cross-Organizational Workflow Management, Proceedings of the 1st International Conference on Electronic Commerce and Web Technologies, pp. 110–121, London, UK, 2000.
11. Mercer Management Consulting and Fraunhofer, Future Automotive Industry Structure (FAST) 2015, 2003.
12. Norman, T. J., Preece, A., Chalmers, S., Jennings, N. R., Luck, M., Dang, V. D., Nguyen, T. D., Deora, V., Shao, J., Gray, A., Fiddian, N., CONOISE: Agent-Based Formation of Virtual Organisations, Proceedings of the 23rd SGAI International Conference on Innovative Techniques and Applications of AI, Cambridge, UK, 2003.
13. OASIS, Web Services Business Process Execution Language Version 2.0, http://docs.oasis-open.org/wsbpel/2.0/OS/wsbpel-v2.0-OS.html, 2007.
14. Vidal, J. M., Buhler, P., Stahl, C., Multiagent Systems with Workflows, IEEE Internet Computing, Vol. 8(1), pp. 76–82, 2004.

Chapter 14
Outlook

Paul Grefen, Rik Eshuis, and Alex Norta

In this book, we have looked at the concept of IVEs, automated support for establishment and operation of IVEs, application of IVEs and research approaches related to IVEs. In this chapter, we put the results described in the previous chapters in a broader perspective by extending them towards the future, i.e. providing an outlook into further developments.

First, we broaden the view by discussing the application of the CrossWork approach in fields other than the automotive domain that we have concentrated on in this book so far. Next, we discuss a number of functional extensions to the CrossWork approach. Finally, we place the entire IVE concept into two broader frameworks by taking a look at the concepts of eCommunities and eMarkets.

14.1 Applicability of CrossWork in Other Fields

In this book, we have mainly focused on the automotive industry as an example application domain for instant VEs and information systems supporting them. Obviously, the approach presented in this book is also applicable to other domains requiring the dynamic formation of business networks for the delivery of complex products and services. To illustrate this, we look below at two broad application domains: high-tech manufacturing and the services industry. The first is a generalization of the automotive domain (as cars are high-tech products). The latter is a broad domain where non-physical products, i.e. services are produced.

14.1.1 High-tech Manufacturing

In most chapters of this book, we have focused on the car manufacturing domain. Manufacturing cars is a typical kind of high-tech manufacturing. Consequently,

P. Grefen (✉)
Eindhoven University of Technology, Eindhoven, The Netherlands
e-mail: p.w.p.j.grefen@tue.nl

N. Mehandjiev, P. Grefen (eds.), *Dynamic Business Process Formation for Instant Virtual Enterprises*, Advanced Information and Knowledge Processing, DOI 10.1007/978-1-84882-691-5_14, © Springer-Verlag London Limited 2010

one might ask whether the CrossWork approach can be generalized to high-tech manufacturing. As the CrossWork approach is centred on the concept of an IVE, the first question is whether this concept is applicable in high-tech manufacturing in general. Let us recall the definition of the IVE concept from Chapter 2:

> An instant virtual enterprise is a temporary virtual enterprise forged with support of automated systems to fulfil a specific business goal and subsequently operated with the support of automated systems.

The main elements in this definition are "temporary", "virtual enterprise", "specific business goal" and "automated systems". Let us next discuss these four elements in a different order.

The "specific business goal" relates to the "temporary" in the sense that an IVE requires a business domain in which specific business goals emerge with a temporary character. In high-tech manufacturing, we indeed see this characteristic, as high-tech products typically have a relatively short economic life cycle, because their nature is for a large part technology-driven and technology evolves in rapid pace. This is evident for example in the electronics and computer industry, where economic life cycles of new products are typically a few months. In the area of very capital-intensive high-tech products, like the aviation industry, we see this a little less – not because technology evolves slowly, but because the products need to have a longer life cycle.

The "virtual enterprise" implies that reaching the business goals requires the collaboration of a number of autonomous parties. This is quite general in the high-tech manufacturing domain, as the high-tech products often have such technical complexity, that no single organization can have all the required capabilities that encompass both knowledge and physical attributes. When we combine "virtual enterprise" with "temporary", we see that the collaboration needs to be dynamic, based on the characteristics of the business goal at hand. In other words, partners in the dynamic enterprise are selected on the basis of product and current market characteristics. Given the dynamic nature of high-tech product characteristics and the fact that many high-tech markets are very dynamic in an economic sense (think of the semiconductor market), this fits high-tech manufacturing too.

"Automated systems" present an innovative and economical solution to labour-intensive information technology. The penetration of the use of advanced information technology in the high-tech manufacturing domain is quite high in general. This does not necessarily mean that the penetration of business process management technology is very high, but it does mean that information technology platforms are present and that openness towards automated solutions should be in good order.

Concluding, we can state that the CrossWork approach appears to be applicable to high-tech manufacturing in general. This more certainly holds for those segments of the industry where products have relatively short economical life cycles, perhaps a bit less for segments with more "stable product lines" as these may imply more stable VEs too.

14.1.2 Services Industry

We have discussed the applicability of the CrossWork approach to the general high-tech manufacturing domain – this as a generalization of the automotive domain has been the original target application domain for the CrossWork project. Both domains focus on the production of complex *physical* products. Next, we pose the question whether the CrossWork approach can also be applied to domains concentrating on *non-physical* complex products. Therefore, we take a brief look into the services industry.

The life cycle of services is often quite limited as competition is fierce in many service markets and service evolution (or even revolution) is therefore important. In many situations, a service offering may even be highly customized for a single client. Clearly, customization of non-physical products is often easier than that of physical products. Consequently, specific business goals with a temporary character can be found in the services industry maybe even more than in high-tech manufacturing.

In the services industry, we see a fast increase of the complexity of services that are offered to customers. This holds in the financial industry, where for example complex leasing service products are offered in the business-to-business market and complex hybrid insurance–financial service products in the business-to-consumer market. In the telecommunication service industry, we also see complex hybrid services, offering for example triple-play infrastructures and complex combinations of value-added services and digital content. In the healthcare industry, complex medical services are made available, composed of possibly many elemental services. This complexity also calls for collaborative business scenarios like VEs, which is no different to high-tech manufacturing. Given the temporary business goals discussed, these VEs need to also be dynamic.

In many service industry domains, for example banking and insurance, the level of automation is high. The reason for this is that many services are indeed information-intensive. This makes many domains in the service industry perfect breeding grounds for advanced IT applications like the CrossWork system.

The conclusion can therefore clearly be that the CrossWork approach is also applicable to the services industry. The production of physical products is not a sine qua non for automated support for establishment and operation of IVEs.

14.2 Functional Extensions of CrossWork

The CrossWork approach as presented in this book covers a broad spectrum of functionality for the establishment and operation of IVEs. However, it does not cover *all* functionality that is useful to support IVEs. In this section we briefly discuss a number of possible important extensions to the CrossWork framework. The discussion provides an idea of these extensions.

In the following three subsections, we concentrate on transaction management, electronic contracting and support for process evolution. Obviously, there are more extensions possible (like for instance electronic payment support and explicit reputation and trust management), but the ones we treat here are a few "obvious" extensions to the approach presented in this book. Thus, the aim of this section is not to be complete, but to present a direction for functional extension.

We place the extensions in the CrossWork architecture that we have described in Chapter 5. We do this in a cumulative way, as this both illustrates the complexity when adding more functionality and provides the opportunities to look at aspects where extensions influence each other.

14.2.1 Transaction Management

Transaction management is used to safeguard the reliability of processes [11]. Originally developed for use in database management environments, it has been applied to business processes for over a decade now. However, early developments, like the WIDE project [5], did not place it in the context of VEs.

One of the first projects developing transaction management for dynamic distributed business processes was the CrossFlow project [3], which we have discussed in Section 2.4 of this book. In this project, transaction management was developed for a dynamic service outsourcing context [8], employing transaction management on two levels; the cross-organizational and the intra-organizational levels. These levels roughly correspond to the CrossWork global enactment and local enactment levels. Following the CrossFlow approach, we could therefore extend the CrossWork architecture with global transaction management and local transaction management modules, as shown in Fig. 14.1 (taking a simplified version of the architecture described in Chapter 5 as a starting point). These modules are connected by a transaction management interface to synchronize their activities.

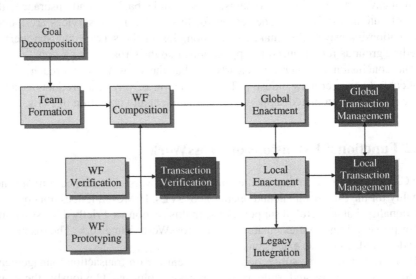

Fig. 14.1 CrossWork architecture extended with transaction management

Note, however, that the CrossFlow outsourcing paradigm is far less flexible with respect to process topologies than the CrossWork IVE paradigm. Consequently, the CrossFlow transaction management mechanisms would have to be extended to be usable in the CrossWork context. Given the dynamic nature of IVE processes, the workflow composition phase would have to be supported with a new module (next to the existing workflow verification and workflow prototyping modules) to verify the transactional behaviour of composed global processes. This is also shown in Fig. 14.1.

More recent developments in the transaction management field take dynamic composition of complex processes as a starting point, allowing truly dynamic composition of transactions. An example is the XTC project [9], in which an approach towards contract-governed transaction support for service-oriented processes is developed. The service-orientation would fit well with the service-orientation in the CrossWork enactment architecture.

In the XTC approach, processes are composed from subprocesses. Each subprocess is coupled to a service module that describes its transactional behaviour. Such a service module is based on an Abstract Transactional Construct (ATC) that specifies an abstract transactional behaviour based on an abstracted transaction model [9]. In XTC, a library is developed that contains a taxonomy of ATCs. An ATC is parameterized based on the specifics of a subprocess. Multiple parameterized ATCs are composed into a Composed Business Transaction (CBT), which describes the transactional behaviour of a composed process, which can be a complex subprocess or a complete process. The way ATCs can be designed, parameterized and composed into CBTs is governed by the Business Transaction Framework (BTF), a conceptual framework that describes the manipulation of ATCs.

To obtain reliable business processes, transactional support for them must be specified in business terminology that is understood by all involved parties. This means that transaction support should be specified at the same level (comparable business terminology) as the process specification itself.

14.2.2 Electronic Contracting

Contracts in general define the collaboration between parties in a legal sense by stating their rights and obligations with respect to each other. We have seen in this book how global process specifications specify the operational collaboration between IVE partners, but these do not provide a legal basis. Contracts can be used as a legal underpinning of an IVE, complementing the operational specifications we have seen before. A contractual context for an IVE can be defined in a single multi-lateral contract pertaining to all members of an IVE or in a set of bilateral contracts that each pertains to the IVE initiator and one other member. To obtain the efficiency required in IVE establishment, electronic contracting [1] should be used instead of traditional contracting. Electronic contracting in its full version includes two main aspects; contract establishment to define contracts and contract monitoring to assess the compliance of contract partners to the contract (i.e. to detect contract breaches).

In the CrossWork approach, contract establishment is part of IVE establishment – more precisely it is the last phase of IVE establishment. From an architectural point of view (taking Fig. 14.1 as a starting point), this would mean adding a contract establishment module between the process composition module and IVE enactment, i.e. the global enactment module. This is shown in Fig. 14.2. Note that it would be possible to place contract establishment "earlier" in the IVE establishment process (e.g. between team formation and process composition). This would mean however, that established contracts must be dismantled in case later IVE activities (process composition) are not successful.

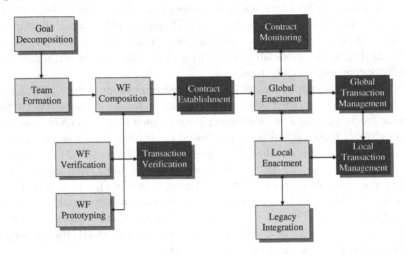

Fig. 14.2 CrossWork architecture further extended with contracting

Contract monitoring is part of IVE enactment. As a contract defines collaboration specifics between IVE members, a contract monitoring module should be coupled to the global enactment module (as shown in Fig. 14.2). IVE-level contracts do not concern encapsulated business details of individual IVE members, which means that contract monitoring at the local enactment level is not required.

Transactional requirements to processes can be stated in contracts between the parties [10] to make them explicitly part of the *business arrangement*. The agreed transactional semantics is related to a specific process-oriented service and is therefore specified in the Service Level Agreement (SLA) that is part of the contract and prescribes the QoS of the aspect under consideration (transactional quality of service in this case, denoted by TxQoS).

14.2.3 Process Evolution Support

Support for process evolution means providing mechanisms that enable processes to evolve during enactment time, i.e. to change the definition of a process instance while it is running. Process evolution is used to deal with changing requirements to process that cannot be foreseen at design time. In the CrossWork context, this means changing a composed process while it is being executed by the global and local enactment modules.

Process evolution may on the one hand be considered not so important in an IVE context, as IVEs have a short life cycle. In other words, at design time it is not required to look far into the future, and requirements to processes can thus be easily foreseen. On the other hand, high time pressure on IVE establishment may introduce *mistakes* in process composition that have to be *repaired* later on, i.e. during enactment time. Also, local processes of individual IVE members may change over time without synchronization within the IVE life cycle. This may certainly happen in situations where members participate in multiple IVEs with overlapping life cycles. The extent to which process evolution will be useful or even necessary depends heavily on the application domain.

Changing a global process during IVE operation implies returning from the IVE enactment stage to the IVE establishment stage and at least recomposing the global process (in a more extreme case even forming a new team). After a new global process has been composed, it must be checked whether the new global process is consistent with the process state that was reached with the old process definition. If it is not consistent, the new process cannot be *installed* in the enactment subsystem, as this would lead to an inconsistent state. If it is consistent, the old process state must be *translated* to the new process definition and *installed* in the enactment subsystem. To provide the process state checking functionality, we introduce a new workflow state checker module into the architecture. This module is coupled to the workflow composition module, as shown in Fig. 14.3.

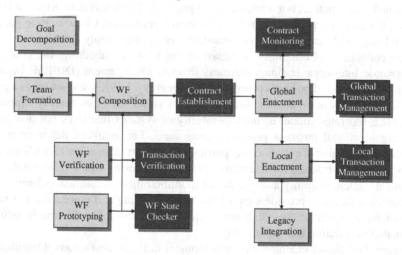

Fig. 14.3 CrossWork architecture further extended with process evolution support

As can be seen in Fig. 14.3, workflow composition and workflow state checking precede contract establishment. This implies that changing a running process may indeed require reestablishment of a contract.

Changing the local process of a member during IVE operation is only relevant to the operation of an IVE if the change is reflected at the external level of the three-level framework, i.e. if the change is indeed visible to other IVE members. If not, changes can be freely performed by IVE members, as their effects are fully encapsulated. If the change influences the external level process of a member, a new global process definition is required. This means that the same procedure, as described above, must be followed as with a change to the global process.

14.3 Placing CrossWork in a Broader Perspective

This section reviews the concepts of eCommunities and eMarkets. In doing this, it highlights their implications for broadening the scope of business activities present within the CrossWork frame of reference.

14.3.1 eCommunities

The notion of (instant) virtual enterprise is closely related to eCommunities [6], which are collaborative, inter-organizational business networks. Like an IVE, an eCommunity is dynamically established to respond to a business opportunity. An eCommunity is a specific collaboration with special operations, agreements and states. An eCommunity is governed by an electronic contract that is multi-laterally negotiated. This contract is a refinement of a predefined business network model that defines the services, parties and roles, plus their interactions. Collaborating parties join or leave an eCommunity either voluntarily or by community decision.

The concept of eComminity is shown in Fig.14.4 as embedding the concepts of Dynamic Inter-organizational Business Process Management (DIBPM) [4] and electronic sourcing of business processes (eSourcing) [7]. While eSourcing is a concept for externally harmonizing business process views, the eCommunity approach supports a federated model of interoperability of systems that does not deal with inter-organizational business process management, but monitors the interactions between the domains of collaborating parties that are part of an eContract. eSourcing provides an infrastructure for integrating business processes with a different degree of mutual content visibility and enactment monitorability. In contrast, eCommunity management facilities provide support for loose coupling and emphasize the need of predefined, dynamic (breeding environment) type discipline for the benefit of automated negotiation and monitoring.

Figure 14.4 shows eCommunity development in three dimensions. One dimension is a life cycle of an eCommunity that has a setup, enactment and post-enactment phase. During the setup phase an offer is made to form an eCommunity [6] that is eventually defined in a BNM. The collaborating parties engage in forming one or many eContracts [1] until signatures exist for them and the eContract(s) are stored. Changes of community members and their relationships result in updates of the

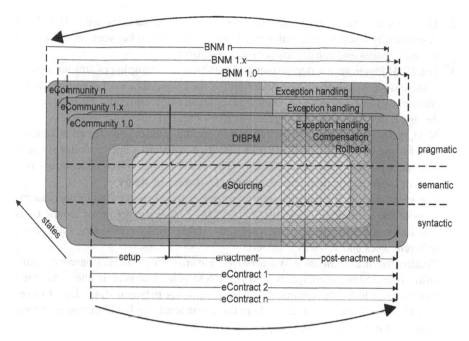

Fig. 14.4 eCommunities development model

BNM, e.g. the service provision is modified, a party of the e-business collaboration changes and so on. Such changes result in a new state of a community, which is visualized by the second dimension in the figure. The third dimension in Fig. 14.4 establishes a separation of concerns with respect to pragmatic, semantic and syntactic issues of collaboration. Pragmatic collaboration captures the willingness of parties to perform the necessary activities. The willingness to participate involves the capability to perform requested actions and policies that dictate whether the action is preferable for a party to be involved in an eCommunity. Semantic collaboration means that the content of a message is understood in the same way by a sender and receiver. Finally, syntactic collaboration means that messages can be transported from one application to another and correctly processed.

As shown in Fig.14.4, an eCommunity life cycle is a series of stages through which business collaboration moves. The specific functional blocks of an information system supporting this life cycle are discussed below, of which all are currently part of the eCommunity [6] concept. The following mechanisms are listed in accordance with an eCommunity life cycle:

1. The life cycle starts with a *BNM former* that is instrumental for the formation of a BNM where defined roles and interactions between roles are governed by policies and consolidated so that the structure and behaviour of a collaborating community is set up. In this case, a first negotiation between potential partners involves comparing and matching strategic and pragmatic goals in the network.

2. The *populator* represents a breeding process where services are selected for eCommunity roles. Here a match needs to be established between the candidate attribute values and constraints for roles in a BNM.
3. The *BNM joiner* goes a step further and establishes a grouping of similar models with suitable transformers and adapters for the configuration of communication channels so that information exchange is understood correctly. Furthermore, a deadlock free message exchange needs to be ensured.
4. Next, the *membership manager* retrieves potential participants for an eCommunity for the defined roles of a BNM based on a service-type repository where providers publish their service offers. The resulting eCommunity contract is a subject for re-negotiation that results in a trajectory of states.
5. The *state support* is a mechanism that manages the change of major reorganizations of the collaboration structure in a BNM. A state is a period where the roles and services of the BNM participants are stable while subsequent states have different roles and services involved.
6. Finally, the *state-transition synchronizer* governs state changes based on transition rules. Some participants that fill BNM roles reappear in the next state, while others leave the community. The transitions between states lead to synchronizations between partners where the constraints in a BNM that govern their behaviour need to be adjusted.

Mapped to Fig. 14.4, the first four dynamic mechanisms form part of the setup phase, whilst the latter two mechanisms form part of the enactment phase. A post-enactment phase of an eCommunity is a dynamic mechanism that results in an orderly termination where the members agree to part, the behaviour governing rules and linked business processes are uncoupled, and the technological infrastructures in the respective community-member domains are disconnected.

The CrossWork approach is overlapping with, and complementary to eCommunities. First, CrossWork can help to define business network models in a semi-automatic way. However, in CrossWork these business network models are the same as the contracts, so no distinction between the two types of models is made. Also, eCommunities are not always explicitly process-based. Using CrossWork technology, eCommunities could use state-of-the-art service composition languages like BPEL and the related tools to support the actual ongoing of eCommunities. Next, CrossWork can benefit from the facilities for trust management in eCommunities. Each execution of a service is monitored in eCommunities. Each party can build a reputation, thus increasing their trust level. Also the context influences the level of trust. Within CrossWork this is used for team formation.

14.3.2 eMarkets

The CrossWork approach as described in this book is based on a rather closed market paradigm: team formation is based on the information about possible IVE members as registered in the market knowledge base (or known to the human team designer). If we wish to move to an open market paradigm, team formation should be based on an open market registry, in which new potential IVE members can register themselves. This ideally implies the use of a third-party broker that acts as an "IVE market yellow pages server". Third-party brokers have been proposed before to link business processes, e.g. in the CrossFlow project [3]. Brokers to link business functions are even basic in the service-oriented architecture, where the UDDI [2] standard specifies broker functionality.

Introducing third-party electronic brokers facilitates open eMarkets. An eMarket is in principle a digital platform where business partners can meet each other to do business, typically in an offer-and-request paradigm. eMarkets can be considered complementary to CrossWork; once interested business partners have found each other through an eMarket, they can use CrossWork technology to actually build an IVE that controls their collaborative business. Alternatively, the CrossWork approach can be extended using eMarkets. Especially the retrieval of team partners can be directly based on eMarkets, i.e. an eMarket could replace the CrossWork market knowledge base.

In replacing the rather closed CrossWork paradigm with an open eMarket paradigm, the trust issue becomes important: How can one trust a potential IVE member found through an eMarket? Reputation and certification mechanisms will be important in this case to select IVE members. Contract support which is already important in a closed market is essential within an open market.

> In summary, the concept of eCommunities highlights broadening of the collaboration between members of a network, thus going beyond inter-organizational business process management. This is complemented by the concept of eMarkets, serving as a mechanism for broadening of the scope of the collaborating network, thus going beyond the semi-closed markets implied by the CrossWork team formation mechanisms.

References

1. Angelov, S., Foundations of B2B Electronic Contracting, Dissertation, Technology University Eindhoven, Faculty of Technology Management, Information Systems Department, 2006.
2. Bellwood, T., Clément, L., Ehnebuske, D., UDDI Version 3.0, Published Specification, http://uddi.org/pubs/uddi-v3.00-published-20020719.htm , 2003.
3. Grefen, P., Aberer, K., Hoffner, Y., Ludwig, H., CrossFlow: Cross-Organizational Workflow Management in Dynamic Virtual Enterprises, International Journal of Computer Systems Science and Engineering, Vol. 15(5), pp. 277–290, 2000.
4. Grefen, P., Service-Oriented Support for Dynamic Interorganizational Business Process Management, Service Oriented Computing, MIT Press, Cambridge, pp. 83–110, 2008.

5. Grefen, P., Pernici, B., Sánchez, G., Database Support for Workflow Management: The WIDE Project, Kluwer Academic Publishers, Dordrecht, 1999.
6. Kutvonen, L., Metso, J., Ruokolainen, T., Inter-Enterprise Collaboration Management in Dynamic Business Networks, On the Move to Meaningful Internet Systems: CoopIS, DOA, and ODBASE, Vol. 3760 of Lecture Notes in Computer Science, pp. 593–611, Agia Napa, Cyprus, October, 2005.
7. Norta, A., Exploring Dynamic Inter-Organizational Business Process Collaboration, PhD Thesis, Technology University Eindhoven, Department of Information Systems, 2007.
8. Vonk, J., Grefen, P., Cross-Organizational Transaction Support for E-Services in Virtual Enterprises, Distributed and Parallel Databases, Vol. 14(2), 2003.
9. Wang, T., Grefen, P., Vonk, J., Abstract Transaction Construct: Building a Transaction Framework for Contract-Driven, Service-Oriented Business Processes, Proceedings of the International Conference of Service-Oriented Computing, pp. 434–439, Chicago, USA, 2006.
10. Wang, T., Grefen, P., Vonk, J., Ensuring Transactional Reliability by E-Contracting; Proceedings of the 20th International Conference on Advanced Information Systems Engineering, Vol. LNCS 5074, pp. 262–265, Springer, Montpellier, France, 2008.
11. Wang, T., Kratz, B., Vonk, J., Grefen, P., A Survey on the History of Transaction Management: From Flat to Grid Transactions, Distributed and Parallel Databases, Vol. 23(3), pp. 235–270, 2008.

Index

N. Mehandjiev, P. Grefen (eds.), *Dynamic Business Process Formation for Instant
Virtual Enterprises*, Advanced Information and Knowledge Processing,
DOI 10.1007/978-1-84882-691-5, © Springer-Verlag London Limited 2010